MAGIC AND MYTH
OF THE MOVIES

By Parker Tyler

Introduction by Richard Schickel

SIMON AND SCHUSTER · NEW YORK

791.43
T983

FIRST SIMON AND SCHUSTER PRINTING

Certain material in this book originally appeared in the
form of articles in the following magazines: *View, Tomorrow, Theatre Arts,* and *The Sewanee Review.*

SBN 671-20545-5 CLOTH
SBN 671-20599-4 PAPER
MANUFACTURED IN THE UNITED STATES OF AMERICA

TO

THOMAS Z. TYLER,

MY FATHER,

AND TO THE MEMORY OF

EVA PARKER TYLER,

MY MOTHER

CONTENTS

INTRODUCTION

As a reader I am peculiarly, indeed fatally, attracted to the special kind of critical daring practiced by Parker Tyler in *The Hollywood Hallucination* and *Magic and Myth of the Movies*. This daring consists of two major elements: a willingness to risk overinterpretation of specific objects (the popular films and film stars that catch his endlessly roving eye) and the courage to build on these fragile and transitory creations a towering theoretical structure (a structure from which, it should be added, one can gain a unique view of the way one of our most significant cultural institutions actually works—or used to work at the height of its powers—on us). There are a few works of literary criticism that are a little bit like Mr. Tyler's books; one thinks of Lawrence's *Studies in Classic American Literature*, Pound's *ABC of Reading*, Fiedler's *Love and Death in the American Novel*. But it requires a very commodious critical tradition, much critical activity, to produce even such a small number of stimulating, intelligently eccentric works. We have not had, in film criticism, anything like the level of activity, or length of history, that can support such work. Indeed, there has been so little basic scholarly activity in film (a situation now, perhaps, beginning to be rectified), so little genuine criticism (as opposed to reviewing), that it is a wonder we have produced even the tiny, standard shelf of worthwhile volumes we now have (*Agee on Film*, Warshow's *The Imme-*

diate Experience, Kael's *I Lost It at the Movies*, and three or four others).

It has long been my contention that Mr. Tyler's two books belong in that select company and that they are the more remarkable in that they were published in 1944 and 1947. For at that time a man attempting to seriously comprehend the phenomenon of film was really working on his own, with no tradition to sustain him, few books and articles to refer to, few colleagues with whom he might conversationally test and refine his ideas. And, worse, as the indifferent commercial reception of these books proved, no genuine audience to address—just a handful of fellow buffs, nuts, fans... you pick the patronizing word.

Indeed, it is as some such character that Mr. Tyler was brought to the attention of the nonspecialist audience recently, when Gore Vidal, in the course of his extended sick joke, *Myra Breckinridge*, seized on *Magic and Myth* as just the kind of work—so intense it often comes close to self-parody—his hero–heroine–whatchamacallit required as motivation-inspiration for his–her–its idiot savantry about Hollywood. If Mr. Tyler's book had not existed Vidal would have had to invent it.

And, in decency, he should have. Except that he couldn't have, for there is nothing in his work with the imaginative intensity, the intellectual daring, of Mr. Tyler's work. I am sure the subject is, or was, painful to Mr. Tyler, since undoubtedly large numbers of the reading public now think of him as an invention of Vidal's. On the other hand, there is no critic in America better equipped to understand and appreciate the irony of this transformation of himself from a living reality into a symbolic fiction.

Indeed, it is one of the basic ironies he explores in these two books. All the movie stars he writes about preceded him in the kind of self-transcendence Vidal foisted on him. Creators of images (usually unconsciously, since they have the fortune or misfortune of looking like our imagined ideal of hero or villain, vamp or virgin) they become prisoners of those images. They come to each new role with bits of gossip about their private selves adhering to their public selves, trailing the bright rags and tatters of previous impersonations, encumbered by our expectations about what the behavior of certain types ought to be in certain situations. So they become creatures at once less than human and more than human. It is Mr. Tyler's prime business to explicate the iconography of these faces and forms—more real than real at first glance, less and less so the more we study them—and it is singular that, a quarter century after he introduced us to the fascinating possibilities inherent in this work, he has found so few disciples. For once we begin tracing out such analyses with him it seems a completely logical, completely natural thing to do.

And so it also is when he begins to work on the cliché that movies are dreams, the studios dream factories. It is, he argues, in the nature of a camera designed to capture *moving* images to create a special kind of realism—*sur*realism— a special kind of naturalism—*super*naturalism. But it is not just technics that impart this quality to movies. There is also the industry as social, commercial institution to consider. With its "mad search for novelty, the iron necessity to keep producing and to find ideas, angles," it unconsciously contrives to create a much richer matrix of meanings—and ambiguities—than, to use Mr. Tyler's example, "the efforts of dramatists to congregate enough words...to permit the curtain to ring down on another Broadway hit" can possibly aspire to. In other words, the drama clearly visible within the borders of the screen does not end there. He alludes to the off-screen drama, much more intense, that may take place between a directorial Svengali and his current Trilby. He mentions how an actor's vocal quality, his accent, may work against the characterization he strives for, may work for it, but always "refuses to be completely absorbed into the artistic mesh and creates a little theater of its own." The attempts to shoehorn "properties" into preexisting mythopoetic screen forms produce yet another interesting example of off-screen tension that is scarcely ever mentioned in formal reviews, yet is acknowledged in the trade phrase "licking the story" (rather as a mother cat licks her newborn offspring into acceptable behavioral patterns), and in our minds as we witness the movie unfolding before us. And then there is the career drama proceeding in almost every film we ever see. For example, Jennifer Jones in *The Song of Bernadette* asking us, after her "novitiate" in B westerns for "strict observance of the occasion" of her arrival in major films, like "a trained nurse admonishing us with finger on lips and murmuring: 'actress winning award.'" And so much, much more that Tyler himself can say better than an emcee can.

What it comes to, in essence, is this: There is the conscious movie, the one the people who created it thought they were making and the one we thought we were paying our way in to see. Then there is the unconscious movie, the one neither makers nor viewers are consciously aware of, a movie that exposes the attitudes, neuroses, desires shared by both parties. This film, if not beyond good and evil, is certainly beyond the reach of "good" reviews or "bad" reviews, beyond favorable or unfavorable criticism. It is not, however, beyond contemplation of the sort Mr. Tyler practices.

And, it should be mentioned, his style is as unique as his subject matter. He has a way of warily circling his prey, surrounding it with speculation, until, weary and frightened by an astute hunter, it falls victim to one of his quick dashes to its most vulnerable point.

I said at the beginning that I am extremely vulnerable to the charm of daring critical huntsmen of Mr. Tyler's sort, inclined to concede them their excesses of enthusiasm, their occasional lapses (even into incomprehensibility). Implicit in their enterprise is their own vulnerability to satirical and parodistical shots of the sort that people like Vidal, with their unquestioned ability to hit the broad side of a barn, can so easily make. Most of the best screen actors and screenplays, the ones we best and most lovingly remember, are similarly vulnerable, as is much of our best literature. In the end, work of this kind lingers in the mind precisely because it opens it up, leaves it speculating, trying to apply radical formulations to new phenomena as they appear.

It is possible, of course, that some of my affectionate regard for Mr. Tyler's work stems from the fact that most of his examples are drawn from a period (the late Thirties and the Forties) that happened to be the most formative one for me as a watcher in the shadows. They may seem obscure or distant to people under thirty-fivish. Yet most of the genres and performer types he discusses are still very much with us. And the processes by which they were created are still very much alive and well wherever people get together and make movies. Styles may change but the basics remain constant. Mr. Tyler may have written these books as the sound film passed through adolescence—age 14–18—but the bending of the twig was by then complete and its maturity was clearly prefigured. And even if the New American Film that one now sees taking shape should totally drive the traditional commercial product from the screen (which I doubt, some form of coexistence being a much better bet) *The Hollywood Hallucination* and *Magic and Myth of the Movies* would remain essential tools for understanding film history. Moreover, the mark they have made on at least some writers about film since they were published would remain indelible, even if, as is generally the case, unacknowledged.

Movies are, no matter what else they may from time to time claim to be, a mythopoetic form, and Mr. Tyler's criticism has, appropriately enough, a poetic quality about it. The critic Barbara Herrnstein Smith has lately defined the poem as an entity which "allows us to know what we know, including our illusions and desires, by giving us the language in which to acknowledge it." That, precisely, is what Mr. Tyler was trying to do when he wrote in his strange, compelling, uniquely rewarding way about films back in the days when we knew no better than to call them "the movies" and pretend their unimportance to us.

—RICHARD SCHICKEL

PREFACE

That the movies offer nothing but entertainment is a myth
in a sense never used or implied in the following pages.
I am not denying that millions of America's movie fans
succeed in finding only entertainment in the nation's
theaters. Aside from the newsreels and the documentaries
given impetus by the war, entertainment remains all that
is consciously demanded by those paying rising prices at
movie box offices. Yet as a fact there *is* more, and that
margin, which I regard as the essence of the matter, is the
subject of this as of my previous book on American
cinema. Patrons of all art media may get more than they
demand as well as less, and since the surplus is not precisely expected, it may register vaguely, obliquely, unconsciously. Especially is this true of the movie audience,
if only because as a large mass it is critically inarticulate.
I hope that my efforts may succeed in giving it some voice
on the positive side—movie reviewers take care of its
voice on the negative side—and I hope also that for the
benefit of students and those hitherto indifferent to the
"folk" art of cinema I may further demonstrate that Hollywood is a vital, interesting phenomenon, at least as important to the spiritual climate as daily weather to the
physical climate. A myth foisted specifically on the movies
proper rather than on the reaction of audiences is furnished,
as I explain later on, by devotees of both stage and novel

who scorn movies as below the serious level—as standing in relation to true art somewhat as the circus does to the legitimate stage. But unfortunately these judges, unaware of the ritual importance of the screen, its baroque energy and protean symbolism, are unwarrantably summary, basically uneducated in the movie medium.

As in my previous book, *The Hollywood Hallucination*, it was not my purpose to provide evidence that American movies constitute high art, so here I have not undertaken to prove what would be transparently false by my own criteria; indeed I often insist on absence of artistic merit just where it is acclaimed by most critics. The proposition I have to offer now is the same I have offered before, but here, I trust, more carefully documented and logically reasoned: the true field of the movies is not *art* but *myth*, between which—in the sense "myth" is invariably used here—there is a perhaps unsuspectedly wide difference. Assuredly a myth is a fiction, and this is its bare link with art, but a myth is specifically a free, unharnessed fiction, a basic, prototypic pattern capable of many variations and distortions, many betrayals and disguises, even though it remains *imaginative* truth. It has one degraded function connected with the idea of entertainment I discussed above, as when the word itself becomes adjectival and is deliberately attached to that pseudonymous Baltic kingdom having no existence saving in fifth-rate novels and in the movies. It is unsound to make a fact such as the existence of the very nation where a story occurs into a fiction, for it is like taking the props out from under a building and assuming it will still stand. No matter how fantastic an action, its background must be firm. It is the status of background that determines the strength of a myth, the status of its perspective in human history.

Essentially the *scene* of imaginative truth, or art, is the mind itself, but in some manner this truth must be objective, capable of projection onto the screen of the world. In a sense man *is* his past, the past of his race, and all the beliefs he ever held. Reality cannot be made up from the material facts of his existence, his immediate sensory reactions; nor can it be fundamentally a world that never was. Certainly man has ceased to believe much he used to believe. "Oh, that is a myth," we say, meaning that even if significant, it is an ideal or an illusion, a thing that has no substance. But psychology has taught us the strange reality of chimeras, their symbolic validity; and comparative mythology has revealed the great persistence of psychic patterns, with special reference to the supernatural, whose continuity in human belief is sometimes surprisingly self-evident. At one time men believed the earth was flat. Today this is a purely ornamental myth; it has died because imagining the earth is flat has no relation to our desires or employments. At one time the pagans believed in Diana as goddess of the moon and the hunt. Today this also might be considered a decorative myth, something in the fairy-tale class. Yet like so many legends it holds a mesmeric appeal for the mind; Diana represents, as a matter of fact, a certain sexual type—the vigorous virgin, the woman resistant to love; and yet according to the legend Endymion made her lose her heart; that is, the man lived who could break down her defenses merely through his physical image. Obviously this sexual pattern is repeated today. The modern belief that the earth is round corresponds to the conditions of our planetary existence insofar as, proceeding on this premise, our astronomical calculations work out. The belief is consistent with *all the facts*. Today the fact that Diana once had for the pagans a reality she does not have for us means merely that the myth lives in another form. It is an ideal archetype, a past of human experience that has its home in the imagination. And yet . . . that which was true once may become true again. What was symbolized by the Diana myth in actual human experience is a permanent legacy of the race. So the essence of myth also has the status of permanent possibility . . . in short, *desires* may have the same power over the mind and behavior, indeed a much greater power, than *facts*.

In the following pages I have occasion to refer specifically to the great researches made in ancient magic by Sir James Frazer. That there are anthropological assumptions contradictory to various of Frazer's own premises is of no importance to the point I am making. In order to explain a single phenomenon, the priest cult of the King of the Wood at Nemi, Frazer accumulated into one work a prodigious array of ancient primitive beliefs and customs suggesting the limitless lineage of the relatively recent cult at Nemi. At this moment, as when his book was written, nobody is a devotee of this cult; nobody believes in the magic of the golden bough that had to be plucked by the aspirant to Diana's priesthood before he was empowered to kill in single combat the incumbent priest. And yet those who do not profoundly know anthropology might be astonished to learn how much of our personal lives is influenced by all the ancient magical and religious beliefs connected with this one cult. The whole history of the decay and fall of gods, the extermination of divine hierarchies, could be told with just the Nemian cult as basis. In discussing in later pages the male comics of the screen who entertained troops all over the world during the war, I show how they may be considered modern medicine men or primitive priests, scapegoats who transferred to themselves the inner fears of the soldier striving to be brave and made cowardice and bravery alike into a kind of joke. Consequently in relation to my argument the myth is not, as a psychological or historical nucleus of fact, necessarily to be judged as true or false, illusory or real, according to its specific labels, its historic status, its literal beliefs. Essentially myths are not factual but symbolic. I assume that movies are essentially likewise.

Into the present book I have put a number of analyses I term "magic-lantern metamorphoses." Not only do these sometimes show how significantly a movie differs from the literary original from which it was made, but also I have tried to reveal that the conscious purpose of the screen story is by no means the true substance of its message. Briefly movies, similar to much else in life, are seldom what they seem. In this sense—being, to begin with, fiction —movies are dreamlike and fantastic, their fantasy and dreamfulness having actually come to the fore at the moment of writing as consciously embodying certain assumptions of my previous book. These assumptions are simple: (*a*) the existence of the unconscious mind as a dynamic factor in human action and (*b*) the tendency of screen stories to emphasize—unintentionally—neuroses and psychopathic traits discovered and formulated by psychoanalysis. Unaware of the precise function of the unconscious mind, Hollywood movie-makers are used to combining their own automatism of mental and physical behavior with that of the characters in their products. However, recent movies with psychiatric themes were *Shock, Spellbound,* and *The Seventh Veil;* recent movies more or less deliberately exploiting sexual symbolism or "Freudian" themes were *Gilda, Leave Her to Heaven,* and *The Dark Corner;* another film, *Out of the Night,* termed a "psychological mystery," dealt with the theme of divination by dream and introduced one of the current "evil" psychiatrists. Meanwhile the verbal psychoanalytical innuendoes in movies have increased with surprising speed. We should remember that a deliberate strategy of the movies has always been, because of popular prejudices and censorship laws, to state certain themes obliquely and to adapt the end strictly to the available means. Movie education in psychology may give cinema expression greater freedom of means, which would be a big step forward, but this would not necessarily lead to the consciousness of art. As I say in my fifth chapter, it is the photogenic quality of the dream that gives psychoanalysis a favored current place in screen art.

Preface

My logical reasons for positing *myth* as against *art*, the *unconscious* as against the *conscious*, as dominant values in American movies, were analyzed in *The Hollywood Hallucination* in considerable detail. The lack of individual control in movie-making in this country, the absence of respect for the original work, the premise that a movie is an ingenious fabrication of theoretically endless elasticity —all these positive and negative elements make for lack of form (or art) and specifically encourage the spontaneous growth of popular forms ("what the public wants"), thus leaving crevices for whatever there be in actor, dialogue writer, cinematic trick shot, or directorial fantasy to creep through and flower. Under such conditions the factor most likely to succeed in Hollywood would unquestionably be the mythic; that is, the basic vestigial patterns surviving in popular imagination and reflecting the unconscious desires and the secret remnants of the primitive belief in magic. It is not news that what is known as superstition has a powerful hold on the popular mind. What is not so generally realized is the extent to which the superstitious stratum of the human psyche lies below the surface, below the verbal and conscious fields of expression, and how great is the symbolic potential of the material there. It is perfectly logical that Hollywood's lust to display the *obvious*, the *sure-fire*, the *sensational*, guarantees for its products the latent presence of the most venerable stereotypes of emotion. Sometimes it is not a case of the survival of ancient patterns per se but of their strictly modern form and the place of that form in movie plot or character pattern;

examples of this are the folk myths of the absent-minded professor, of the efficiency expert, and of the eccentricity of genius—all considered in the chapter on schizophrenic motifs.

Naturally when I ally myth with superstition I am taking not only Frazer's view of the profound interrelatedness of myths but also Freud's view that beneath the upper levels of the mind lies a vast human capacity to think in terms of frantic passions and above all in terms of symbols. Even ten years ago it would have been thought impossible by movie moguls that a surrealist artist, Salvador Dali, should be employed to devise images to portray movie dreams, which in turn are subjected to psychoanalysis, a clinical process that provides the solution of the plot. In *The Hollywood Hallucination* I wrote of Hollywood's "Surrealist Eye" as an integral part of screen technique just a little before one of the companies was ready to welcome Dali as a employee.

The fundamental eye trickery that is a genius of the camera—you see the object, yet it isn't there—came to the fore in the movies and ever since then has mocked with its dynamic plasticity the very form from which it developed, the still camera. Today the movie has all the flexibility of the novel as well as the vision and speech of the stage. In striving through imaginative works to create the illusion of reality the movie screen must constantly transcend its own mirror nature of literal reflection. Camera trickery is really camera magic, for illusion can be freely created by the movie camera with more mathematical accuracy and shock value than by sleight-of-hand magic or stage illusion. The very homogeneity of cinema illusion— the images of the actors themselves are illusive, their corporal bodies absent—creates a throwback in the mood of the spectator to the vestiges of those ancient beliefs that I discuss in detail later in the chapter on supernaturalism, such as beliefs in ghosts, secret forces, telepathy, etc.

Moreover, the movie-theater rite corresponds directly to the profoundly primitive responses of the audience; the auditorium is dark, the spectator is relaxed, the movie in front of him requires less sheer mental attention than would a novel or stage play—less attention because all movement seems to exist on the screen; even the background changes easily, quickly; the whole world moves around the spectator, who is a still point. From the capacity of the screen for trick illusion, plus the dark-enshrouded passivity of the spectator, issues a state of daydream, which I termed in my previous book "the daylight dream" because it occurs in the dark: the screen is the focus of light, while the spectator is conscious in a darkness of the bedroom. It is in daydreams that magic seems to operate, in daydreams that things begin to seem rather than to be. "The movie theater," to quote directly from my previous book, "is the psychoanalytic clinic of the average worker's daylight dream." It is likewise in the process of psychoanalysis, where the *part*, truly recognized as symbol, transforms the meaning of the whole. The movie process is a complex myth of sheer synecdoche. People go to the movies merely to see a favorite player, or for the locale or period, or for the genre, or because they are bored almost to death. How, under these conditions, can anyone hope to appreciate the *whole* movie, especially since, to begin with, the movie can hardly be considered a whole?

No longer does man believe in myth or magic. No! For magic has been sifted and reorganized into science and governs only his material world, not the realm of his spirit, while comparative mythology and anthropology merely comprise school subjects. The sects of Christian religion have organized Western man's spiritual beliefs under one heading: the myth of Christ. Yet Christ's myth too can be related to pagan myths. The very fact that for children the Bible itself is but another series of fairy tales, weighted but little by a sense of historical fact, alone demonstrates my point as to the basic importance of myth with regard to popular or folk art. Our imaginary lives as children survive in us as adults and enrich our subsequent natures. So the fairy-tale lives of primitive races, our ancient antecedents, survive in the religions we formally believe in today as well as among those tribes still unassimilated to modern civilization. I do not claim any absolute value for the myth and magic of Hollywood or for those modern vestiges of the old Greek divinities I have dubbed "the gods and goddesses of Hollywood." On the contrary the principle I mean is one of relativity and metamorphosis rather than absolutism and changelessness: just as a word has synonyms—and antonyms—so has a myth. In psychoanalytical symbolism, the deepest symbolism of the mind, the identity of objects is established by a complex frame of reference in which an image may represent one of three objects or all three objects at once. If, then, I say that the actors of Hollywood are an enlarged personnel of the realistically anthropomorphic deities of ancient Greece, I do not indulge in a mere bit of verbal humor, satiric or otherwise; on the other hand neither am I proposing or assuming the existence of an unconscious cult of supernatural worship. I feel I am but calling attention to the fact that the glamour actors and actresses of the movie realm are fulfilling an ancient need, unsatisfied by popular religions of contemporary times. Those men and women who perform for us are human, as we are; they have homes, children, love affairs; they suffer and die. And yet a magic barrier cuts across the texture of our mutual humanity; somehow their wealth, fame, and beauty, their apparently unlimited field of worldly pleasure—these conditions tinge them with the supernatural, render them immune to the bitterness of ordinary frustrations. It does not matter if this thought is a mythological exaggeration. It is a *tendency* of the popular imagination. The secret of the power of Hollywood gods and goddesses is that they seem to do everything anyone else does except that when they die—in movies—they die over and over; when they love, they love over and over. Even as the gods do, they undergo continual metamorphoses, never losing their identities, being Rita Hayworth or Glenn Ford no matter what their movie aliases. And like Jupiter in the modern comedy, *Amphitryon 38,* they can condescend, even be ridiculous. All that the public demands is what it always gets—the power to make and break stars—but gods have always led basically mortal lives.

Lastly, in this and my previous book, do I have *a method*? Not in the sense that I am selling ideas, nor above all, is mine a method by which one can test the high or low esthetic content of a given movie; in the magic-lantern metamorphoses I do not analyze the best movies as the *artistic best* but as the *mythological best*. If my method is worthy of a label, it is "psychoanalytic-mythological," often socially angled. I have invented little or nothing. I have merely applied it to new material and formulated in accordance with the reapplication. That I speak metaphorically, in dream symbols, and, as in the climactic chapter, in terms of my own "hallucination," is a fact I wish not only to admit but to proclaim. Yes, I have made up a collective myth of my own, and I confess that in so doing I have plagiarized Hollywood exhaustively. If I have interpreted many things as dreams are interpreted, I cite as belated authorities recent movies of psychoanalytical themes and dream-symbol material. Indirectly, however, I have only been obeying Hollywood's own law of fluidity, of open and ingenious invention. If I have formulated an element of moviedom to be known as "the supernatural hush" and interpreted it as applicable at once to the hush of a cathedral, the hush of a psychiatrist's clinic, the hush of an isolated lovers' session on Riverside Drive, and the hush of the studio while Jennifer Jones does a scene in *The Song of Bernadette,* I feel that I am defining a quality of the movies as one would classify an acidic combination

in the laboratory. And if in one of the magic-lantern metamorphoses internal movie meanings are discussed in terms
of doubting the evidence of the senses, I am merely following the technique of psychoanalysis as well as paralleling
legal criticism of circumstantial evidence of crimes: *things
are not always what they seem.* I hope to have revealed a
deeper sort of truth than that to be found on surfaces and
at the same time to have assembled here a little mythology,
a kind of concordance, showing the frequently unconscious
magic employed by Hollywood—a magic of dream creation that far transcends its literal messages.

MAGIC AND MYTH
OF THE MOVIES

1. CHARADE OF VOICES

VOICES IN THE NIGHT

Relatively few movie patrons become analytical enough to be aware of the voice as an independent medium of artistic illusion on the screen. Yet, if we disembody it by shutting our eyes in the midst of the theater twilight and render it a purely aural force, emanating from night or nothingness, we can isolate it and catch in its dynamic structure factors we did not suspect were there. These voice factors seem the more piquant, perhaps, as we anchor them again to their origins by opening our eyes and measuring the degree in which they duplicate or echo, rather than qualify, the vocalists' visual presences. Of course the voice has considerably less responsibility in the movies than it does on the one hand on the stage and on the other on the radio—for obviously disparate reasons. On the stage it must bear about two-thirds of the illusion; on the radio all . . . *all*! Certain Hollywood voices already had good training, in the strictly elocutionary sense, because they were those of actors who had started in the legitimate theater. Ronald Colman proved again in *Kismet* that these vocal instruments, with their evident tattooing of drawing-room comedy with shadings of Hamlet's soliloquy, are distinctly identifiable, mostly because of their Britishness, and highly distinguishable from such workaday American voices as those belonging to the three Roberts—Taylor, Young, and Montgomery.

VOICES FROM THE SILENCE

The advent of the talkies gave fresh opportunity to those cinemactors whose vocal cords contained unexplored reaches of eloquence, while a definite quota of studio population promptly lost their jobs as a result or hung on till they scratched the then unreliable sound track and automatically faded. I recall how throughout an entire picture Priscilla Dean screeched like a cockatoo till it seemed certain someone would clamp a net over her. But strangest of all, a certain rising young Broadway star revealed superb screen diction, as I had anticipated, but also a vocal quality that was like a much-worn child's phonograph record at its highest pitch.

Moreover, the talkies took down the bars before musical comedy and set up house for tightly synchronized music scores on the same sound track as the voices. The red carpet thus unfurled was trod and made dusty and frayed by the feet of Jeanette MacDonald, Bing Crosby, and a cavalcade of unnamables. Flush with the microphone was also heard a sort of two-dimensional opera, allowing the more physically birdlike Metropolitan stars to reveal more pointedly whether or not they were capable of purely histrionic flights. None achieved a better mark than "whether," and most were "not."

Charade of Voices

To the front in sophisticated cinema sound devices is the vocal chorus, often quite unseen and indeed merely an extension of the orchestral score, which the advent of sound made a much more accurate means of accompaniment. Music now fills in all stretches of movie action in which the actors do not speak, and sometimes it is in the background even when they do. Frequently a soaring chorus will be introduced to help the climax of a picture, especially where the emotion is one of hope or triumph, something opening on "new horizons." The remote implication is that the desired outcome has been brought about by divine favor and that the chorus thus manifesting itself at the end is a heavenly chorus. After all, the voice, especially in choral volume, is no more artificial an aid than symphonic music itself. Recently *narratage,* the voice of a storyteller, usually one of the actors, has found favor; and it is plain that, however weakening this and other sound effects are to the pure cinematic principle, the screen has gained a fresh psychological dimension, which, as the indirect narrative, was always the property of the novel, and profits from the extra musical harmony that the sympathetic storyteller imparts in collaboration with the music score.

Such plural vocalizing, however, is beside the present examination of the rôle of the actor's voice as attached to a visible personality. In this situation the voice is not a mere medium for speech, normal or raised in song, and

3

assuredly in prose it must be a medium for a definite personality. The fact is that especially in the movies the voice often—as things in Hollywood are wont to do!—contracts the hallucination of a license sometimes little justified by taste or reason. With or without the permission of the actors to whom it belongs, it may behave like a bird out of its cage.

THE VOICE

No actor suggests this situation more strongly than one who seems to reverse it and to belong to his voice rather than be its possessor. I mean no other, of course, than he who goes by the curt cognomen of The Voice. He also reverses many a personal chronicle of the screen by having practically originated as a voice and gradually added to it a body. For he had reached the radio state of perfection even before he had made many personal appearances of importance. Having created such a thick curtain of sound before his concrete image, he had reduced the thing called personality by a rare and highly artificial simplification; on the stage he might have been a sort of Aladdin's lamp, from which, when it was touched by the conductor's wand, issued a vocal cloud that held the dim shape of a skinny youth in a demi-zoot suit. Here is something as startling and intriguing as the phenomenon of ventriloquism; indeed I think that if it be examined with scientific detachment in its more candid aspects, Mr. Sinatra's face will reveal a trace of Charlie McCarthy's. Charlie, too, has a detachable voice. I don't hint that young Sinatra does not deserve personal credit for every note he paints in such colorful glissandi. The miracle is that he *is* the source of the sound.

A very neat little myth burgeons forth in the train of such lyric magic. The Voice is the ventriloquist; Frank is the glamourized dummy, fortunate victim of a supernatural sort of hoax. Every bobbysox admirer of Frank's has a pragmatic notion of what I mean. It is just as if the sweet-expressioned but rather homely boy sitting next to her in class suddenly poured forth a torch song in tones hitherto thought the exclusive property of Nelson Eddy, Dennis King, or brotherly Bing Crosby. It somehow partakes of the marrow of the schoolgirl's dream that a voice dripping with the most nectarish sauces should originate in a diaphragm over which the suitable screen would seem to be a large school initial surrounded by a sweater. That the vocal phenomenon is, rather than a croon, actually a beatified groan lying precariously in the upper register is not precisely an accident. Anyone born with an adagio epiglottis like Frank's has a rendezvous with destiny.

Because as a matter of fact The Voice is that of the teenage Romeo who, with opportunities unrationed, was thrust into the spotlight vacated in the suburban lanes and ballroom crannies by the eligible young man gone off to war —the neighborhood Tyrone Power or Robert Taylor who abdicated the civilized sex struggle at the behest of Uncle Sam. Strip Sinatra to the skin, and probably you will find someone who is an ugly duckling to the football squad and the track team, but who, challenged by a profile or a biceps, will answer back fearlessly in a voice like a swan's neck. . . . Personally I think it is the rarest bleat that ever climbed with justifiable optimism up the throat of a man thinking of love. It makes little difference what songs he chooses or whether on the screen he is visible from the neck or the knees down. On his lips is the theme song of a boudoir Tarzan—not everything he might be in weight, it is true, but swinging, if the lady has a radio, from end to end of the Hit Parade and naked to the larynx. . . .

At one moment of his career it appeared that Frank wanted to act, whatever that connotes, whereas his producer wanted him to sing, while his only class rival, Bing Crosby, wanted to sing in defiance of Hollywood ukase that he act. I take no sides in these divisions among professional egos and their sponsors. Yet Bing, as another example of a personality nurtured into prize quality by main vocal force, seems to have outgrown his first period and to be causing Hollywood to think of him as a heart-winning mime, maybe with point. But if I had the alternative of being cornered by Voice Bing or Man Bing in an empty theater, I'd settle for "A White Christmas."

VOICES THAT LEARNED TO SPEAK ENGLISH

The personality of the individual, however, is not all that hangs on spoken syllables of the silver screen. Besides characterization of individuality and agedness, the latter demanded sometimes of a young actor, there is racial, regional, and national characterization. The problem of handling foreign stars was capable of helping to handle itself, for American movie audiences take easily to the glamour and spice of foreigners, including their accents. Therefore it was only automatic, for reasons behind and in front of the screen, to choose for foreign actors a fable either with a foreign background or showing the star surrounded, so to speak, by a familiar plot and a strange country. It was interesting to observe that when Garbo was called upon to say a few hundred thousand words, they managed for her to begin with doing a character whose social origin as well as whose nation accounted to some degree for the huskiness and abysmalness of tone that went along with her broken accent. Her accent was literally correct; that is, she was of an immigrant Swedish family, the Anna Christie of O'Neill's play of that name. It was a hit picture, largely because Garbo was enough of an artist to equate her personal style and acting with her voice; and incidentally her Anna remains one of her top performances despite a stubborn subjectivism, conceivably a spite campaign against her own Hollywood profession, which has prevented her from ever conceiving a part with proper objectivity. Previous to Garbo's talkie debut audiences were in the dark about the quality of her voice. But when it came, I was one of those ensnared by its bitter-chocolate color and notes that fell as securely into place as major chords on a harp.

American movie fans were soon educated to the fact that foreign actresses, exclusive of the British, who illustrated the opposite end of the scale, were inclined to speak with a delightfully dark brown taste. Dietrich's voice was charming and remains so, subtly weighting the fluffiest phrases with a pleasantly meaty content. Set at rather too low a key, Claudette Colbert's voice has found much favor for its vibrancy and good-sportiness, yet it is patently spoiled by nasality—not only the congenital kind but the cultivated sort of ambivalence between lower throat and nose that betrays a submerged but overflowing self-conceit. In color—or should I say Technicolor?—it is a sodden biscuity brown. Among foreigners, Elisabeth Bergner's voice is, like her acting style, brilliant, her accent being pure ornament. Luise Rainer's voice and accent, which seem to have departed from the screen, are also full of charm—perhaps a little too sentimental, a little cindery with tears, as Cinderella's must have been.

Of course just as at the introduction of sound there was the problem of proper speech articulation, foreign actors went through apprenticeships of qualified satisfactoriness until they eliminated the illusion of speaking broken English. Gradually, if an actor was seen enough and could make himself verbally plain enough, his accent was accepted as a convention. Yet for the screen and its mediocre standards of acting the addition of the voice, regardless of the subordinate problem of foreign accents, meant broken pantomime. If one sees the extraordinarily talented Lillian Gish in Griffith's *Way Down East* (1919), wherein her performance told everything in pantomime and very good pantomime, one can realize that the shifting of part of acting responsibility from pantomime to voice entailed laziness in the craft of screen acting, a deterioration in gesture and in everything that makes the actor an eloquent moving image. Indeed in Miss Gish's late acting days, when she must use a voice none too attractive or effectual, she seems commonplace and has evidently quite lost her touch . . . or was it Griffith's touch?

It is difficult to tell whether producers may not urge a star to maintain a minimum of accent to keep her foreign glamour. But the cases of Ingrid Bergman and Hedy Lamarr, when compared, show that much the better actress of the two, Miss Bergman, has an accent that stands in the way of her complete charm in that it appears and fades, roughens her quality, and actually causes her to muff words. Miss Lamarr's accent on the contrary never seems in the way but makes her speech a sublime sort of baby talk, as though she had just caused a marshmallow successfully to melt in her mouth. Miss Rainer's early accent was embarrassingly thick. As appurtenance to a comedy actress such as Carmen Miranda a thick accent pointing a broad sensuality makes for fun. A rarity in a foreign actress is Simone Simon's soprano speaking voice coupled with a charmingly suppressed accent. Her quality was particularly well used in *Curse of the Cat People*, in which she appeared as a fairy spirit, a child's imaginary playmate. Both her accent and preciously feminine voice with its hint of feline purr lent apt charm and exoticism to the rôle.

When we come to the foreign gentlemen, we find much less variety of voice than among the ladies, partially no doubt because there are not so many of them. Outstanding in Hollywood are the Sir Galahad organ tones of Charles Boyer, without which, in my opinion, he would be a strict mediocrity. Jean Gabin is a much better actor than Boyer, and when his voice not so long ago was revealed in English on the American screen, it maintained its interesting texture, one of more individuality than his rival's, sonorous as the latter is. Peter Lorre's German accent has a lot of color, enhanced by the personal quality of his voice. Equal difficulties appear among the men incumbents of English-speaking rôles. A competent actor, Conrad Veidt, could never make his English smooth. With respect to the French visitors, their normal speaking pace at home is somewhat faster than that in American films; so sometimes their speech in effect does not sound so uneven as it might if the American pace were more rapid.

VOICES THAT FIRST SPOKE ENGLISH, INCLUDING THE BARRYMORE

The convention of the British accent is of course universal in the English-speaking theater. So many well-known actors and actresses have crossed from Liverpool with secure faith in the future of their voices on the American screen that listing them would have no point. So far as the talkie went, Englishness lent not only fine vocal quality but an accent that brought elegance of social tone. The character of the quality was squarely divided between that appropriate to drawing-room comedy and that appropriate to Shakespeare, with the former of course the really utile weapon. Perhaps still the most individual in English character is the voice of Charles Laughton, although its overliquescence makes it sound sometimes, and not necessarily aptly, as sentimental as a flute or as self-pitying as an oboe. I investigated some of the consequences of the reign of the genteel British voice personality in my previous book on the movies. But I did not take cognizance there of the vocal tradition of the American stage, the Barrymores, all of whom have graced the movies with their silent and sounding presences.

Perhaps no more memorable voice has come to the screen than that of Lionel Barrymore, at least the elder Lionel, for the perfection of the talkies came somewhat late for the younger. This voice, despite the corn it must continuously shuck, is obviously a fine instrument; John's, clinging to youth and romantic comedy simultaneously and unable to forget that it too had a deteriorating profile, seemed a pale imitation of his elder brother's. John's voice was always subtly playing its own part; it was a narcissistic voice with ill-concealed contempt for the churlishness of those who could resist its manners. Hence, when John Barrymore used to suffer on the screen, one felt that his voice suffered rather than he. It was a voice that felt at home apparently only in Hamlet's black or Romeo's heliotrope, and yet when cloistered cozily in such heavenly precincts it proved that where one desires to be, and is, is not necessarily where—to others

11

—one seems at home. A bizarre auditory memory of the screen, for me, is *Twentieth Century*, in which the late Carole Lombard and the late John shrieked at each other periodically for half-a-dozen reels. It was difficult to believe that even in the service of a satiric comedy an actress and her director—the rôles played by the stars—could enter into such a marathon of slanging one another and call it life. But the film was amusing because it hinted the possibility of a voice complex as a prominent theatrical neurosis.

Exotically enough, the third member of the Barrymore "royal family," Ethel, lent her famed speaking talents to a recent movie, *None but the Lonely Heart*, in which she played an old cockney woman. I have always thought of Miss Barrymore as primarily a diseuse rather than a Duse. In this cockney rôle she is ill from an incurable disease, and although she plays a mother, she seems far more a Monument to a Mother. As an inert image she was very effective; as an animate image she was utterly without distinction; and as a speaking image she mixed her cockney accent with a dramatic style that suggested Clytemnestra rather than the kitchen. I admit that Miss Barrymore succeeded perfectly in looking ill. The coached dinginess of her tones, however, could not conceal the registry of dramatic diction, just as though it had come from the holes of some muted pianola record. Would it be barbarous to suggest that Miss Barrymore, in reference to the voice complex mentioned above, was concealing a dropsy of the vocal chords; that her voice had the apathy of an acrobat who has been told that, for reasons of health, he can no longer perform his favorite tricks? In view of the fact that Miss Barrymore's rôle was not in any really proper sense *acted,* especially in the sense that an actor *plays with others,* perhaps it is just to assume that she has a theatrical neurosis of the vocal sense. Now that I think of it, Miss Barrymore is the perfect image, in *None but the Lonely Heart,* of someone suffering from manic depressiveness of the larynx. Another actress in the same movie June Duprez by name, apparently French and for this film apparently a school-educated cockney, had an accent that placed her nationality out of this world—and by "out of this world" I don't mean so relatively familiar a part of geography as heaven.

No English player of fame has essayed the American screen in cockney rôles, I believe, but Gracie Fields, whereas from Ireland we have had at least two talented actors, Sara Allgood and Barry Fitzgerald, as well as the superb Irish-inspired acting of Scotch Victor McLaglen in *The Informer* with its brace of top-flight Irish rôles.

VOICES PLASTIC AND MADE PLASTIC

Victor McLaglen is a most fortunate and exceptional instance in the rich schedule of foreign duress on the duties of American- and English-born cinemactors, which sometimes provokes, from the knowing, faint ironic smiles. Not long ago Greer Garson plunged her bird-of-paradise tones and accent into the problem of being a nineteenth-century Middle Westerner; she just managed to keep her chin above disaster. It isn't ladylike for a screen actress to retain a trace of anything so local as a Brooklyn accent or a Southern drawl—for obviously practical reasons, of course. But men like Bogart and Robinson, even when not doing gangster parts, can do as they like with their accents, which are just plain American. Only the comedy lasses can go without having their accents lifted or getting the hooks off their consonants. Indeed, accent on the screen as in life is an index to social standing and educational background as well as a geography weathervane. On the Hollywood flickerscope American business men are usually not allowed to have Boston college-bred accents unless they are patently over thirty. As a rule the regulation romantic hero in his twenties finished college where he was born, although usually he also seems to have sneaked in a couple of profitable years at dramatic school and gained there first grip on what might be termed the well-dressed accent, the old masters of which are William Powell, George Brent, Ronald Colman, and so on. Today Fredric March, too, certainly rates postgraduate status, but I can remember very well how his voice grew up from picture to picture. Two male voices with an ingratiating and native nap are those of Joseph Cotten and Franchot Tone, both of them rather better than nice clotheshorses, chiefly because of their aural charm. Cotten's rich carpety crackle fairly emits sparks of sex appeal, whereas the drawlish tones of Franchot are mellowed with a Scotch-and-soda flavor that makes them very smooth young-man-of-the-world. Simply and solely as linguists, a Briton, George Sanders, and two Britain-inspired Americans, Laird Cregar and Orson Welles, deserve some of Mr. Winchell's orchids. That each gentleman's voice is—or was, in the deceased Cregar's case—superior to their lines has been announced every time they opened their mouths.

VOICES FROM VALLEY, MOUNTAIN, AND PLAIN

Regional characterization means, to American actors, doing hillbilly, Deep South, or cowboy parts; mostly directors have little trouble casting, for in Hollywood and elsewhere there are special courses that prepare for such contingencies. Some voices are naturals, such as that of the late Will Rogers and, better still for Hollywood guile, that of Gary Cooper with its flavor of cured rawhide and lingering tobacco. The American screen does not lean heavily on accent to portray regional and national character, however, but wisely enough prefers to let a polite illusion exist about this form of realism as about so many others; after all, the realities of voice form only one element of the whole charade. Especially when a star actress must essay a Deep South part, the shift from the normal way of speaking to that prevalent generally below the Mason-Dixon line has no more validity than this very line; an outstanding instance was Bette Davis' characterization of the heroine of *The Little Foxes*, which was fully as much a characterization of Tallulah Bankhead, who filled the stage part.

15

It happened that Miss Bankhead could fall rather easily into the fur-lined accent of the South, since she hails from Alabama. But it is also a fact that she served long terms on the English and American stage, so that it was possible sometimes to catch alien nuances in her accentuation. What developed in consequence when Miss Davis stepped into the vocal tradition of the rôle was that she imitated the London-overlaid accent of Miss Bankhead's South. . . . It may be hard to believe, but I think a proper linguistic analysis by those who have heard both ladies in *The Little Foxes* would confirm my opinion. Like American actresses who play Germans by producing a mild little accent, actors and actresses forget their vocal make-believe, especially at the high points; if no one on the set has objected, no one in the audience is supposed to notice.

TATTLE-TALE VOICES

Voices that tell on their owners, whether actors or not, are sometimes the creation of a situation in that person's life. In Bette Davis' case her success in the rôle of Mildred in *Of Human Bondage* created her screen personality, of which her voice is now the indispensable symbol. Mildred's whining, snarling, shrewish tones have never left this actress' linguistic manners. Among feminine character categories Miss Davis exemplifies the sarcastic woman, the legendary cat of colloquial esteem, and her rôles are selected to utilize the native quality of her voice, which, even in its pleasant moods, secretes those cynical harmonies that express a sophisticated, neurotic, artificial kind of femininity.

An artificial style may hint of multiple character reality; Jean Arthur's voice, dedicated exclusively to rather wacky comedy parts, is professionally cute in its sweet femininity, which ranges disconcertingly from *do* to *do* on the scale. Its shopgirl personality has lots of spunk, however, which seems the real base, so that when Miss Arthur essays the coy and helpless feminine, she seems to be posing, more or less deliberately according to the occasion, as a sissy. The opposite of a sissy feminine voice is Margaret Sullavan's, so husky with "human sympathy," as I believe it is called, that I have sometimes imagined its quality the result of a sort of fatigue, as though the lady had been carrying around a man-sized load of sentiment too long a time.

Hollywood's voice factory is an efficient institution. Its ideal is the sleight-of-accent adeptness that distinguishes Paul Muni. Some actors have quick-change vocal apparatuses. The voice of Ann Sheridan, for instance, is a peeling voice, just as one speaks of an eating apple. Let her roll back its ruffles, and you find, as was demonstrated in *The Doughgirls,* the voice of a lady wrestler.

FUNNY VOICES

Some of the voices of which I have spoken are doubtless capable of evoking our own raised in laughter, not only by

17

their verbal delivery but by their uniquely suitable and expressive quality. Some Hollywood linguists may be said to live off their voices because they're funny voices. Marjorie Main, with a facial expression like dry ice, has a gravel-shod voice with the emphasis of a stamping machine. Her success as the mother who denounced her son in the stage version of *Dead End* first brought her to public attention, and as a result she played the same rôle for the screen. However, beyond this bit of tour-de-force her rather villainous sincerity was unadaptable to Hollywood requirements; consequently they isolated her voice, let her cultivate its coal-bin croak, and asked her to be someone with a cynically humorous view of life. This made her a first-flight comedienne. In her duets with Wallace Beery in a film called *Rationing* she sounded like an ungreased coffee-grinder sparring verbally with a greased one, which was Mr. Beery.

Voices such as those of Zasu Pitts and the late W. C. Fields are unforgettable, because of their quality and also their pace and the way in which they are integrated with the actor's personality. The late Edna Mae Oliver had the same sort of voice, and the teamed voices of Laurel and Hardy somehow seem natural correspondences. Arthur Treacher, specialist in butler rôles, and Ed Wynn have voices artificially and rigidly inflected to suit their acting personalities. The trade-marked voices of comedians, indeed, entitle them to laughter from the audience at the first sound, even before their initial speech—be it merely five words—is finished.

VOICES THAT NO SPEAKEE . . .

Inevitably the assumed accent would find its hardest test on the screen with respect to racial characterization. In fantasy and romance almost any kind of ritual charade will suffice the flat luminous shadows of Hollywood. . . . An amusing one occurred in *Kismet*, in which the young sultan, who masqueraded part of the time as a gardener's son, was played by James Craig, a young man with some kind of Middle Southwest drawl, a genuine lulu. It was piquant to think that the accent might have been assumed to supply an *equivalent* for that of a common or "provincial" Arab, but this proved to be illusion, since Mr. Craig talked exactly the same way when he duly stepped back into his palace or spoke from his public throne. Hence one movie convention might be conceived as obtaining in the palace, another over its backyard wall. Really to justify the internal inconsistency presented by Mr. Craig's accent in conjunction with the accents of others in the film one must delve to a profounder and nonlinguistic level of symbolism and say that Mr. Craig is the wish projection, tall, strong, and good-looking as he is, of American boys from eight to eighty years of age who have read the *Arabian Nights' Entertainments* and imagine themselves as its heroes—with, as in dreams, the local accent retained intact. In the same picture Dietrich as a blonde harem queen had to be accounted for in a country of damsels with coal-black tresses, so she was made out to be a gift, on tentative terms, from conquered Macedonia; thus through Technicolor coincidence, one might say, the estrangement of La Dietrich's still pleasantly German accent in Arabia is symbolically accounted for. Sometimes certain studios acquire stories with a foreign setting simply because they have a lot of foreign players idle on their payroll whom they want to utilize all at once. Although supposedly all of one nationality, it makes no difference whether they have come from Macedonia, Germany, Arabia, or France with their accents tagging behind them. . . . Basically they're all so many Chinese laundrymen to the majority of the great movie public!

When, as happened in *Dragon Seed*, Hollywood has the double difficulty of drama and Chinese drama, it has a genuine linguistic problem that cannot be ignored. In this movie, although all the characters are Chinese or Japanese, only minor parts were filled by actual members of these races—unless, as may well have happened, the presumptive Japanese were really Chinese. It was an undesirable contingency that, although Katharine Hepburn's features lent themselves well to Mongoloid interpretation by the make-up artist, her inherent vocal make-up—of the pronounced dramatic-school type, indelibly personal, and Bostonian to boot—resisted deportation to a foreign hemisphere. At times one caught its familiar little singsong quality helping the illusion of Oriental speech as Occidental ears hear it, but its Hepburn trade-mark always tagged the illusion. Katharine's is a voice of schoolgirl dreams, and no amount of implicit cinema weddings ever quite make it into the Voice of Experience.

In the same movie something parallel happened with the voices of the Chinese-by-courtesy Walter Huston and Akim Tamiroff, which remained respectively American and Russian. The studio adopted the superficially intelligent device of using for all a formally Anglicized vocabulary, holding suggestion of ceremoniously Oriental turns of speech. At least this imparted some unity, but, as merely formal, this unity engaged in a perpetual struggle with the disuniting principles of the separate accents. I wonder if the unity would not have been aided by consistent adoption of a clarified, even poeticized pidgin English. This may well horrify those who will instantly say, "But these people are not supposed to be Chinese laundrymen living in America!" To which I would counter: "True. But neither are they supposed to be Americans and Americanized foreigners acting in a movie laid in China."

AND THE VOICE OF LAUREN BACALL

I had not heard Lauren Bacall's voice until I saw her in her first picture as Humphrey Bogart's leading lady in *To Have and Have Not*. There is something foreign about Miss Bacall's linguistics in the way that the foreign inheres in continuously strange things that have somehow taken root among us or hang onto the fringes, such as phonetic spelling, Basic English, and Esperanto. What a tantalizing problem the lady's voice was for me till I had solved it by analyzing her curious personality! An embodied manner-ism rather than an actress and suggestive in face and figure of another suddenly successful schoolgirl, Katharine Hepburn, Miss Bacall yet seemed far less fresh, less breathless and individual, than Miss Hepburn was in her first screen appearances. For one thing she recalls other young and notably undistinguished actresses, such as Gene Tierney and Rita Hayworth. In some curious fashion she seemed to have all the poise of a veteran until it registered that this poise was basically self-conscious—stiff, superficial, and monotonous.Then I began to see what Miss Bacall was about. The rôle in the movie might have been written by herself and was certainly acted in bland disrespect for any indication in the script that her Slim was a certain type of person. I am sure that many a Hollywood actress who remembers her earliest desire to reach Hollywood heights in the first pitched battle, without a difficult apprenticeship, envied Miss Bacall her calm deadliness and equipoise on the tightrope of her first big rôle. It would seem that this young actress, from the distance of dramatic school, had worshiped such glamourous, sophisticated, and despotic queens of movie love as Garbo and Dietrich and perhaps some of the crisp and mellow sirens of the French screen; she had decided that beyond question she could be just as glamourous, sophisticated, despotic, crisp, and mellow as they, and why not? She possessed enough of the juice of confidence to feel quite at home when the opportunity came to show that she felt domestic—and how!—in the presence of a hard-to-get leading man such as Humphrey Bogart. . . . Meanwhile I was still transfixed by the conundrum of her voice, almost without inflection, low and lazily paced, with a pleasant burr of the Dietrich sort but not classifiable as to its true sources. Yet it happens to have a perfect index. I can imagine the triumph in Miss Bacall's youthful mind when she saw her film tests, those that perhaps won her the job, and reassured herself: "There's the evidence!" That she approached Hollywood with a certain Machiavellianism, I think, is shown by the mild Mephistophelian peaks of her eyebrows. Yet all of us are human; the most sensational military plans, even if the army wins, sometimes go kerflooey. Miss Bacall had evidently intended her voice to give notice that she was a Garbo to the gizzard, hard to get, and not going to let Humphrey triumph at the first shot. But certain laws of reality modify the most talented strategies. Miss Bacall might not have bothered to consider that she was in a movie or that Humphrey Bogart couldn't just as well be called "Humphrey" or "Bogie." She might have considered that she was what she was—an ambitious young actress trying to make a big impression on a Hollywood hero. And it seems no dislocation of genuine reality to conceive this scene between Mr. Bogart and Miss Bacall as virtually that between a young actress asking a big star for a chance at acting a part in his next picture and even—as Miss Bacall does in the movie—putting on a little act of being pathetically broke, stranded, and with no future. By no means of course do I imply that this was the case but merely that the structure of Hollywood reality is such that a little charade of this sort with symbolic content might easily occur as a routine even if involuntary collaboration between actor, director, and script-writer. It happened that despite the smokiness of Miss Bacall's voice and its insolently shaded surface it revealed, just as Dietrich's or Mae West's reveals, its underlying incendiary motive. . . . A sudden illogical breakdown took place in her carefully conceived delaying action à la Garbo. Her schoolgirl emotionalism rushed to the fore. This was too good an opportunity to miss—and lo! she reverted to movie type and became the vampire, cynically exultant on the doorstep of her triumph. Humphrey gives signs of being snared . . . and Miss Bacall has a permanent job as a siren. It was amusing to notice, however, the almost inadvertent revelation of a certain entirely unaffected emotion on Miss Bacall's part, of a sort that can only be described as "hot." Even though the act has been staged and Humphrey, despite reflexive squirms, is apparently in the toils, she cannot resist carrying the plot's action a little ahead of itself and showing how jealous she is and is going to be of other women in her man's life, looking upon "incidents" as no more than opportunities to express the down-to-earth status of her love. Then during the course of the picture Miss Bacall sang. Her voice was dry but heavy, like a cordial. But still conceiving her as the stage-struck imitator of Dietrich, I heard only the shadowy resonances of Dietrich's voice—and then a little later it burst on me. Miss Bacall, despite her cosmetic coating of sibylline trance extending from stem to stern, is actually in voice and personality a torch singer with a trace of the low-down blues in her temperament. So I saw her as a kind of monster, with a special, fire-extinguisher kind of charm. The flat, low, uninflected voice was simply a de-chemicalization of the rampant and fiery juices in the vocal equipment of such unrestrained ladies as Gertrude Niesen. Then, because I had recently heard the song, "Patty Cake Man," I recalled the precise intonation and quality; they existed in the voice of Ella Mae Morse, the Cow Cow Boogie Girl . . . here was Miss Morse's looping contralto lyricism lassoed into tacit, sophisticated prose; I offer Miss Morse's record and Miss Bacall's movie as evidence. It was as though Miss Bacall had by some extraordinary concatenation of circumstances fallen heir to an experiment similar to those so frequently seen in "scientific" thrillers.

As an Ella Mae Morse personality she was injected with a Garbo serum, which took sensational effect but not rapidly enough. Before the new personality could set, with its somber sounds, mysterious poise, and skyscraper chic, the old personality broke through, asserting its vocal and temperamental heresies and giving the home-town girl—a New Yorker, I believe—a place in Hollywood heaven. Result: a new star, Lauren Bacall.

THE VOICE OF ANTICLIMAX

After writing the above I learned with a degree of amused surprise that Miss Bacall's singing voice in *To Have and Have Not* was not even mechanically produced by herself. A Hollywood columnist reported that it was that of a boy cleverly dubbed in. I could not see that this assumed fact disturbed even a comma of my analytical reconstruction of the essential Bacall. But it did exaggerate the dimensions of the synthetic screen personality known as Lauren Bacall. That Hollywood has its peculiar magic and myth is the theme to which I dedicate this book; hence I enthusiastically welcomed this fresh piece of evidence, only to learn eventually that indeed the voice was dubbed in but was that of an anonymous young woman noted for her masculine vocalistics. I would say now that Miss Bacall's analytical equation balances even better, with Cow Cow Boogie the power of every integer on both sides. Her Hepburnesque Garbotoon, clearly confirmed in her subsequent pictures, equals Dietrich travestied by a boyish voice.

Yet could we have supposed that in 1946 Hollywood would leave a trick in Walt Disney's factory unturned to magnify the dimensions of its vocal myth? After *The Three Caballeros,* Disney's nadir of bad taste, in which Mickey Mouse, Donald Duck, and Joe Carioca, a parrot, court and cavort with the photographed flesh of human females, one was justified in any expectation for the future. Not that *The Three Caballeros* failed to illustrate a sexual charade in terms so blackboard that it would be useless to rehearse them. A later Disney, *Make Mine Music,* although it included a visual crime exposing two ballet dancers, not in person but via silhouette, also had a dahlia of a voice charade picked fresh from the magic garden of movie inspiration. It is a skit called "The Whale Who Wanted to

Sing at the Met," starring the voice of Nelson Eddy in all the singing parts. Its imaginative premise devolves on the possession by a whale—quite a cute little whale, though bigger than the Met stage—of a trio of human voices with which he can sing all at once. One admires the super-Arabian Nights prodigality of the inventors of this fable, who assigned to a whale not only human vocal chords but three sets of them. When Tetti-Tatti, the great impresario, sets out to find the singing whale, Willie finally sees the chance to realize his life's ambition and grasps it; swimming along by the yacht, he serenades Tetti-Tatti.

But Tetti-Tatti is only human, not a whale, and evidently not conversant with the esthetic conventions of Disney animations; hence, a rigid logician and philosophic naturalist, more or less, he has concluded that Willie has swallowed an opera singer, and desirous of saving such a brilliant talent, he orders the yacht's gun fired at Willie. It is hard to understand how Tetti-Tatti imagines that a living opera singer can be liberated safely from the dead body of a whale. But perhaps, even if not a biblical fundamentalist with Jonah in mind, he is as temperamentally unbalanced as some of his stars. In any case the sailors, sympathetic to Willie's silvery tones, refuse to fire the gun. Then Willie, to increase his impression on Tetti-Tatti, lets go with his trio of voices. This, sadly enough, serves only to triple the impresario's determination to shoot Willie, since now he feels he can save three singers—a tenor, a baritone, and a bass. At last the frantic Tetti-Tatti has to fire the gun himself. Willie is hit. He sinks. His life is ended. But Willie's

27

voice, magically enough, continues and multiplies into a chorus of voices that goes singing eternally on.

First I was struck with the fact that never before had I found it bearable to listen to Nelson Eddy. Yet as Willie he had a naïve coquettish charm that seemed quite pleasing. Willie's ambition to sing at the Met, lodged in a whale's body, seemed most understandable, and when he died, I was saddened. Then I began brooding on Hollywood's vocal charade and the neurosis of its vocalists, and then Willie's three voices and the ensemble of voices came back to me —and the obvious satire of his bulk on the bulk of opera singers in contrast to the charm of their voices. And then I thought of Nelson Eddy's implicit ambition, like that of every serious singer, to perform at the Met, and I realized that it was only common sense to suppose that this was Nelson Eddy's charade. Nelson Eddy is not a whale but a man who, in the opinion of his admirers, ought to sing at the Met.

But naturally a hitch in the reasoning appears. What has stood between Nelson Eddy's person and the stage at the Met? Not his face or figure, for he is a streamlined rather than whale-lined figure of a man, but the very voice that fictionally arouses Tetti-Tatti's crusading zeal. So a paradox is here; "The Whale Who Wanted to Sing at the Met" is another movie myth. It is not Ezio Pinza or even Nino Martini whose voice is dubbed in for Willie's but literally someone who has never gained laurels at the Met. So what have we? Surely a parable, a moral tale, of real folk caliber. Many a person physically more pleasing than

90 per cent of the Met stars has spent his or her life being trained to sing grand opera. But no soap. Radio, yes; concert performances, perhaps; the movies, if lucky. But the Met, no! The ironic twist to Disney's miraculously deft little fable is that the physical-vocal ratio of frustrated Met aspirants is inverted in it. Willie, theoretically, has the right voice but the wrong figure, as well as—it is only factual to add—the wrong species.

Is it revenge on whalelike Met figures that streamlined non-Met singers want? This Disney fable affords them their revenge. And even if Nelson Eddy had no direct hand in this inspired charade, its inventors are speaking for him and his wistful class, the ones with fine figures and good-looking faces but with voices that do not make the grade. Very well, in the dream world of these beings, forever barred from the Met by a fortuitous idiosyncrasy of the vocal chords, might not the guilty impresario, Tetti-Tatti, assume the aspect of someone tricked by a quirk of nature into turning criminal and destroying the whalelike beings whom in his right senses he allows on the stage at the Met? At the same time what pathos inheres in the subjective dream transposition of the frustrated singer, who imagines his own voice substituted for that of the human whale who really sings at the Met . . . his own voice, which must perish beyond the paradise of the Met's golden precincts because of Tetti-Tatti's mad hallucination. The Disney fable works out perfectly as dream symbolism. The sense of doom it is that causes Tetti-Tatti at once to recognize the merits of disappointed singers and to destroy them. This sense of doom belongs to the frustrated singer dreamers—indeed, in terms of Willie's infinitely multiplied voices, of all the singer dreamers who wanted to sing at the Met and, beautiful as they might be, never have.

Surely Nelson Eddy's Met-angled voice is par excellence the Voice of Anticlimax to end the Voices of Anticlimax.

2. HIGH, LOW, COMEDY JACK, AND THE GAME

The most traditional conception of the comedian is that he is low. He was the king's shadow and parody, the unserious essence of the king that by some dialectic law of nature came to his rescue in his darkest moments and by pointing out the ultimate absurdity and vanity of life afforded him a salutary detachment, a respite that psychologically caused him to bear misfortune or anxiety with more grace. Therefore the most beautiful clown I can think of is the Fool, companion of Lear; for seeing the mad old king, the Fool knows his liege is beyond the medicinal aid of comic philosophy, and so is humbled—having been robbed of his own meaning, comedy, in the presence of a victim deprived by insanity of the noble significance of tragedy. Lear is a poor, bereft person in great trouble, a man fallen lower even than the Fool, not only because he actually has fallen from a great height but because, being completely irrational, he does not know he is being a fool. Here the Fool, like the king, is thrown out of his job.

In modern civilization and especially in the movies the low estate of clowns is a lucrative profession and therefore raised to such a lofty commercial level that it is quite natural to call Chaplin, for instance, the King of Comedy. If the clown has any socio-psychological function, it is no longer to console kings, for clowns are not privately maintained even by industrialists or financiers, whereas public careers are automatically open to them. But naturally a still deeper reason exists for their absence from the ranks of domestic retainers. Their lowness would provide no really dramatic contrast with the natures of their masters. All that personal power in society today can command in the way of the clown is the stooge, often on the surface a quite serious character whose status is not actually that of an employee. But a stooge essentially is only a clown's servant—the butt, the foil, of the master comedian. On the American screen there used to be a rather mediocre comedian who had a string of stooges; at one point of his success he abandoned them, but their training was good; they managed to stage an amusing act of their own, and they are performing today under the professional name of The Three Stooges. Through his mask of the perennial underdog the truly great clown achieves a subjective independence of style in his profession of art.

I recall a French movie, whose title I forget, in which one can see the origin of all modern clowns and the prototype indeed of all movie comedians of today. He was a Frenchman of the sixteenth century whose rhymes used to delight the Parisian populace and help them to forget they were hungry. The plot of this film was concerned with how this idol of his people, a tailor by vocation, a poet and singer by avocation, mediates between the rebellious anger of the populace and the haughty indifference of the nobles until his tricks actually avert a revolution. The point was that he loved fun and had a sincere, albeit realistic, admiration for the aristocracy. In the end he proves entertaining not only to *hoi polloi* but to the palace gentry. But he is paid, you may be certain, by the queen's lover, the cardinal. Here the clown was servant to the noble class as in olden times, but in this case he was an economic stooge. Diplomats and other strategists, we may note, employ less obviously comic stooges.

It seems not farfetched to draw a general parallel and say that Chaplin and the numerous latter-day galaxy of funny men, in making millions laugh, help them to bear their troubles, especially their economic troubles. After all, this is a function which is not exactly news. Movie comedians such as Bob Hope and Joe E. Brown were among the most active and indefatigable of entertainers at army camps. And they repeated the ancient pattern of distracting the mind from the serious and troublous matters on which it was engaged. Comedians, along with singers, were most frequently called upon to entertain soldiers and sailors, not only because one-man shows such as Hope are much more portable than whole casts and orchestras but because Hope and others like him are spontaneous, funny, ad lib, and become pals across the footlights with their hordes of listeners. They knew what made the common man laugh and momentarily forget the seriousness of the fighting job he had to do.

Our democratic structure is such that it reinstates with reference to the clown a tradition much more ancient than the relatively recent divine right of kings that developed the institution of court fool. Even in the democracy of ancient Greece, not so very distant from us, kings and heroes and the gods themselves were not immune from travesty as the butts of satire. Those who govern today are denoted as "public servants," "servants of the people," etc., and we know how viciously they may be caricatured by political rivalry in the guise of newspaper cartoons. Among the most primitive tribes of the earth even up to this time a king is much more a real public servant than many may imagine. Once in human history kings almost everywhere were literally the prisoners of the people, while priests and generals were their jailers. Life has revolved similarly with the institution of the medicine man, the ancient magician, who was likewise a public servant, often imitating the duress of his clients in illness or childbirth and so lightening their physical and mental burdens. The modern clown is the inheritor of part of the medicine man's rôle as public benefactor, and in societies of high cultural development in the nearer centuries he has continued to relieve tension, caused by high matters and the tragic aspect of destiny, through mimicking them as though they were shallow affairs. His ability to do this according to his own tradition is an idiosyncratic immunity to normal human feelings, the clown being, generally speaking, too ugly, deformed, or foolish to have serious sentiments.

At one time the king himself was a magician, but with the advent of a planetary religion placing all power in an invisible, remote, and omnipotent being, not human at all, the king became the victim of tragic destiny by his persistence in keeping a vain supernatural image of himself. Therefore his mimic or stooge, the medicine man, was divided in two; in one personality he was the court physician with the specifics of medieval medicine, and in the other he became the fool; thus one was the minister to the king's physical being, the other the minister to his spiritual being in its worldly aspect—since in its supernatural aspect it was supervised of course by a prelate of the church. The court fool was the king's personal property—as close or closer, as such, than his own queen.

Today the generic clown as public entertainer is the circus clown, whose fantastically painted face and professional costume separate him from the civilized human being and render him a sort of savage mask and fabulous apparition. But it was a natural consequence that we should have got, eventually, a Canio, the wearer of a disguise, a character who inevitably passed from the modern operatic stage to the movies—and, in the latter, with what ineptitude! The clown of *Pagliacci* is the naturalization, so to speak, of the commedia dell' arte myth of Pierrot, whose heart is broken by Harlequin's sweetheart, Columbine; for the brokenhearted clown is not elementally a mimic, a pure professional or eccentric, as the ancient myth of the clown implied, but a real man, whose heart may be really broken—an amateur as well as a professional. Still another example of the naturalization of the clown is the modern play, *He Who Gets Slapped*, likewise Hollywoodized. It is quite logical, therefore, that Chaplin himself, the great wistful clown of the movies, should have added to his repertory a film called *The Circus*.

Chaplin has been greater than any of the others, not

only because he is a greater pantomimist than any comedian I know of but because he is the strict humanization, in mythical terms, of the traditional clown. His history as a movie mime bears increasing witness to an accent on a serious or relatively realistic treatment of pathos and the emotion of love, with its concomitant of chivalric courage. As his pictures became longer, he could the better introduce such a theme and tone into the more involved plots. But as a matter of fact I feel that the more serious treatment, parallel with a certain modernizing, proved a loss to Chaplin's art, because his best pictures in my opinion are *The Gold Rush* and *City Lights*, which come at the beginning and end of his middle period, before he began to invest his work with what might be called conscious social content.

In *City Lights* there was a most revealing master-slave, knight-clown relationship brought down to the present and showing the split that may occur in aggressive ruling-class personalities as the result of ambiguously acquired temporal power, a split that accounts in our society for the more usual symptoms of megalomania. In this movie Charlie was a tramp who ran into a rich man in his cups and who became the recipient of his kindness to such an extent that he found himself established in the man's home, but finally emerging from his alcoholic bout, Charlie's patron sees him with detestation as great as his former love for him and drives him out. The comedy of alternating drunken affection and sober aversion continues to the bewilderment of Charlie, with many hilarious chases and

embraces. The analysis is fairly simple: the gross culture
of the class of rich men in our time, with its necessary con-
cessions to money standards and materialistic thinking,
engenders an inner spite toward easygoing, humorous fellows who take life lightly—that is, fellows epitomized by
Charlie's tramp, who can't seem to earn a decent living;
when in their cups, however, these hard-boiled, well-upholstered gentlemen relax and think up dreams of a truer
grandeur wherein they can regard poor fools as symptoms
of cosmic irony and as delightfully amusing, because by
them they measure their own high estate. However, in the
arid chambers of complete sobriety or modern common
sense, Charlie becomes a moral allergy, there being no
room for him in a society which binds wealth to poverty
in so mechanical, direct, and compromising a manner.
The point is that there is actually not complete forgetfulness of his drunkenness in the turncoat behavior of the
rich man toward Charlie, although the simple convention
of the comedy would make it seem complete, but rather a
fatal memory by whose dim dream he accurately measures
his present state; for he sees Charlie as two people, and
both are himself: one is himself before he made or inherited
all his money, and the other is the part of himself that,
languid, human, smiling, and ironic—like Charlie—had
told him unavailingly that material success was all too
much trouble, all too ephemeral. That easygoing self he
all too coldly destroyed, but he hankers for it whenever he
gets drunk, which indeed may be why he does get drunk;
and lo!—it happens to appear incarnate in the little tramp,

Charlie! Yet Charlie seems to him, after he has sobered up, the self he relentlessly drove out, and, some compulsion arising, he must do so again, especially as the tramp is a phantom of the class created and maintained by inordinate wealth. Here the rich man, thrown out of his job of magician-king, a supernatural being, is forced to drive the true clown out of his life, for he evokes only memories of his former forgotten glory, when he hallucinated his grandeur so successfully that he could laugh at it with his fool.

In considering Chaplin we must not overlook the basic things about so universal a comedian. First, he is short— and in the literal sense of stature therefore is *low*. One cannot conceive a tall comedian very well, unless a comic butler, and I note that of tall comedians only one stands out in my mind, and that is a woman: Charlotte Greenwood, of stage and screen; but after all, excessive height in a woman is correspondingly as absurd as excessive diminutiveness in a man. Moreover, Mr. Chaplin is no Adonis even out of his comic mask. Yet his private life tells us bountifully that he has always been filled with the tender emotion and that his filmic amours are no mere professional charade. As Charlie, the early screen figure, he is a homely, quaint little man, very shy of women, to whom, however, he is very sentimentally attracted. He is as chivalrous as Don Quixote—and indeed is a curious compound of Don Quixote and his servant, Sancho Panza. Of the fusion of the Don's romanticism with Panza's servility and gross humanity a sweet clown was born. I should mention that Chaliapin, acting Quixote in a little-known English movie, gave a truly resplendent performance in what was a rather mediocre production. We well know that Quixote is the knight rendered comic through anachronistic manifestation. From the Don's viewpoint the common sense of his servant is as incongruous as his own conduct is in the eyes of Panza. But this means ironic comedy, a genre very alien to Hollywood. In that fabulous and Gargantuan hamlet on the West Coast ironic comedy takes place only in life. It is poetically ironic that Chaplin's own life should have provided one of the leading examples of this several years ago in the charge of paternity lodged against him in court by an unfortunate young woman. Chaplin's chivalry myth of the Wilson, Harding, and Coolidge eras became more and more pathetically frail as the stuff of life until, seen in the transparent and slightly cruel high lights of the Roosevelt era, it was almost nonexistent. However innocent Mr. Chaplin may be—it seems the law was helpless to pronounce him actually so—it is obvious that he is only human and that while living much in the public eye as a modern man and a great professional, he is subject to the hard logic of these realities. His artistic mask of the modern clown (Quixote-Panza) has been rudely broken, and he becomes, his chivalrousness assumed, a Quixote caught in a trap typical of the Panzas—the nonidealistic middle class; so in a sense the Cervantean comedy achieves a peculiar echo in modern life. As a public servant Chaplin erred; he permitted his professional myth to be marred in the eyes of millions by exposing that he is also a man and modern. It was prophetic when Chaplin said, "The tramp is dead." He might have said, "The Don is dead." For how can he ever again fly with all the courage of Mickey Mouse to save and forever after succor the honor of some charming damsel—and receive as a result the wholehearted tribute of sympathetic laughter?

The classic early comedians of the movies—Buster Keaton, Fatty Arbuckle, Harold Lloyd, Chaplin—were or would have been exempted from the drafting of comic talent for troop entertainment "in person" if for no other reason than that they are not, or were not, gagsters; their art originated with the silent screen and is, or was, closely connected with action and situation. Fred Allen, Jack Benny, Bob Hope, Joe E. Brown, Red Skelton, Danny Kaye, and the rest, are zanies with varying degrees of talent who are abstracted smoking-car entertainers, outfitted with grimaces and gestures rather than anything that could be known by the dignified name of comic pantomime; Hope, Skelton, and Kaye have their mannerisms and their numbers, but it is not the same thing. Certain animated animal inventions of pen and ink are so much funnier on the screen than anything a human professional clown can invent today that not the least comparison between them is justified. At the same time it is evident that the human clowns love their work and assuredly are sometimes funny.

Radio and movie publics combined, the most popular of the clowns are Hope, Benny, and Allen—all famous radio men, inheritors of the vaudeville tradition of patter, funny sayings, gags, and puns that intersperse song or dance routines. Yet these particular mimes can neither sing nor dance; they are the M.C.'s, pure and simple, who have somehow managed to make the true performers their stooges; Allen and Benny, with their vocal buffoons of the air waves, are top examples. If we look at life for their counterparts, we find at a place little removed, vertically speaking, a woman—Elsa Maxwell; in short, the professional hostess. When Allen and Benny perform on the radio, they are bringing into the home the life of the party, which the home's gatherings lack. Yes, professional performers have superseded the local gagsters, the small-town funny men; and what were these performers at the army camps but temporary professional hosts?

Such hosting clowns resembled, too, the local faces; in other words, they have no motley but what some whim of nature may have given them, such as the bags under Allen's eyes and Jimmy Durante's ex-nose. I wish to point out, incidentally, that great professors of fun like Allen and Benny confirm their parallel with the medicine man of ancient times and religions as no great exaggeration; they are fun doctors—Allen, for one, is a savant in his field—and they have a suave bedside-blues manner. But Benny and Allen are mummies in comparison with the lively gait in grimace and gesture characteristic of Red Skelton, Bob Hope, and recently Danny Kaye.

If we compare all the comedians, who have moved in on Hollywood and made it their own, with a far more subtle jester, a pure pantomimist, an individual case, Jimmy Savo, we are on a different level of art. Savo's pattern was a little gauzy for movie patrons; he did not succeed in

Hollywood, although in New York, on stage and in night club, he seemed able to carry on. Here again is the professional triumph of the hard-boiled, closer-to-life of comedy art over the pathetic and fragile cartoons of more genuinely theatrical clowns. Savo has a marginal relation to Chaplin and such other comics as Hugh Herbert, the schizophrenic fussbudget, and the late W. C. Fields, the Dickensian red-nose, in what may be called the Milquetoast motif in modern humor. And now we come upon pungent juxtapositions in our foray into high, low, comedy jack, and the game. . . .

One of the great characteristics of the fool, a part of his natural unfitness, was that, unlike his masters, the king and the knight, his blood was presumably mixed with water. He had the opposite of a warrior's courage: he was a coward. As we know, the classic comic heroes of the slapstick screen—Chaplin, Lloyd, Keaton—all had innate courage if also physical and temperamental drawbacks. Chaplin especially tried to crossbreed the knight and the fool, unite chivalry with the craven and eccentric. We realize that traditionally the underdog rises up, the worm turns. But this is not the professional essence of the matter. The rôle of the clown, mythologically speaking, is still to provide a contrast to the knight, to illustrate by a kind of magic that the knight may project on the fool—who accepts it—every base qualm or cowardly quaver and thus purify his knighthood. So what did we have in the army camps where performed movie comedians like Hope and Skelton, whose dominant make-believe characteristic is identically a jittery sort of cowardice? We had the fool, as of old, continuing his inheritance from the medicine man and purifying the knight, reassuring him that he is bold and brave and nothing else, that only fools—the mentally or physically deficient—are cowards.

It is curious and instructive to note the extent to which the effeminate is also identified with the traits of the fool. For women and fools are traditionally—even if, today of all days, anachronistically—often lumped together: "only a fool or a woman," etc. Part of the routines of Hope, Skelton, and Kaye is female impersonation, merely a logical extension of their character idiosyncrasy of cowardice. I recall that in one movie the talented Skelton gave, without benefit of costume, a pantomimic imitation of a young woman arising from bed in the morning and performing her entire elaborate toilet: it was extremely funny and authentic; and in the same movie he joined a ballet class of young women and vied with them in pirouettes, leaps, and *entrechats*. He was far more graceful than some of the young ladies, although presumed, considering his football player's physique, to be excruciatingly inept. In fact the hard-boiled quality of all this, the palatable flavoring, is that gents such as Hope and Skelton are huskies, their physiques thus belying their unstable guts. Oddly enough, concomitant with the gelatinous state of their courage—incidentally, I think that Hope wins the chocolate cake for sustained trembling—is an almost pathological susceptibility to the ladies; this trait stresses the little-recognized tradition that the tender emotion is incompatible

with the warrior's character. At any rate, so far as the blood
of comedy jacks is concerned, Sparta may be considered
as perpetually at war with Athens: the virus of war and
abstinence versus the virus of art and love.

Danny Kaye, outstanding recent arrival in the realm of
outfacing the camera, is slender, unlike his brother Panta-
loons of similar type, and has a more varied repertory
than any of the other male comedians who carry onto the
set a white rose in their lapels and a red one in their hearts
—or would it be vice versa? Like his female counterparts
(Joan Davis, Betty Hutton, and Cass Daley), Danny sings,
dances, and has a stylized violence that is foreign to the
Milquetoast mold. It is not that he is so much a coward—
like the others, he is capable of spasmodic bravery—as
that he is temperamentally uninterested in militancy, in
being the professional modern knight, the soldier; hence
his first movie, *Up in Arms,* in which he plays a hypo-
chondriac with the draft-board jitters, is in exactly the
right groove. Although the military pattern is inescapable,
Danny with every ounce of his pacific nature strives to
negate it, so that, although ostensibly the Army normalizes
him, he is like a butterfly perpetually trying to extricate
itself from the severity of the martial cocoon. During this
travail his soul has the shakes. Mr. Kaye, who possesses a
rather charming if beak-nosed boyish countenance and
blond curls that he arranged on his forehead, has created
an ingenious style to illustrate himself. The point of his
charade personality is that he is not cut out to be a soldier
but to entertain soldiers and so makes visible, if not always

comprehensible, the propaganda that male comedians rightly belong on the platform at an army-camp show rather than in the audience. Indeed the explosiveness of his fun is curiously suggestive of a "medical *dis*charge."

Surely no comedian has ever appeared on the screen who revealed without subterfuge a more obvious fixation on the camera than does Kaye—so much so that once in *Up in Arms* he literally flung himself in its face. His proclivity was crystallized, no doubt, through experience as solo entertainer at resorts and night clubs before going on the New York stage. But Mr. Kaye, unlike more craftsmanlike clowns, has somewhat neglected to adapt himself to the convention of the spectacle and remains, whenever he can show it, someone who is playing directly and self-consciously to the audience. He seems to be aware of the increased size of movie-house audiences, to imagine not merely hundreds "out there" but many thousands, and to have a global sense of the visual scope of his own comedic spectacle.

Kaye's madness, a kind of elephantiasis of the funny bone, stands in single rivalry with the concerted goofiness of the unique Marx brothers, a wily galaxy of clowns whose art has the rare virtue of complete informality. Kaye never relaxes. Groucho, Chico, and Harpo seem to be relaxing all the time; only Groucho, significantly cast in the burlesque mold of the great thinker, the brains of the outfit, has any calculated style: he is a satire on the household philosopher, the phony with his feet on the fireplace fender and not a dime in his pockets. Obviously this clown knows nothing, knows that he knows nothing, but knows enough to know that the pretense of knowing something is universal and, carried through, gains universal respect. The Marxes are patently a team in every sense, a smooth-as-silk protective association of cowards and fools who invariably, by their outrageous lack of conventionality, bemuse and foil the rational and orthodox maneuvers of their opponents. The Marx brothers exalt fake and dishonesty; they represent the clown as charlatan; because their idiocy always works out, in the plot and situation sense, to be wit, to be effective, they are ethically forgiven. In some strange way they all seem part of the same organism, to be one personality split three ways. Groucho is mind, Chico body, Harpo the mad genius of love and music, a Chopin among Harlequins. Groucho and Chico are higher and lower elements of the common instincts of self-interest; Harpo is the moon and the stars, the idiot son who charms and disarms with his art—an expression of euphoria—and who stands closest to his mother's heart. The Marx brothers are the arch misadventurers. They even provide an echo of a Shakespearean triumvirate: Prospero, Ariel, and Caliban—Groucho, Harpo, and Chico being the burlesques in the order named. Harpo's concupiscence, one feels, has a harmless symbolism, is mere air, being the unreckoned playfulness of a virtually supernatural idiot. There used to be a fourth Marx brother who made the professional trio a professional quartet. This fourth man was pure convention, pure necktie salesman, pure subway sheik. In essence he was the association's manager, the titular M.C. who never emceed—a mere symbol of his brothers' realistic connection with life. When he passed away from the quartet, however, he was magically revived in such men as Hope, Skelton, and Kaye, whose genius is individualistic, a stylistic projection of commonplace qualities in the male. Therefore Messrs. Hope, Skelton, and Kaye may be interpreted as the fourth Marx brother on his own as entertainer—and not doing badly. Among other movie teams is one classic example, Laurel and Hardy, and two modern: Olsen and Johnson, of *Hellzapoppin* fame, and Abbott and Costello. Their scintillations, duet and solo, are uneven, but doubtless as clowns Laurel and Hardy, though now rather outworn, are superior to the others.

The trio of comediennes I mentioned above—Cass Daley, Joan Davis, and Betty Hutton—are half sisters in art to Danny Kaye. Most conspicuous in their style is, of course, violence—a violence that makes it irrelevant to decide whether or not they are portraying ladies, with all that the term implies. I think that sometimes they can be very funny; Miss Davis is the only one who embellishes her routine materially by dancing, although Miss Hutton is able to take terpsichorean measures. Miss Daley's face relates her a little to the movie traditions of Louise Fazenda, Marie Dressler, and Polly Moran, but modern glamouriza-tion has made her almost femininely attractive. Such daft damsels as these modern three count horsiness as very much a part of their stock in trade; indeed Miss Daley was once a perfect yodeling cowgirl for the screen. Also part of their stock in trade is their panting efforts to get and hold their males. More so than in the case of the corresponding male mimes, likewise inveterate chasers, these comediennes' styles are systematizations of mere sexual frustration, song and dance being weapons to transfix and magnetize the desired male object. The grossness and violence become laugh-getters through the logical incongruity lying in the transfer of aggressiveness from male to female. Innately the female feels the dislocation involved in any excessive energy required to attract the male, and her spiritual horror of her unnatural rôle creeps into her style, whether actress or not, and modifies its essence. In the professional style of these ladies, giving us leave to think of them colloquially as "tomatoes," is a subtle parody of the awkward, the typically Western, male in a state of love. To arrive at a parallel phenomenon of female aggressiveness and violence we should have to go to the insect world of the bee and the praying mantis.

We all know, and according to our natures hold in differing degrees of credence and sympathy, the comic-strip myth of a caveman love. We also know the extent to which this has been exploited in movieland's characterization of gangster heroes; I need mention only Cagney, Robinson, and Bogart. Misses Daley, Davis, and Hutton may be called caveladies rather than cavewomen, for their styles are compromised, there being limits to the humiliation of the sexual ego. A specialty of Miss Hutton is the song routine in which she sometimes practically knocks herself out. The meaning of such ditties as but the preliminary measures of Cupid leaves no room for doubt. Miss Hutton in a way seems far too attractive to go to such trouble as this type of exhibitionism, but her professional clown's mask is nevertheless that of the sex-hungry female, put to much constraint to land her man in a climactic clinch and resorting to the refinement of a vocal and manual charade to get her message across. The term "clinch," borrowed from the lingo of prizefighting, is here much to the point. For Miss Hutton's most famous song is a symbolic round of fisticuffs in which the singer hints by analogy and more direct forms that toughness in the amorous male is as welcome to her as tenderness. It would seem, according to common sense, that there are much more efficient and obvious ways for a woman to communicate that she has a taste for being taken by storm. But our local civilization has suffered materially from its puritan heritage. The thunder and lightning, the cannonading, of Miss Hutton's song style suggest that it may be a mere reflection of a social pathology of sex necessitating that the female deck herself with unambiguous advertisements to make the sluggish male aware that, if he chooses, it isn't necessary to go through all the polite forms of wooing or even to respect the supposed fragility of the feminine emotional structure. But I may hazard that the esthetics of Miss Hutton's style is even more complex than this. A contrary sort of violence, that of the gangster's militant love-making, may be based on the theory that he thus mechanically extends his real war-making; a pattern of violence is etched in his blood. Correspondingly Miss Hutton has a song, performed with overwhelming approbation, in which sex is bluntly, albeit metaphorically, identified with murder. We may even have a subtle hint in this song that the murder metaphor refers also to the accessory device of contraception. The Hutton comedienne is a persuasive hieroglyph that symbolizes something deeply ingrained in modern morality: the commoner man's subconscious impulse, when a girl evades or refuses a kiss, to knock her out, take it, and have done. His anxiety psychology makes the identical assumption of La Hutton's chanteusing; that is, underneath, the woman really wants the kiss but is held back by a stupid taboo, which may even provide the occasion for a subconscious invitation to violence. One wonders, in view of the stunning success of Miss Hutton's epileptico-mimetic pantomime, if both sexual parties are not peculiarly right. After all, fashions in love do follow fashions in war, or vice versa. In the medieval days of chivalry war was inseparable from ceremony, often involving personal honor and personal love; during the Crusades knights went to war in honor of their ladyloves; moreover, in tournaments, gentlemen periodically tested the caliber of their loves against one another at the point of the lance. Today, when war is far less a personal and ritual affair and has no direct connection with a high and serious love, we should not be surprised at the violence and crudity with which love itself is sometimes expressed—or that this should often, especially with regard to the play of words, take a comic aspect.

Comedy itself is a game, the traditional game of life played on the level of philosophic cheer, with the emotions as strictly ambivalent counters, its tears being those of joy, chagrin, or a transient grief. Perhaps laughter is less close to life as it is lived in the heart than are secret, terrible tears and the solemn trying to do things and get places. Assuredly, however, screen comedy has a much higher esthetic rating than screen drama, whose sentimentality and dishonest mummery are so often ruinous. Especially in the figure of the solo comedian, the pure entertainer, rather than the comic hero with his Chaplinesque ambiguity, screen low jinks deserve royal-flush prestige and the best prizes of Hollywood. Yet comedians in Hollywood are almost completely ignored for the regular acting awards. Perhaps comedy seems not arty enough, seems too closely wedded to the everyday chore, even to that of the comedian himself, to be hailed as exceptional or superlative. In a sense this is quite true. A great comedian of Hollywood always does his act, goes through his business, everything being entirely expected and perennial—that the most popular dramatic actors, willy nilly, do the same, is less widely recognized and assumed.

Chaplin's full-length mask is but one of a familiar repertory of screen motleys, current or historic, that outlast 95 per cent of movieland's seriously composed faces. The idea of the mask, the unchanged and unchanging dominant expression, calls to mind the classic device of actually using a mask, a false face that obliterates the clown's own features. In respect to comedy it provides the *Pagliacci* pattern implying that two realities exist in the representation: art and life, or specifically laughter and tears. In classical Greece the tragic mask existed too, since at that time visual

51

artifice in connection with the actor was valued on a higher level than on the popular stage developed later.

If we think of the masks of tragedy and comedy that were familiar decorative motifs to the Greeks, we think of two fixed expressions, one an inversion of the other, the tragic mask having the corners of its mouth turned down, whereas the comic has the corners turned up. A modern theory of laughter has it that the historic root of its physiology—the opened jaws, the sudden inhalation and exhalation of breath, the upturned corners of the mouth, and the jerky palpitation of the diaphragm—originated from the hunger cry of the jungle beast and implied the presage of food in the flesh of its victim and the licking of the chops that would follow the meal; that is, the anticipated sensation of well-being, whose dynamism caused the animal's mouth to curl up in a smile of contentment. We all have a vivid memory of the image of the animated-cartoon tiger smiling like the cat that has eaten the canary. This image is assuredly as much a comic mask as the most conventional ever designed.

Modern comedians have a facial physiology depending on basic animal fear and exuberance as well as on irrational animal well-being (euphoria). Danny Kaye's frenzy of impersonation, which seizes him, in *Up in Arms*, while waiting in a movie-theater lobby, is the same sort of self-knockout pandemonium that takes hold of Miss Hutton, and their comic masks during these performances were each, in the sense of the traditional contrasting masks of tragedy and comedy, about half comic or happy and half tragic or dismayed—the latter being a straight travesty of the tragic mask. Symbolic as they are, there is little difficulty in orientating such plastic masks to signify an analogy to the theoretical origin of laughter: the modern masks signify the savage appetite for adulation that inspires so many entertainers. In imitating, among others, Carmen Miranda, who shows more of her teeth than any other singer, Mr. Kaye logically portrayed an omnivorous desire to annex all his rivals' aggregate publics, and accordingly in Miss Hutton's case the reluctant male is virtually a symbol of those indifferent prospective customers who haven't yet bought tickets to see her. . . . Study that wild glint in Mr. Kaye's eyes; he seems quite prepared to devour the camera at the first hint that such a feat would be applauded! As modern knights and versions of feudal lady-lords, comedy jacks and queens, professionally inspired, stalk the game of the movie public in the mantles and motleys of strange descendants.

So it was far from being a coincidence that in his third starring vehicle, *The Kid from Brooklyn*, Danny Kaye took the part of a balmy moron who is illegally manufactured from a milkman into a mauler. As "The Tiger," Danny's public acclaim goes to his head and he literally makes a circus of his bogus ring-career; the metamorphosis from obscurity into blinding fame closely resembles, with its grotesque effect on the subject, what might happen to an actor during a parallel metamorphosis. At one point, Danny's original nature (that of the calf-eyed milkman) has to be resurrected, and therefore his rascally manager upbraids him for having become a heartless bonebreaker—

a "beast of the jungle." Miraculously, a mounted tiger's head is handy, and Mr. Kaye goes through a meticulous experiment before a mirror to discover if perhaps, after all, the milksop may not really have become a man-eater. The analogy between the comic mask and a snarling tiger, fangs exposed, here becomes more than metaphorical: it is as close as nature can permit.

3. MAGIC-LANTERN METAMORPHOSES I

Dorian Gray, Last of the Draculas

The consciousness of being hunted, snared,
tracked down, had begun to dominate him.
THE PICTURE OF DORIAN GRAY

The original conception of Dorian Gray's picture is one of metamorphosis by magic, being based on the savage superstition that an image of oneself or one's reflected image is the same as oneself or actually one's soul. Hollywood's version of Wilde's late Victorian fiction classic came to us through special dispensation, and therefore it is a pity that Albert Lewin's cherishing production did not prove the masterpiece that seemed possible. The result merely proves that literary reverence on the part of movie-makers should be intelligent as well as ardent. Yet the theme holds such an intrinsic magic that the production would have had to be positively barbarous for nothing at all to have come through triumphantly.

Hurd Hatfield's face is a remarkably successful feat of Dorian's visualization from all viewpoints—from that of casting the mythical features of Sibyl Vane's Prince Charming and Wilde's youthful dandy to the art of the make-up man, who gave Mr. Hatfield's fortunate features a mellifluous quality, especially the melting eyes and the turned-up corners of the mouth, which have a fugitive hint of the

55

Mona Lisa's smile. Although one might be impelled to scout such obvious accent on the purely photogenic, as though Dorian were being screen-tested, the image is distinctive enough to cling to the montage continuity of the film. No one need discover that Dorian is a version of Narcissus, suggesting, as though he had been cursed by a god, a psychopathological interpretation. The point is that Mr. Hatfield is a poetical realization of a legendary image brought up to date by Wilde. While devoid of mature accomplishment as an actor, Mr. Hatfield deports himself with apt economy and an accurate feeling for the somnambulistic quality of Dorian and furnishes, for this beholder at least, an insight into the nature of the original Narcissus myth.

Mr. Hatfield's features have the expressionless quality of those persons, women as a rule, who wish to preserve their youth by not exercising their facial muscles and so creating wrinkles. At the same time these features are not frozen, as usually is the case with such women, but contain a sort of internal mobility like the mysteriously alive waters of a still fountain. So we may conclude that the presence of the water mirror in the essentially adolescent myth of Narcissus is based on realistic observation and is a mere symbolization of the quality that may inhere in the face of a beautiful adolescent, male or female. It was not that Narcissus saw his face in a still fountain but a still fountain in his face. He is a symbol of arrested development, and his face, like Hurd Hatfield's as Dorian, is peculiarly sightless, as though indeed he saw nothing unless he looked in a mirror and there saw the still and fascinating fountain of himself.

Now that this has been said, one has to cast about for something else in the Hollywood lens to make a show of really virtuous seeing. There are good photographic touches, but these are routine filmic adventures in the incidental dramatizing of vision. At least these—like a man's writing Dorian's name and address on a wall in the slums, thus giving him away to Sibyl's brother, who wants to avenge her death—belong to Hollywood and are none of Wilde's. As to the general justice done the original story, the scenario department has taken advantage of simplifying pictorial devices. No doubt the initial strategy of having Lord Henry Wotton pursue and catch a butterfly in Basil Hallward's studio while chatting with Dorian on their first meeting is first-rate montage à la Eisenstein but rather third-rate poetry and something at which Wilde would have been shocked. But considering the problem that it was necessary to portray the relationship between Lord Henry and Dorian in some neat, pocket-sized way, perhaps the heads of Hollywood should be complimented for their ingenuity. Lord Henry poisons and immobilizes Dorian with the exquisite tip of an idea as deftly as he drowns and immobilizes the butterfly without harming its wings.

This little device, travesty as it is, has the appropriateness of spanning several oceans. The British globe conquerors are noted for stalking game in foreign parts, and the drama of hunter and hunted is likewise sympathetic to an American society settled among savage aborigines and in love with sport. The butterfly Lord Henry catches is, as he remarks, a rare specimen, and therefore it is a foreign element stalked and trapped at home in England. Since it is true that Dorian and all he symbolizes in Wilde's esthetic are an importation in art for which their creator was forced to pay the most exorbitant duty, perhaps another hit-and-run idea should be chalked up for Hollywood. I must add that George Sanders as Lord Henry, fruit-fondling and bouquet-savoring as he is portrayed, hardly has the physical style that Wilde implied in his prose. Yet when one considers how the selected assortment of epigrams might have been dealt out by a lesser actor, perhaps one should simply fold one's hands and be grateful.

The dilemma of Wilde's classic in the shambles of Hollywood must be taken by its exotic horns. The truth is that despite the fact that thousands, perhaps millions, of people everywhere have read and enjoyed *The Picture of Dorian Gray* as a sort of adult fairy tale, it is foreign not only to Hollywood and America but to the country in which it was written and from which it has a necessary imprint—England. By and large Wilde accepted the values of his time and on the surface dealt with the most obvious conventions of morals and sentiment. But, as is well known, he did so as an ironist of a particular sort. If Wilde is not one of the greatest artists, it is only because he did not go sufficiently into himself, as did Proust, who also dealt only with the conventions of his time, but who lived in a much superior society and was a truly profund self-investigator. Sensing not only the basic contraditions in the behavior of British society, which he pinned to prose in epigrams as iridescent and pointed as the wings of butterflies, but also the oppressive stuffiness of the average British character, Wilde nevertheless determined to make a social success of his work. But his genuine instinct of poetry was faced with a temptation to compromise. And as he always yielded to temptations in the end, he yielded at once to the biggest one of all. Hence he was empowered to develop one of his most deeply ingrained talents, the essentially ambiguous form of the aphorism, which connects itself with nothing in particular and everything in general, and especially of the paradox, which cuts its own roots from beneath itself. Dorian is Wilde's paradox in its most elaborate and significantly imagined form, since in *The Picture* much more than in the plays, even *The Importance of Being Earnest,* Wilde made an attempt to concretize in realistic form his conception of the relation of art to life. When in the original story the painter of the portrait, Hallward, protests to the scoffing Lord Henry that Dorian is truly in love with the actress, Sibyl Vane, to whom he intends being married, Lord Henry replies that both art and love are merely imitation.

But we must remember it was Wilde who originated the formula of the imitation of art by life, which is but another expression of the art for art's sake doctrine of the late nineteenth century. Hence Dorian's love is basically that sort of imitation; he seeks to practise love as a lifelike form of art. This, suggesting as it does the first romantic impulses of sensitive schoolboys who fall in love with actresses, is consistent with the conception of Dorian as a delayed adolescent; he is actually twenty-two when he falls in love with Sibyl. But here, at the crucial point of Wilde's fable, is just where Hollywood goes most outrageously wrong. For the screen Dorian has been made to fall down and worship—not a beautiful girl who enacts the Juliet and Miranda of Shakespeare, as in the original, but a doll-faced chit who sings a sentimental beer-hall ditty of the period, "The Little Yellow Bird." The juggernaut of the American moral system has been at work behind the scenes of movies and men and at the appropriate moment manifested itself. That triumph of the morality of esthetics over the morality of the average citizen, to which Wilde dedicated much of himself and which he epitomized in the figure of Lord Henry, has been ignored, and in its place we find triumphing, in the movie-lot *Dorian*, the backstairs romancing of the average citizen against which Wilde was specifically aiming his shaft. Implicitly Dorian becomes in the movie a typical young man about town who consistently goes whoring and gains an evil reputation as a seducer of wives. It is assuredly love versus morality but by no means on the level where Wilde conceived the conflict. Shakespeare's poetry was essential to Dorian's original illusion of love, and it is unpardonable for Hollywood to have omitted this essential.

The whole thesis of Wilde's art was the reality of make-believe not merely in childhood but in youth and manhood too. Naturally the dramatic stage was a symbol of the supremacy of make-believe. It was not Wilde and the *Yel-*

low Book group that created the decadence of the nineties, but they who gave it its only good reason for existence. The make-believeness of Wilde finally became the make-believeness of J. M. Barrie and A. A. Milne, but in itself it had the stature of a profound intuition about art, for, as Wilde understood, art is not only the medieval artifact but also the sum and essence of man's imaginative beliefs, the stuff and form of the spirit. This idea, since the halcyon days of primitive man have gone, has become increasingly foreign to the human race itself, and, England being a particularly modern stronghold of the human race, it was especially foreign to England, a place where a classical education found fruition within the walls of a university and thereafter died unless it became a means of livelihood as the intramural education of others, on many of whom, however, it would duly wither and perish once they stepped into the world. Even Yeats, who came across the water from the west, was, with his Irish fairies, thought a fool by most. Tempermentally Wilde was a strategist superior to any of his contemporaries, especially since his peculiar situation practically forced strategy upon him. Under the influence of the classicist, Pater, he was attracted to the idea of pagan love as well as pagan philosophy—and we must not forget that the ideals of Greek antiquity tended to exalt the male above the female not only in mental but also in physical beauty. But Wilde was intelligent enough to realize the great danger of making such emotions into more than obscurely elegant pieces of pseudohistorical research like *Marius the Epicurean* with its fragile fiction and immense coating of erudition. Wilde was too impatient to bother with much erudition, too realistic to confine himself to historico-literary symbols. He determined to be an up-to-date anachronism, and that is precisely what his Dorian Gray was. In his acts—and he was interested in nothing but action, primarily in the social sense—Wilde had to move behind a screen. He moved behind the screen of imaginative concepts but in the very heart of society, behind all the outposts of the enemy camp. He moved secretly because he was a trespassing hunter of a unicorn whose existence was not even acknowledged by the authorities and that Wilde himself regarded as an ideal only: the purest personalized symbol of pagan love. In this aim Wilde was the prince of an alien and socially aggressive esthetic philosophy, and Dorian Gray was his Mata Hari, a man in the service not of another country but of another sex.

I could not help noting that in certain scenes of the movie Mr. Hatfield's face and manner of speaking strongly suggested the romantic adolescent style of Katharine Hepburn —by which, of course, I mean no disrespect to either! I well remember the amusing and rather appealing novelty of Miss Hepburn's streamlined angularity of both figure and speech in *A Bill of Divorcement,* a movie version of Clemence Dane's play . . . her immobile upper lip and active lower lip, in the English style, between which sound issued often muted—sound which was a sort of dramatic monotone suited to expressing adolescent simplicity, laconicism, and pathos. It is not only that the structure of Mr. Hatfield's face is similar to Miss Hepburn's but that the use of his lips and a muted monotone also resembled hers. Psychologically these features of style are symptomatic of suppressed emotion and a hopeless kind of compulsion. This is quite appropriate to Dorian's prolonged adolescence and his tactic of concealing his internal feelings by a neutral, formal sort of monotone. I mention this only to show that by happy coincidence screen history provides a handy index to the effeminate defensiveness of Dorian's style. His is a passive, dreamy mask, which, like Miss Hepburn's, is that of an inwardly tortured but proud and strong adolescent who feels sorely victimized.

Yet because of Dorian's effeminacy it must not be supposed that Wilde was double-dealing to make his hero— symbol of the beauty he most admired—fall in love with a woman and remain to all appearances woman-loving. That is exactly what Wilde meant, for it is logical to his chosen artistic scheme. Despite obvious sensuality, in great part sensuousness, Wilde's elevated nature had its ascetic side, and in identifying esthetics with the ascetic he was following classic Greek thought in general and Plato in particular. Physical beauty in all was primarily an esthetic object, and in men, from the viewpoint of other men, it would seem that it could provide no more than an esthetic object. But the bridge between the esthetic and the ascetic-sexual had been provided by the example of Socrates, who, according to Plato, loved men supremely and personally but not physically. The resemblance of Lord Henry to Socrates is not to be overlooked. Both were primarily ironists, both connoisseurs of beauty; and both assumed the

rôle of social philosopher. But even more essentially both
dealt in different fashions with the paradox, Socrates with
the logical paradox and Lord Henry with the social paradox. The result was that both set any naïvely positive conception of values at naught. Obviously, although the movie
hints less of this than does the prose story, Dorian is the
youth with whom Socrates-Lord Henry is Platonically in
love. And implicitly it was Lord Henry's counsel to Dorian
that loving women was of little importance, indeed that,
taken too seriously, it was a sort of vice. Chastity in men
was a virtue because it reserved them as esthetic objects
for those other men who could in this way appreciate them
on a plane higher than the physical, on which women appre-
ciated them. But Wilde recognized the typical adolescent
illusion of the male that it is everything to love a woman,
and in a sensitive male this would take the form of identifying women especially with the heroines of poetic drama
and legend. It took only an ordinary realist to measure the
difference between actual women and the poetic shapes into
which the adolescent imagination might project them.
Dorian ritually goes through such a disillusionment by
pertinently picking a dramatic actress with whom to fall
in love. Indirectly Wilde recommended through his story
the precept of abstinence from women, because Dorian
observes that as soon as Sibyl falls in love with him, a real
man, she ceases to be a good actress and her enactment of
stage love becomes cheap and artificial; thus the inference
is that as soon as love becomes real, it is inevitably vulgar-
ized. One is astounded to observe that on the contrary in

the movie Dorian is disillusioned *because the girl is willing to accept his love out of wedlock.* The movie's bourgeois slander of Wilde's conception is thus logically extended.

Not only does Hurd Hatfield create the first male erotic somnambule who is a beauty rather than a Dracula, or such as the denizen of Caligari's cabinet, but he is the first great lover who, despite all Hollywood handicaps, manages to seem more loved than loving. Here, willy-nilly, Wilde's conception triumphed. For the whole meaning of Dorian's life is that he is the detached *object* of love, not its *subject* —the beloved, not the lover. There is no pretense in film or original story, after Sibyl Vane's suicide, that Dorian has the least emotion of genuine love; all that he does— and it is supposed to be very base—is the negation of love by sensuality. It is not even that primarily he is an image of youth and beauty in his own narcissistic mind, but that he is an image of youth and beauty in someone else's mind. Here the screen contributed the inevitable poetry of its medium to the vision of Dorian, moving faultlessly, smoothly, seemingly without sound, through the rooms of his private mansion, where he dwells as a bachelor and apparently orphaned. Dorian lives in an empty house, which only the eyes of a lover may visit. That this abstracted conception of Dorian as a moving, beloved image in someone's moving, loving mind, is the essence of Wilde's story is proved, I think, by reference to the general facts of life—and here I may pick on America and the American stage rather than England and the English stage. Wilde thought of Dorian as an actor, just as Dorian thought of

Sibyl as an actress, and today, if a real woman were to fall in love with Mr. Hatfield after seeing the movie, she might experience a disillusionment parallel with the original Dorian's.

Besides being an Adonis, Dorian is portrayed as a particularly heartless Don Juan who grows old cantankerously and ungracefully, not to mention also in a most paradoxical fashion. But if we look at an American Adonis from real life, John Barrymore, a man who displayed not only enduring regard for his love life but, where this aspect of his private life was concerned, a stubborn individualism and negligence of public opinion, we find that his psychological conduct differs from Dorian's not at all, but that by no means did his soul grow old as Dorian's did with its corresponding patina on the face of his age. While in public and private life Barrymore inveterately assumed the rôle of the great lover, it is obvious that his face at fifty, though not what it was at twenty or thirty, certainly was nothing like Ivan Le Loraine Albright's staggering rendition of the transformed portrait of Dorian, which literally is that of a fantastically balmy and nasty old man. Despite the ravages of time and an emotional mode of life, the great profile stuck to John Barrymore, even when on the silent screen he had a parallel metamorphosis from Dr. Jekyll into Mr. Hyde—a fable closer to Hollywood than Dorian's. But the great fullface of Dorian, as lush as a tea rose, is utterly absent from the portrait of his aged soul. One wonders if Wilde's imagination, feverish as it might be on such a point, would sanction this horrible example of a Dracula to end all Draculas. Moreover, it is rather painful to state that after Dorian's assassination of the portrait has rendered it young again and rendered him the old and repulsive image of the portrait, the glimpse we are permitted of Dorian is provided by a dummy—the full-length dummy rigged up by the Albright brothers to pose for their painting! The Hollywood skeleton cannot be kept in the closet; it *must* fall out.

What have we, then, in this mere effigy presumed to be Dorian, whose soul is liberated when his body dies, according to the Hollywood, Wilde-derived convention? We have indeed, as everyone expected, the end of the movie. But we have more. We have that potent tradition of Hollywood art that will not relinquish its mythology to potent literary art even when Hollywood conspires against itself. Throughout, Mr. Hatfield's Dorian is visually a lamb, handsome with an inveigling dewiness and strangely enough wearing a collar very much like that of the Sinatra of today, albeit the ends of Dorian's bow tie are tucked under it rather than left outside. Dorian is an image indeed that may have earned, by the time this is in print, the worship of the more ethereal among the bobbysoxers and those Vassar students who are supposed to take their classics more seriously than they do the movies. But to put it in bluntly Broadway terms, he is—as some New York lambs reputedly are—a wolf beneath the wool. Time and space collaborate with time and space, and we see the Americana show its unmistakable stripe in Dorian's immaculate Mayfair tailoring . . . he was a creep all the while! And as we well know, Hollywood has the undisputed monopoly of all varieties of creeps—from the wolf in Disney's *Little Red Riding Hood,* through Frankenstein's monster, Mr. Hyde, Dracula, the Wolf Man, and Lennie of *Of Mice and Men,* to the panty-waist Jack the Ripper of Laird Cregar, and Charles Laughton posing in liquor. To this numerous and impressive group must be added frail Dorian, who, like the Werewolf of London, practiced his foul deeds in the murkiness of back streets.

That the latest expression of American primitive art, that of Ivan Albright, should have been enlisted in the service of another creep carnival, however liveried it may be with polite conventions, is more than matter for the simple shock that turns a man over in his grave. It is proof of Hollywood's commendably alert, albeit limited, imagination. The art of the Albright brothers, especially that of Ivan, is super-realistic in its accentuation of naturalistic detail under sharply dramatic and weirdly colored light —usually, one imagines, supplied by a daylight electric bulb hanging close overhead. Every puff, excrescence, wrinkle, protuberance, and loop in flesh and fabric receives individual attention in the work of Ivan, to whom entire credit for the painting is given, although he was assisted by his brother in its execution. No doubt it was the thoroughness of Albright's style of painting, making corruption, age, and sloth so literally present, that appealed to the imagination of the Hollywood artificers and won for the Albrights a fat sum for their labors and an adventurous trip to the lupine land of American art. Under their hands

Dorian turns out to be a scrawny old wolf with a potbelly, clothed with apocryphal festoons of sometimes shocking nature, cloth and articles of furniture sharing in the kind of swelling and cracking one associates with the decay and disease of the body. Another cinema inspiration is that both the original Dorian portrait, a tepid affair, as well as the Albright portrait burst out in the fireworks of Technicolor from a previously dun screen; although art is implicitly offended, one cannot help reacting with a certain thrill. It is the way one usually reacts to zombies and werewolves from the jungles adjacent to Sunset Boulevard. Ivan Le Loraine Albright has given us in his portrait of Dorian the wicked, a compelling version of the American moral jungle from which fundamentally all famous creeps must be said to crepitate. The painting is so full of accentuated detail that, seen by the camera so fleetingly in proportion to its elaborate content, it remains strangely vague, almost as though it were in motion—just as the hunter imagines that the animal somewhere behind the forest screen is seeking to hide. The painter in the story, Hallward, whom Dorian murders out of paranoiac terror, imagines from the beginning that the painting has a life of its own. This is the alien life of the hunted from the viewpoint of the hunter. All human or semihuman monsters, those dwelling in the brain as well as in the organic world, are hunted and hunter at the same time. So it was with Frankenstein's monster and with all the others that Hollywood has taken tenderly to its jungle. . . .

Even when he was a charming youth, Dorian Gray as a

literary hero was a monster for the British public, to which Wilde with a measure of audacity introduced him. In truth he was the hunted, ideal object of Wilde's insistent esthetic quest, which he dared to prosecute in the midst of life itself, even while believing that it was only ideal. Yet when in a work of fiction Wilde chose to thrust this image into the scene of a society in which its reality was not to be found, he understood the paradoxical logic that such a fabulous being, lost in the actual pitfalls of society, must carry within himself the seeds of the gross decay of the sexual that was the social destiny and that Wilde saw everywhere around him in the vulgar and stupid rather than imaginative and esthetic pursuit of women by men.

Wilde's rightness in judging the basic primitivism of sex in modern society was carried forward logically by Bernard Shaw, who added the paradox of portraying women as the unscrupulous hunters of men. Wilde considered the London of his time a civilized sort of jungle, a city which had its private jungle in the East End and its hidden East End in many a fashionable drawing room. Resistance to the esthetic formulation of love, as typified by Dorian's adoration of the personified heroine of Shakespeare, Wilde considered monstrous and evil. It is the same resistance to art that in Hollywood makes Dorian into a nephew of Dracula and Company, as it made him into something parallel in Wilde's story. Instinctively Wilde with good reason feared the operation of social law and the pressure of its taboo upon the submerged ego. For he himself, if we are to believe all the evidence, was not exempt from the operation of

sexual law that he visualized in *The Picture of Dorian Gray.*
. . . Thus, if the art of the story has been lowered by the
movies, its moral denouement has been strong enough in
essence to survive. In the less lovely and unhappily rather
commodious region of the American psyche Dorian is
every leading man, magically transformed by cinema art
into the beast "under the hill," once pictorially initiated by
Aubrey Beardsley as the stunning young god and now pictorially given the finishing touch by the Albright brothers
as the awful old man.

4. SUPERNATURALISM
AT HOME

No doubt there were parents, sweethearts, and wives of our
military who found genuine consolation in turning to a
Deity from whom special consideration might be wooed
for particular fighters in the field or for the American
troops and their allies as a whole. And some may pause
to ask for divine mercy on all killed and killing. Christmas
and Easter during world wars become more solemn times
than usual for ritualistic worshipers, the atmosphere being wrought with more complex spiritual significances. But,
when asked to consider the realm of being or appearance
known as supernatural phenomena, as we are whenever we
see certain kinds of movies, our sense of belief is placed in
a different position from that when we kneel in prayer or
invoke perhaps the image of a grieving Deity, perplexed
by the wayward life of this planet but as remote from us
by and large as if He were some farther moon.

In my previous book on the movies I pointed out that
the adulation, often so shockingly naïve, given to movie
stars independently of their screen rôles and only as personalities, provided a basis for thinking of them as semi-
divine, a vestigial form of the pagan divinities of classical
Greece. By the supernatural phenomena of the movies I
do not mean anything of that sort here, although I would

call the supernaturalism of the screen a factor contributing to the popular illusions concerning it. Here I principally mean to separate the creative order of the supernaturalist means from the essence of the creation, so far as concerns all personal factors, the actors themselves, and to conceive the supernatural fables of Hollywood as bona fide creative offerings, destined to be accepted as true or untrue representations of the orders of reality—part of such orders being of course the spiritual orders.

It is amusing to note the supposition of the most sophisticated cinema reviewers, most of them nesting in Manhattan, as to the premises for belief in regard to the supernaturalist offerings of Hollywood. Since the advent of Frankenstein's monster among the silver shadows of the screen and his perduring and high success in a continuous wave of reappearances and generic imitators, reviewers have decided that it is just too much for even a decorous show of sympathy with the extremist fantasy conventions of the movies. At first, because the industry must go on—and will, no matter what reviewers say—it was deemed proper to fall into the mood, especially since there was a precedent of a certain literary prestige in *Dr. Jekyll and Mr. Hyde.* Yet it was obvious that in regard to this fable both ethics and psychology as techniques of understanding provide explanations of the Stevenson fantasy as mere literary symbolism. Hence the emphasis, so far as successive movie renderings of this fable went, was on the powers of the leading actor and the cleverness of the theatrical effects. Yet patience, courtesy, and the mood of sympathy gradu-

ally wore out as virtually dozens of examples of supernatural horror art stalked and lunged across the screen
at regulated intervals. The mystery murder, during the
thirties and up to the present, was infiltrated with frequent
and strong doses, in powdered and liquid form, of the
supernatural—or at least the preternatural. Elsewhere in
this book I have listed a number of the higher ranking
personnel evoked during this proceeding. Here I want to
consider the principles of their manufacture and the justice
of their claims to belief.

Readers may think me absurd to bring up the issue of
actual credibility of such supposed phenomena in ostensible
representation on the screen. They may side with the reviewers above mentioned that one must either accept movie
supernaturalism as latter-day examples of fairy tales for
adults, with 1947 tongue in 1947 cheek, as forthright laugh
festivals with no symbolic overtones, or simply pronounce
them phony art. As to the phoniness, often nothing could be
phonier than the everyday realism of Hollywood artifice,
as witness *The Postman Always Rings Twice.* As to the
laughter, of course that may be sour. Nowadays reviewers
rather generally have adopted a simple little formula for
discussing monster mummery, a formula consisting in
clever sarcasms about the efforts of such films to be frightening. What they refer to is of course that in the more
routine or Grade B offerings inexpensiveness is usually
synonymous with crudity, and little trouble is taken with
illusion. I imagine that subconsciously the sophisticated
incumbents of reviewing jobs conclude that if movie-makers

are so cheap as to sabotage something requiring expensive and ornate vindication, having so little logic of its own, such loose pandering ought to be rebuked. I feel, however, that simple-mindedness reigns in place of supposed sophistication. The mistake made by disgusted reviewers is to assume that the object of supernatural horror in films is to frighten, in any serious sense of that infinitive. One might think that Hollywood producers considered us children who would hide under the seat as soon as the Wolfman or Dracula appeared. The mechanical psychology of reviewers is that of the recurrence of childhood fantasy when we were frightened by witches and giants in fairy tales. Obviously we are no longer frightened by these figurations, not merely because we do not believe in their reality, but because we are profoundly skeptical—even if they or the forces they represent exist—of their power to influence our daily lives. Perhaps our modernism is a trifle facile in this respect. At one time some of us were frightened by policemen, but unless we can be called fugitives from justice in our adulthood, the sight of a bluecoat is apt to be reassuring rather than frightening in questions of danger and safety, life and death. Civilization, like time, marches on.

When Hollywood fantasies of the supernatural and the preternatural are weak and boring to see, it is not because they fail to frighten. Nobody goes to the theater to be frightened. Most, including children, go to be thrilled. The esthetic thrill of fear, of mock fear, is pleasure. It may be conventional to have contempt for those adults childish enough to shudder with pleasure at the sight of a lovely, seminude woman helpless in the arms of an irresponsible and repulsive synthetic man. But the obscure processes of sadism are certainly not contemporary news. Admittedly contempt for this sort of thing is the critical device not only of taste but also of an age of reason and materialism; critics may think it merely the maintenance of a high intellectual tone to sniff at low-grade popularizing of emotion, adjudging the popular pleasure in screen monsters as moronic. But the naïvely susceptible in movie-house audiences are actually more sophisticated than the critics who, with contemporary naïveté, play the straight rationalistic ticket. Whether it be Gargantuan ape, as in the entertaining *King Kong,* or some variety of synthetic man, the creature whose destiny it is to frighten everyone in the movie is really only a symbol of the unconscious life, rendered titillatingly subconscious by the screen image. A fear, after all, is sometimes but the formal inversion of a desire. The rationalistic fallacy is that the chosen conventions of art must cross the footlights to be believed. Art, this fallacy says, must come to us to be believed. But the wise know that we must go to art, for it is much older and more centralized in space than we are. *We* must project across the footlights. Art must *be.* Reviewers are too jaded and debilitated to project themselves. We must be the ghosts amid the reality of artistic fantasy, not the fantasy of the screen the ghosts amid our reality. In other words, some basic and common *spirituality* must exist to support belief in any manifestation of spirit, no matter how outrageous or symbolic in form.

II

Doubtless when the conventional ghosts of today, those that purport to be the manifestation of the human dead and therefore not in any sense monstrous, appear on the screen, their critical recognition may be called democratic in its tolerance. It would be rude for a strictly materialistic, atheistic, or agnostic reviewer to flout the movie carrying them as mere outdated nonsense. It would offend believers of various religious shades. But nicety in observation of customs in actual society should not necessarily extend to critical manners in the judgment of art. Again, the ghosts are conceived as among us; that is, in a time of modern skepticism such as ours, it is hard to believe the more imaginative conventions of art, which, merely as part of their technique, materialize what is conventionally agreed upon as immaterial in fact. The decay of religious belief is a familiar theme in serious modern thought. In the Western world religious belief in this sense signifies the mythological assumptions of Christianity. But the arc—the rise, maintenance, and dwindling—of religion should be held in a certain contradistinction to the arc of magic, whose vestigial beliefs persisted in religion. Therefore readers should not be too much surprised when, in opposition to naïve materialistic psychology, I invoke the human inheritance of primitive magic psychology, whose belief in the spiritual far outdistances, in planetary depth and range, anything that the average kneeler in church may now claim.

It is true that today the scientific size of the universe is greater than anything that primitive man could imagine, but this is only because of a change in the very conceptions of size itself. The very fact that primitive man could not imagine the universe added to its size. The savage in very distant eras had no instruments of measurement, no standards of size. The universe then was truly illimitable, not in the modern sense of the theory that it is expanding but that, in lacking any notion of distance in empty and outward space or indeed any clear definition of the exact limitations of matter itself, very primitive man could measure time and space (reality) only by inventing its modes of operation from his own imagination. In the tenets of sympathetic magic—imitative and contagious magic—which Frazer has explained, pure spirit was supposed to annihilate space as the electrical energy of radio and telephone does today, and to do so by its own power, not with the assistance of mechanisms. Thus spirit was an incalculably effective but real extension of the desires and purposes of matter. Primitive man believed that the sun shone, the rain fell, crops were bountiful, hunters were successful, enemies died, and women were fertile, only because he himself performed certain symbolic actions imitating these processes or maintained a king or magician who would see that the natural results materialized by his peculiar power of dictation. Thus man himself was the spiritual center of the universe, without whose perpetual vigilance the material universe would not only fail in its life-giving functions but totally disappear. I remind the reader that it is the same

human race that today has super-sophisticated reviewers
and sub-naïve movie patrons . . . and I remind myself
that, before I could possibly have heard of such ideas as
those having to do with primitive magic, namely when I
was about eight years old, I had the strong suspicion, in
broad daylight, that when I turned myself completely
around, the section of the world that was then invisible to
me behind my back disappeared, and it reappeared only
when I turned around again. I used to try to catch the
world stepping back into place by turning around suddenly!

Modern reason has proved the fallacy of the supposi-
tions of primitive belief simply by referring to the un-
deniable fact that when the seeds of modern religion
appeared and absolute spiritual power was lodged in an
unseen and immaterial god over whom man had no control
but whom he had to propitiate in his own behalf, natural
phenomena continued in their accustomed rhythmic, dis-
harmonic, but constant manner without the existence of the
magic rituals previously deemed necessary. The spiritual
center of the universe was radically reorientated, and man
became a being materialistically defined and of considerably limited power over his natural destiny. But it must
be pointed out that theoretically this did not lessen the
amount of spirit in the world, theologically speaking, but
simply re-established its order and technique of manifestation more realistically in human understanding. Kings were
no longer supreme symbols, and after Christ only the pope
of the Roman Catholic Church and the greatest saints were
accorded anything equal to the superstitious veneration

given ancient kings and magicians. It is notable, however, that in his transition from magician to pope the priest attained a much more arbitrary and self-willed power than he had had in ancient times. Only the kings of Egypt, the Far Eastern potentates, and the tyrants of Greco-Roman civilization—in other words comparatively recent rulers— have wielded similar power. The absolute power of an individual as seen in the modern institution of dictatorship seems to have reached its last stage.

The grounds on which movies are said to fail in their hypothetical mission of frightening has a root that penetrates deviously into the ancient past of magical belief. For primitive man was frightened by everything; that is, he considered it only common sense to take the most extravagant precautions against the eventuation of what today we should call sheer impossible nonsense. For instance, the ancient savage believed that the spirit of a killed animal had the power to persecute its human killer and that the killing of either man or animal was fraught with the greatest danger, not only for the victim, the murdered, but for the victor, the murderer! Today a vestige of such fear exists in the consciences of murderers who regret their crimes, even if only through fear of social vengeance; indeed, the ghost of a murdered person is a widely recognized convention as symbol of bad conscience in the murderer. We must bear in mind that everything with primitive man was personal and individual, and the community was unified, an entity, merely because everyone had the identical things to fear. Thus killing an animal for food, and to a certain degree even cutting down a tree for firewood, was considered a crime for which due expiation must be made, even if it were only asking pardon of the tree beforehand. In the film, *On Borrowed Time,* based on the play of the same name, a tree is possessed by a revengefully egotistic spirit, the devil himself, and engages in a duel with human spirituality for the life of a little boy. Here modern rational convention, the growth of scientific reason, was ignored completely in favor of savage superstition. Yet it seemed legitimate art, and no one became outraged in behalf of good form.

Many modern movies illustrate the latter-day vestiges of very remote but serious beliefs of mankind that now have the appearance of mere symbolic fantasy. But now let us look closely at the means that the technical medium of cinema has developed for exhibiting or creating the real illusion of such unrealities as these conventions of art. The miracle of the moving photograph had hardly dawned before men intuited its most far-reaching capacities of illusion. No sooner was life in movement reproduced in effect than cinematographers took the utmost liberty with the scope possible to cinematic illusion. There was a *Trip to the Moon* (Georges Méliès, 1902), not unlike a modern revue of the Follies type in its bizarre imagery, artificial effects, and mixture of decorative femininity and low comedy. Then there was the serious or journalistic side by which the respectable public was acquainted at a distance with *Intimate Scenes of Convict Life* (1905), all acted out by solemn-faced mummers. But most significantly, in the last year of the nineteenth century, when science was about to take command of the world, Méliès made a film entitled *The Conjuror,* in which the tricks of stage magicians, such as that of appearing and disappearing persons, were counterfeited by purely cinematic manipulation. In this sense the cinema or moving photograph actually achieved the same effect of interchangeability between matter and spirit that the ancient savage supposed to exist in reality. It is meaningful to recall that one of the ancient magical beliefs was the soul as shadow and reflection—the identity of the life principle of a human being with his shadow thrown by the sun or his image in water. Even in this century urban Chinese are found to be afraid of having a camera set before them, since apparently they believe that it is an evil eye or a machine that will rob them of their souls and cause their death as a result. Is it any wonder, therefore, that some of our most worshiped film actresses seem to be sleepwalkers, the mirages of souls incarnate, their own shadow selves, rather than real women? And those creatures known as zombies, the living dead of the West Indies, the body deprived of its individual soul, do they not have a place in the movies that might be defined as prophesied, inevitable, even scheduled?

There are those who believe the movies can be nothing but a show, a glorified sort of circus, a human drawing-room menagerie. The object of such an institution could only be the creation of fun—and thrills, such as the hallucinative cavalcade of circus clowns, the incredible but visible performances of balancing high-wire acrobats, and

82

the man who really gets shot out of a cannon. When one considers that any effect possible to physical reality or illusion can be perfectly achieved by the movies through artifice or contrived illusion at much less risk to human life, one wonders exactly what it would take to frighten cinema reviewers besides a direct threat to their own lives such as an earthquake, a bombing, or a fire. No one who remembers he is sitting safely in a movie theater, under normal conditions, can expect to be genuinely frightened by movie make-believe. Yet the imagination, to be as free and elastic as it should be in a state of health, must react directly in the esthetic convention to the display of supernaturalist vestiges in the movies, or its owners declare themselves once and for all as revolutionary old maids, so reasonable and modern that before retiring they don't look under the bed for a burglar or Veronica Lake.

III

Miss Lake is one of the most naturally supernatural of screen apparitions. Her record as a feminine hant, calculated and uncalculated, is impressive. Originally she appeared with one eye and both shoulders covered by a cascade of luminous blond hair, as undulant as a long waterfall and suggesting a slit Ku Klux Klansman's hood. Her features, assisted by the magic art of the make-up man, are what is known as photogenic or camera-natural, and under the proper lighting and in the proper degree of repose they cannot be distinguished from those of a shop-window mannequin. Yet she is a living woman. Although she is living, I have found something suggesting fright about her even in those rôles in which she pretends to be a usual biological phenomenon. For instance, if there was ever a mannequin gangster, he was Alan Ladd in *The Glass Key*, and if he ever reached for the upper crust and took down a mannequin moll to load his mannequin gat for him, she was Veronica Lake. What in a less preternatural atmosphere might pass for restraint is in Miss Lake simple lack of animation; one is startled that she can talk. Mr. Ladd, whose personal charm is considerable, played his gangster rôle as though indeed it were a hard-boiled egg. So far as I could make out, the stiff upper lip characteristic of gangster stamina extended to the rest of his face, and aside from an occasional flutter of the eyelashes or a twinkle of the eye, denoting the presence of animal intelligence, all he moved with any elasticity was one side of his handsome mouth to let the words through. The fact that Miss Lake in her charade as a society girl freezes up at first on Mr. Ladd, who manages with a superb display of histrionics to look slightly miffed, produces the effect of an interview between freshly made zombies.

The sources of these precise effects is unquestionably partly the nature of the movie camera and the necessity to use make-up with its attendant effect of artifice, especially if for some reason a lot of it has been used. Miss Lake, however, has lent her remarkable talents also to the filming of an all-out, albeit humorous, tale of the supernatural,

Thorne Smith's *The Passionate Witch*, renamed for cinema consumption *I Married a Witch*. In New England at one time one might be burned as a witch if a person of repute swore with enough emphasis that one had been seen in a state of witchery. The wrong family was burned when they touched that of Miss Lake; she and her father, played by Cecil Kellaway, manage to make their homes in wine bottles till a suitable opportunity arrives for revenge on a living descendant of the person who swore with emphasis, etc. Thorne Smith was not a serious writer, but he had talents, and here his manipulation of the incest theme with a supernatural-fantasy framework is more than ordinarily amusing. Free of their bottles only when they emerge as vapors and materialize in human shape, daughter Veronica and father Cecil are spirits in a double sense. The implication in vacuo is that they may have taken to drink as a refuge from their incestuous impulses; anyway they are great pals. One may recall the magic hocus-pocus of the first movie years and discern the elementary appeal of this device, toying as it does with a supernatural belief as old as thinking man. Daughter and dad, who is a confirmed toper, decide that their duty is plain, and they set out to ruin the young scion of the family responsible for their disgrace. It is also plain in all the overhanging fates that the young people will fall in love with each other. Once Veronica is alienated from her parent, the problem for the prospective bride and bridegroom is how to get rid of the drunkenly revengeful and now doubly embittered pater. The plan decided on and executed with a little strategy is very funny, of noble inevitability, and of supernatural harshness; the old man is corked up in his bottle and put on the whatnot in the young married couple's home, where he provides an object lesson on alcoholism for their off-spring when they are old enough to understand. I might also remark that a tree is the original anchorage for the spirits of father and daughter, as well as the scene of a heart-rending interview between them when the young man tries to rescue the girl from eternal consignment to the spirit world. "Super-fairy tale," to classify this type of film, would do as well as "supernatural."

Thorne Smith has also provided patterns for other prestidigitations for adult libidos: the Topper sequence, with its routine sex intrigue transposed to the fantasy life of a middle-aged man by using the convention of the ma-terialization and dematerialization of spirits, and *Turn-about*, a delightfully forthright little essay on the exchange of secondary sexual characteristics between husband and wife. So far only *comedic* manifestation in the supernatural genre has been specifically considered. The fact is that no matter exactly what the fictive conventions be—what atti-tude of belief be taken by those in the story toward the supernatural phenomena—we are meant to laugh if that is the only alternative to being genuinely frightened. It is a golden rule that one can always laugh at the misfortunes of others, provided those misfortunes are of the "just sup-pose" variety. There are times when the phenomenon is so supernatural that a direct reaction is forced from the audi-ence. When Frankenstein's monster walks, the feminine shrieks from cinema-house balconies are those of the sex-conscious, and as for the howl of the Wolfman, every boy of sixteen in the audience is sophisticated enough to regard it as merely another formal and fortuitous expression of his restless libido . . . and accordingly with the titters and catcalls that respond to the outlandish fix in which the young couple of *Turnabout* find themselves. Of course, there are a few chills—but how far is a thrill from a chill? Only a second's saunter. Just as the source of supernaturalist feelings and superstition is hysteria and the human depths that hysteria releases, so the esthetic reaction to them partakes of hysterical elements.

A most interesting parallel in movie history was presented by the appearance of *Turnabout*. Artificial fantasy as this fable is, considering that its scene is here and now, the invention is so good and the symbolism so sound that it decidedly comes off. The plot arises out of the simple and not too uncommon situation, promoted usually by sexual boredom, when husband and wife find themselves wishing each had the other's responsibilities rather than his own —which might be a mere symbol incidentally for wishing one another at the bottom of the ocean. An alert Oriental god, whose statue happens to be sitting in the couple's bedroom, has harkened to their despair and granted them realization of their first wish. Naturally this wish turns out to be the exchange of personalities mentioned above: ostensibly the exchange of moral responsibilities peculiar to each sex but subconsciously perhaps an expression of latent abnormal impulses in both partners. The young husband becomes the incarnation of that compulsiveness toward feminine mannerisms, gestures, and vocal habits that characterize a certain type of homosexual, while the young wife blooms into the horsiest variety of female with a corresponding opera baritone. Since talkie magic allows the voices to be dubbed in—that of the wife in the husband's case, that of the husband in the wife's case—we have a realization of ancient magical belief in the guise of modern make-believe, and the same ambiguity and ambivalence of spiritual essences are revealed that modern psychology, especially psychoanalysis, has uncovered in present-day civilization. The principle emphasized is not that *matter* and *spirit* are as identical as primitive man's psychology supposed, but that *subjectivity* and *objectivity* are ambivalent. Indeed savage magical principles, mentally applied, form the basis for the fundamental imaginative devices of art: metaphor, symbol, and analogy. From this view supernaturalism becomes a mental convention only, a conclusion that of course shelves the question of the independent existence of a world of spirit. We might extend, however, the identification of the supernatural principle of old with, let us say, the homosexuality of today as far as we like. How can we account for certain homosexual illusions of identity unless we assume that by *imitating* the female the male believes that he *becomes* the female, thus automatically and unconsciously practicing the imitative variety of sympathetic magic?

As we may learn in the movie realm from a marvelous film, *The Dybbuk,* made by the Warsaw Art Players from

S. Ansky's play, homosexuality is not the only basis for the expression of this sort of sexual supernaturalism. The religious sources of this drama are profound, authentic, and traditional, coming down to the present day in Europe, so that we are not dealing with the arbitrary and relatively trivial inspirations of modern scribes. A young and over-zealous adherent of the mystical Chassidism is the son of a man who has made a pact with his dearest friend that the boy should wed his friend's daughter. But the boy's father has died, and now the friend, become worldly, prosperous, and covetous, wishes his daughter to marry a rich man's weakling son. The poor young student, thwarted and passionate, makes a pact with Satan to die and reappear as a dybbuk or spirit capable of possessing another's body and neutralizing its will. A quite wonderful atmosphere is evoked by this film, which there is no reason to describe here in detail. What happens is that the young lover's dybbuk enters his beloved's body as she stands reluctantly at the open-air altar to be wedded to another. Thereafter all possible inducements, including the frightful orders of a great and venerable rabbi that are issued in the synagogue, are directed at the dybbuk to make him leave the girl's body, which stands wavering and wracked as he makes his refusals through her lips. Interesting to note is that artistic discretion has designed that the actress in the girl's rôle use her own voice, deepened and hoarse, for the dybbuk's replies; this heightens the reality of this supernatural event; for to have used the dead young man's voice might have seemed a shade artificial. The dybbuk rejects the most sacred threats until, when all are despairingly certain the girl is doomed, pity seizes him, and he departs. As he leaves, the girl sighs profoundly. Now seated on some steps with head bowed, she lifts her face and asks, "Who sighed?" I cannot recall a more elevated moment of poetry in the movies.

This film provides the same mechanism of a man's spirit in possession of a woman's body as appeared in *Turnabout,* although here under entirely different spiritual conditions. The illusion of identification with a beloved object is a common enough manifestation in modern love of the poetic type; the lover Proust offers an impressive instance. We do not have to regard a dybbuk as a very outlandish or anachronistic phenomenon; indeed the phenomenon of possession in hysterical types, especially women, is well known in modern medical history, and in the Middle Ages, when it was a definite religious expression, it was quite frequent.

IV

Nothing Hollywood has done can compare with the seriousness of *The Dybbuk,* but naturally the American screen city has produced a large number of ghost stories of the straight type; that is, conforming more or less with latter-day popular Christian conceptions of life after death. Yet the fact is, though some of these movies suppose that ghosts are often benevolent and in accordance with the desires of the patrons of spiritualistic mediums manifest themselves as familiar beings to their loved ones, film ghosts as a rule— just for the spiritual hell of it—are costumed with the traditional trappings of hants or beings suspected of venting on the living in a rather uncritical and careless spirit any residue of ill will left from their former life, especially since by ancient tradition a ghost is a rather haughty and mannerless creature, incapable of appreciating the natural qualms of those still in the mundane state. Since it is felt that those ghosts impelled to return to earth find their immateriality a handicap, at least relatively when brought again in contact with the world, they resent the absence of their former carnal pleasures. That their peculiar state of mind opens the way for practical jokes, not always perfectly kind, is shown by the capers of Topper's friends, the Kirbys, whereas the opposite, an intent of the deadliest kind, is revealed by the wronged spirit of *The Invisible Man*, also serially movieized.

It is fairly logical that, confronted with mere intimations of ghostly presences without their explicit declaration of identity and purposes, people should be frightened of ghosts. The good-evil ambiguity of ghostly being was illustrated by the melodramatic thriller, *The Uninvited*, wherein the hallowed paraphernalia of ghosts, such as wailing at night, frigid perfume, the ability to wither things, and materialization as a vapor—in fact, everything to make them repellent—are played up as strictly the properties of an evil ghost, since the benevolent ghost, a woman, falls victim to mistaken identification and is suspected of desiring to murder the young heroine, when actually she has returned only to foil a wicked plot of the living, aided by the evil ghost, to deal the same fate to the heroine, her daughter, as was dealt to her: death by violence. Presumably ghosts have difficulty in making themselves known for want of spiritual co-operation on the part of the living. Here the spiritual phenomena, including a distinguished performance by a Ouija board, is almost strictly bona fide and no doubt sends a good proportion of the audience out of the theater properly heated by chills and wondering wistfully if ghosts after all may not really exist. Incidentally a witty play on the capacity of militant ghosts to frighten humans, originated by Oscar Wilde in *The Canterville Ghost* as the capacity of frightened humans to become militant ghosts, was duly carted to the screen and accorded the most expensive hamantics by Charles Laughton as the spirit who redeemed his mundane cowardice.

As for serious religious fantasy of the supernatural, I doubt if the American screen has more pretentious efforts than its two versions of Sutton Vane's *Outward Bound*, its filmizing of Thornton Wilder's *Our Town,* and the super-distance-going *The Song of Bernadette.* A neat device of the stage play of *Our Town* was to present ordinary materiality, the set, etc., as ghostly, namely nonexistent, and the human spirits as material objects. What the screen lost in abandoning this poetically apt device it gained in its natural translation of bodily substances into illusory and formal ectoplasm. James Wong Howe's photography was superb in quality and the movietone as a whole felicitous. Yet these tribal ghosts who take leave from vigilance over their own graves, where they are living and speaking tombstones as opaque as they were in life, to superintend the continuity of their descendants' affairs seem to me essentially boring, mainly because their spiritual substance is one of unimaginative conservatism. Historically and sociologically, they suggest totem poles, being symbols of paleface clans that watch over their traditional households. But to admire such loyal ghosts one would have to admire wholeheartedly—as I do not—the traditions of such households.

The weightiest burden placed by Hollywood spectacles upon modern credulity occurred in *Outward Bound* or, as latterly done, *Between Two Worlds*. Originally this fable did not mince either spirit or matter but represented the beyond as a sort of continent that one reaches by transoceanic liner, the only difference between the so-called living and the so-called dead being that the latter live the rest of their eternal lives as they were physically at the moment of their death. Of course it is easy to interpret such an invention, one quite ingenious in its way, as an allegory of a moral nature, preaching a very ordinary and, needless to say, creepily bourgeois variety of ethics. Life after death is revealed to be in fact nothing if not Protestant, with authority bureaucratized among the clergy, its apparent form oddly resembling the commissar system under current Communist dictatorship.

The examiner literally has the function of a spiritual immigration officer who assesses your moral baggage and decides the degree of punishment or reward for your mundane behavior and the form such punishment or reward shall take. If you are a callous financier or a fashionably frivolous matron, you may expect a very nasty look indeed, mayhap a publicly administered quip, and the book read to you right out of the prop room in Hollywood. If you are just a cynical and romantic newspaperman whose indiscreet conduct has caused big business or crooked politics to ruin your career, you may find that you are John Garfield, after all, and quite willing to let motherly Sara Allgood (Mrs. Midgett) keep house for you ad infinitum. I confess that the acting talent and some shrewd direction, which contribute to the eloquence of this boatload of cinemash, came as near to frightening me as Hollywood supernature has ever done. If my hair didn't stand on end, it wasn't because I didn't go under a wave of gooseflesh whenever I was recalled to the basic bone of the movie's spiritual message.

v

The Song of Bernadette by Franz Werfel has been given visible flesh by Hollywood with what might be called great tact rather than great art, a tact whose distribution is a leveling agent, simplifying through both reduction and heightening. This reverent handling of a best-selling novel about a saint whose sainthood was infused with a certain melodrama of belief and disbelief is a luminous example of the most mature craft of Hollywood in accenting good manners, observing a genteel formal pace, and employing pure artifice to obtain effects hankered after by drama-minded and sentiment-slanted directors. I mean in sum and substance the craft that may prevail likewise for a simple farewell between a man and a woman, a farewell that must show, let us say, that they may never see each other again, and wonder if the parting should occur. . . . The voices must be in just the right key—the same key that pervaded *The Song of Bernadette,* one of reverence toward sentiment; there must be the given positions of the two players and measured pauses, and the words must hit precisely, so that everything will seem solemn and important and injected with the proper degree of spirituality. It is the sort of scene that happens in every third screen drama, and it is this special mise-en-scène, this form of ritual and refinement, that is glorified so studiously in the picturization of Werfel's novel and appears in the symbolic rôle of the supernatural. . . .

It is true that Bernadette, the peasant girl, has a vision, which she declares is that of the Virgin and therefore supernatural. This is the kind of pattern that may touch the heart of the sincere believer in Christian religion, but its strict orthodoxy is its limitation; for as a matter of fact one cannot call contemporary interest in saints very powerful outside the serious influence of the Catholic Church. At any rate, in this story we have to face the fact that the official church was highly sceptical of Bernadette's authenticity and thus, before the miracles were accomplished, placed the peasant girl in a class with superstitious believers in ghosts and even with rank frauds. The truth is that official religion is opposed to the supernatural as an arbitrarily manifest force simply because it fears those very magical instincts which make possible so-called naïve belief in supernatural agencies. If Bernadette's vision had not at last been pronounced authentic, the question would have lain open as to whether Satan might be the next to appear to her. For Bernadette is a leftover from the female ecstatics of the Middle Ages, and these ecstatics, who claimed immediate and personal communication with supernatural or preternatural persons, were a source of concern to the Church, owing to their individualism, which seemed to make them prey to evil forces as well as good. That Bernadette was not an ecstatic—suggesting far more the idyllic rusticity of Millet's "Reaper"—but that she asseverated her vision and its greatness with patient simplicity and decorum bothered her interlocutors as much as Joan of Arc's great steadfastness bothered hers.

We cannot avoid noting the parallel that presents itself here in the shape of pure atmosphere; it might even be called an analogy with supernatural or ghostly presence. As soon as Bernadette makes her claim, she is treated like a mental patient, which in a quite basic sense she is, and thus by a certain circuitous but sure-footed way through the purlieus of Hollywood illusion *The Song of Bernadette* is possessed with the spirit of the generic mise-en-scène I described above: the sad and dramatic farewell. It is the "tread lightly here" of cinema sentiment: "Spirit at work." Human nature, in the state of apprehending the super-realm of spirit, of things above common perception, is in as delicate a condition as someone who has suffered a severe accident or shock or is about to give birth. Is not this a literal echo of the danger in which ancient and even modern savages supposed themselves to exist on all the most important and critical occasions of their lives? Truly in *The Song of Bernadette* it is the solemn hush of a cathedral that suffuses the feeling of the story, but in depth of quality and poetic tone it seems materially no different from the solemn hush that sets in within Hollywood's sound-proofed studios when they decide to take the scene. The actors are at once in a delicate and a sublime condition; they must obey the inner self, the soul, that tells them they are not Helmut Dantine and Andrea King for this perilous moment but Martin Richter and Lisa Dorn . . . and every word and gesture must be right and done as rehearsed. Indistinguishably the same physical texture of spirit dominates the corridors of the private pavilions in a hospital or a fashionable psychiatrist's office. Silence is sacred. The striking thing is that Frankenstein's monster stalking through the fields may evoke the same special hush as Bernadette walking with her vision, the same hush that surrounds the notes of her song. How these things are to be artistically or morally judged seems to have little to do with what may be termed the awed silence they command in the spectator.

When Bernadette's faith in her vision leads to the phenomenon of miracle, it becomes socialized, and mass faith carries her to sainthood. Dramatically and pictorially, the sight of cripples throwing away their crutches and going off crying and laughing and giving thanks has obvious virtues apart from a definition of the source of the transformation. Actually the spiritual structure of novel and movie alike is extremely common, almost journalistic, for invention has been paralyzed by the sacredness of the subject and by the obligation, doubly felt by the movie, to keep it all orthodox; that is, one of the proved formulas. Consequently the miracle therein appears as one of the weakest forms of supernatural manifestation so far as man's spirit is concerned, for it is purely arbitrary: the faith of the cripples needs authority in order to operate and cure them of affliction. Naturally, when Bernadette's authenticity became popularly recognized, official religion could not hold out, being unwilling not to include in itself all recognized authority. In molding the supernatural into so specific, traditional, and limited a form as the Lourdes miracles of cure the author, Franz Werfel, unwittingly conspired with Hollywood to cement further its authoritarian formalism concerning the sacredness of human sentiments on all levels. One might protest: Werfel was helpless, like many another author who is lured by gold. But was he so coincidental a conspirator? The movies have achieved wide and potent fame. Wasn't Bernadette a peacetime Joan of Arc, even a post-peacetime Maid? And wasn't the psychology of the movie's spiritual atmosphere enmeshed with the popular sense of war antidote, a feeling against killing and maiming, since Our Lady of Lourdes became the patron saint of a resuscitation of spirit through the restitution of normal limbs? Peace, the normal pace of life, the relaxing rhythm of alternate rest and activity, the ritual

98

embodied by all elaborately arranged movie scenes of sentiment, were these not supernatural indeed in a world paced by war and perpetual social crises? Sometimes the silence in the movie theater seemed fabulously exempt, and, as we snuggled into our seats, feeling that we in American cities were safe from bombs, the sense of some unnatural taboo might well have invaded us. Those actors on the screen, so careful and conscientious, privileged to choose an exact pace, allow an exact pause to dissolve, and never hurry . . . they seemed to have a supernatural leisure, to exist in the fabulous, sublime time of art. . . . I thought it too bad that Bernadette should have been played by Jennifer Jones, a young lady who is more attractive and appealing than a real Bernadette could have been; for, having previously supplied the feminine interest in Grade B horse operas, Miss Jones dilated on the deferential silence by inflecting it to her novitiate on the screen and asked us for a strict observance of the occasion as though she had been a trained nurse admonishing us with finger pressed on lips and murmuring, "Actress winning award."

VI

Despite spasmodic inspirations such as *Curse of the Cat People,* regrettably not quite so well done as its scenario warranted, and despite productions that have a genuine even if sometimes clumsy poetry and humor—René Clair's *It Happened Tomorrow* probably hits the high point in efforts of this kind—Hollywood's wrestling with the artistic problems of supernaturalist fantasy is sordid to watch, being, when all is said and done, so limitlessly far from being solved with a Dantesque majesty. Inevitably, on the other hand, American films have discovered exactly the right formula for the entertainment of ghostly processes on the unequivocally lower platform of art. This consists of the comparatively sophisticated marriage of the primitive devices of cinema trickery with a resuscitation of the primitive psychology of magic that I have been stressing. Certain films, such as *Gildersleeve's Ghost* and Olsen and Johnson's *The Ghost Catchers,* nailed something neatly by hanging their eerie rigadoons onto the rational premises of criminals trying to frighten legally interested parties away from inherited caches or criminal hideaways. *Gildersleeve's Ghost* had a luscious blonde beauty who kept luring the comic lead into hefty and spine-tingling kisses only to dissolve her shapely avoirdupois without notice. Still more amusing was the fantasy involved in *The Ghost Catchers,* where an unseen, soft-shoe dancing ghost who was a gentleman of the nineties resisted all 1944 efforts to rout him from his former home until he had unleashed on him and his heavenly music (" 'Way Down upon the Swanee River") a full jazz band and a ballet of jitterbuggers who even infested the air over the most august bedsteads in the great mansion. At this he raised the white flag of his klan, which fluttered madly above his invisible presence as he flowed down the stairs and exited by the front door. Magnanimously he returned later, even materializing in seraphically white tails, to aid the hapless tenants, walled up in the

100

cellar by the crooks who would have liked to confiscate the fine wines there. Here one could perceive the justice of being frightened by concrete phenomena of a supernatural type, for even the hopelessly naïve can reason that all visible phenomena have sufficient causes thereof, and if the chicanery isn't supernatural, it must certainly be natural. The purely natural, purely human, and purely ulterior motive is perhaps the most subtly fraught with danger ever known and rightly frightens us all. It is unreasonable to think philosophically of the ulterior motive as supernatural, and yet isn't it common sense to be on guard against what operates in the dark, for then its nature partakes of the dark? What we call the supernatural the primordial savage originally intuited as virtually the subnatural or subterranean—or in terms of more modern myth, as the black art of the devil. . . . It is no fiction for children that the devil's disguises are multifarious and extremely mutinous, being, one might say, far better equipped with invisible zippers than was Mary Kirby when she showed Topper how a lady duly dead can unzipper her material being and become the nude landscape even more easily than she could formerly unzipper her girdle and become her nude self. In this simple trick of the cinema, this ungirdling of the illusion of flesh, this demonstrating of the invisible existence of spirit independent of matter, does it not suggest, with more rudimentary eloquence than religious teaching does, the lightninglike nature of the spirit and its defiance of what we know as physical law—even if in the end it must obey a physical law?

101

5. FINDING FREUDISM PHOTOGENIC

There was a great temptation for me to tack this chapter onto the previous one, inasmuch as the surviving mystery of the soul and the transformed practice of magic (clinical psychology) have together induced Hollywood to tackle the existence of psychiatry, head on and long after it has become a social institution. Naturally, just as with the stage and the novel, the screen has a valid problem concerning the interest of psychology as a form of analysis explaining the deepest human motives rather than leaving them implied. The great artistic convention is that characters express themselves completely in conscious thought, spoken words, and physical behavior, so in one respect it is somewhat like cheating for the author as psychoanalyst to explain to the reader or spectator by means of what, dramatically speaking, amounts to asides. Interesting it is that the best-known American dramatist, Eugene O'Neill, found modern characters so complex to convey theatrically that he made the aside or monologue into an important convention (*Strange Interlude*), thus echoing the stream of consciousness or interior monologue made famous by James Joyce's innovations in the novel. The implicit factor of such modernism of technique is the constant elusiveness of human motive on the one hand and its ultimate static mystery on the other. The function of art, however, is generally accepted as communication, not as inscrutable symbol,

102

and there's the rub. . . . All art in the final analysis is to be subjected not only to standards of plastic beauty but also to criteria of relevance and intellectual clarity.

When Aladdin and other *Arabian Nights* heroes desired a genie's services, a lamp or a ring was rubbed. This produced magic consequences of practical glory and the fulfillment of desire. In the preceding chapter I called attention to the fact that with the same ease as legendary magicians the movies may produce illusions, either as esthetic means of communication or, the reality of this illusion being recognized, as illusion within reality, as when ghosts or hallucinations are the subject matter. I made the point, moreover, that in respect to the hypothesis of another world of being, with which this world is merely in spasmodic and doubtful contact, we have to reckon with a good-evil dichotomy not only because ghosts have evil intents but because of the preternatural world of demons as distinct from the hereafter of the Christian heaven; that is, otherworldly visitants may also come from hell—from below rather than from above. An idea whose perennial fascination has been generously recognized by Hollywood is that phantoms and such may emanate not from a place outside the person meeting them but from inside him; that is, they may be hallucinations of a sick brain. This is the twilight sphere of speculation about mental phenomena that psychoanalysis took for its own and set in order. Possessed persons became not victims of magic or of the devil but sex neurotics and psychopaths. What psychoanalysis accomplished in the sense of social therapy—if this term be permissible—is the inclusion of nervous cases, dipso-maniacs, and would-be suicides in the classification of those curable through dream interpretation and clinical rites. Controversy, to be sure, exists as to the ratio of successful cures in all branches of psychiatry, including Freudian psychoanalysis, but even if all the evidence we had were limited to two films issued in 1946, *Spellbound* and *The Seventh Veil*, there would be proof conclusive that Freud did not probe our dreams exactly in vain. Psychoanalysis is now part of the social texture, and if it is an overadver-tised product of capitalism, it is likewise a clear-cut de-velopment of practices sanctified by an ancient planetary record. I have already discussed the comedian as medicine man and as the fool of chivalric tradition. As a serious per-son the psychoanalyst is a direct return to the intellectual magic of the true medicine man.

The chief reason why it has taken Hollywood and the British movie city, Elstree, so long to find Freudism photo-genic may strike the cerebral tympanum oddly. This reason is the sound of big, strange words. After all, "psycho-analysis" actually has six syllables, and even now a vox-pop reporter requesting a patron of *Spellbound* in the lobby afterwards to spell "psychoanalysis" might easily throw said patron into a panic. "Psychiatry" has two syl-lables less than "psychoanalysis"; yet I remember vividly a screen comedy drama in which someone, with an apolo-getic smirk, made a point of its polysyllables. It is a plati-tude that in the dense ranks of the American people learning is considered an unnecessary affectation. But time

trudges on. And the pressure of the enlightened classes—
or is it the magic of advertising?—makes people tolerant
and even interested in the wonders of the psychiatric clinic.
After all, think of the incredible sale of the *Gypsy Dream
Book*! The interpretation of dreams indeed is far older than
seventy generations of grandmothers. The Sibyls did it.

Perhaps the fatal step toward serious treatment of a
psychoanalytical theme in cinema was actually taken not
in Hollywood itself but in the United States Army, when
it labeled so many supposedly normal and useful citizens
psychoneurotics that people got the vague but persistent
notion there were facts at home that had better be faced.
Part of the success of Dali's surrealism in Hollywood,
primerfied as it was, undoubtedly must be ascribed to the
well-known morbid curiosity of faithful newspaper readers.
Magazines such as *Life* and *Look* have beaten the way to
the semi-reading public with flashy spreads of soldiers
under shock treatment, and even before that Hollywood had
girded itself to present the problem of the returned soldier,
suffering from battle nerves as well as from mutilation,
and Hollywood has religiously presented it. The shock
aspect naturally was right up Hollywood's chromium-
plated alley, and, as if in echo of all the old sensational
effects, a movie duly arrived with the curt tag, *Shock*, treating in a manner as novel as the atom bomb the phenomena
of temporary mental derangement and the dirty Machiavel-
lics of a licensed psychiatrist. The girl and golem formula,
which had its most shining accolade in the classic *Frankenstein*, was here simply converted into the scandalously

opportune terms of a returned soldier's wife as victim of a vicious psychiatrist whom she has seen commit a murder; the doctor tries to prove her insane and almost succeeds in making her so. Here likewise of course was the stereotype of the murderer busy covering up his tracks by the most unscrupulous means. It is not at all insignificant that in a precursor of this film, in which a man is cured with shock treatment by a dangerous serum, the inoculated patient, a victim of amnesia, is started by the serum back at human scratch, so to speak, and we see his silhouette on the sickroom wall going through wild anthropoid motions that apparently put the seal of science on Darwin's theory. But one may be sure he comes out of it all as cute and harmless as Van Johnson.

The psychiatric academies, one may generalize, have come out of it with a far greater triumph than art when we consider the most serious examples of psychoanalytic films. Therefore one wonders that *Shock* should have earned an official protest—as though the "new science" should not produce individuals as false to the Hippocratic oath as so many plain medicos have proved to be both on and off the screen. One cannot help recalling *Kings Row*, not only its sadistic surgeon but also its noble pioneer, the young doctor headed for Vienna. Well, he has arrived . . . back in America.

Perhaps I may be thought to aim at the impression that *Spellbound* and *The Seventh Veil* are phony psychoanalytics. They are not; that is to say, not in the common-sense aspect. Yet *The Seventh Veil*, Elstree's product, although less melodramatic than *Spellbound,* has a mental doctor who is not of the Freudian orthodoxy but relies on a calming drug to help his patient tell her secret thoughts and life history; she is in a dream state rather than being one who tells her dreams, and what the doctor does is to take advantage of a condition of shock to lead her to her true desires by autosuggestion. The young lady is a musician who has been tutored from an early age by her male guardian; the latter, driving her to sacrifice fun and even love for her art, has proved a grim taskmaster. When finally she wins her moral freedom after attaining artistic success, her guardian apparently is willing for her to lead her own life, and so she rushes to seek the young student she has been prevented from marrying. But the delayed affair does not work out, if only because now the student is married and has a pair of children. Nor does a more strenuous episode with a romantic portrait painter turn out fortunately. The young woman's collapse is precipitated, oddly enough, by an automobile accident that occurs on a marriage elopement with the said portrait painter. Her hands burned, she acquires the fixation that she can no longer play the piano. However, as an experiment under the drug proves, she can play. And yet all at once with a sob she grows limp and turns away from the keyboard. The doctor divines love as the source of her dilemma, but steadfastly believing that music will furnish the clue to her cure, he continues the drug treatment and autosuggestion through music. In the climactic experiment he puts on the phonograph the record of a piece she performed for her guardian when as a schoolgirl she first met him. Indeed the man of science has guessed correctly—but so, I would hazard, has the little girl in the front row!

When at the end of the climactic sequence she has to choose among the three men in her life, gathered considerately at the foot of the staircase, the young pianist runs to her guardian. This occurs only a moment after he has shut himself in his den in the belief that he has lost her. The trouble has been that fear of her guardian—a very pleasant-looking fellow, by the way—has prevented her from recognizing her love for him and him from pursuing his love for her. Well, the conditions of this failure to transfer mental therapy brilliantly to the screen should be self-evident. *This* film should be protested by Freudians and other psychoanalysts. Certainly it is not that psychiatry is without a real plot agency here or that it is not the doctor who arranges fate; such rudimentary requirements are met. But it is that psychiatry has been utilized as but another instrument for adjusting a dilemma story so trite that the doctor is a mere foil for the preordained happy ending. How many times, one might specify, have we seen on the screen a lady in the distress of not being able to make up her own mind? Usually her psychological struggle is perfectly conscious even though she may have psychic repressions; in *The Seventh Veil*, however, psychic repression is almost 100 per cent. And how many times have we witnessed an accident whose threat to the life or good looks of the victim has brought the loved and loving one posthaste to the bedside, a gesture by which—surprise!

108

surprise!—all existing barriers are swept aside? Could it be that this is a way of psychoanalyzing not a lady but a deus ex machina, a way of saying that the deity who presides over frustrated lovers is more complex than his traditional surface? But this is to do little to exploit the specific powers of psychoanalysis. And how many times, again, has a movie reserved its climax for the love-choice scene? Alas! it is the same old story—plus the news item of mental therapy. Perhaps it is only fair not to discount the prestige given the lay reputation of psychoanalysis in this film through such means as English accents, tony manners, and the introduction of the reverential hush at psychological moments.

I cannot help thinking nevertheless that when it came to treating what may be succinctly put as "the lady in the dark" theme, the American movies have been more hep to the intrinsic psychological value of this theme by making the lady's soul—to invoke the authority of an American versifier—a circus. Although an Englishwoman, Gertrude Lawrence, played *Lady in the Dark* on the Broadway stage, an American, Ginger Rogers, played the rôle for Hollywood. Assuredly Miss Lawrence was more *Vogue*, but Ginger was there with the elephants and the acrobats. That the benighted lady should have worked on a fashion magazine was perfect, since the attention to apparel—that which disguises—absorbed her thoughts to the critical exclusion of what apparel could conceal: the male torso. Of course the catch was that Torso with a capital T was not really what the lady was in the dark about—a quirk very possibly meant to be a lewd innuendo that psychoanalysis holds the theory that all women yearn primarily for what must be conveniently labeled caveman sex. Oh, the subtlety of such a *left*-handed tribute to psychoanalysis!

It is hard to believe that a metropolitan lady earning a large salary for her talent at fashion editing should not know the main entrances and exits of a psychiatrist's office even before going there; at the same time *Lady in the Dark* was useful for showing the brief *fouetté* it is from the ballet to the circus, where indeed Zorina once performed in an elephant ballet staged by Balanchine. For the dream sequence in *Lady in the Dark* is nothing other than a fantastic circus. We cannot pretend that there doesn't exist an American superstition larger than life to the effect that a woman is slightly affected to dance *sur les points* and a man slightly effeminate to dance beside her; yet blown up to Madison Square Garden dimensions, anything can happen and be tolerated. After all, the circus is a place where high-wire acrobatic tension is on a par with orgastic potency and where a man being shot out of a cannon is, rather than a dream metaphor, a crude existential fact. If the dream appears in *Lady in the Dark* as a fashion-styled circus, it is a modern wrinkle proving psychiatry can be fun so long as you maintain your sense of humor—so long, that is to say, as it has the status of an exotic importation, such as the half-man-and-half-woman from Australia. When it is treated seriously on the screen, psychiatry must serve merely as the base for home-cooked art.

The Oriental spice in *Spellbound* was supplied by the

imagination of the surrealist painter, Salvador Dali, who
—under the supervision, we are to assume, of a psychiatrist
—designed the suspect murderer's dream visions, which,
analyzed, lead to the revelation of the actual murderer.
Almost at the same time as *Spellbound* was issued, a Fred
Astaire film, *Yolanda and the Thief*, had an amusing
dream sequence in the form of a modern ballet; the most
interesting point is that whereas the hero of the latter
movie could hardly be expected to have such dreams, Mr.
Astaire himself might have had them. The choreographic
fantasy comprises an obstacle dream, and though the hero's
path is directed toward a fair young lady, conceivably Mr.
Astaire's path, subconsciously, might be directed toward
the classic heights of legitimate ballet; in fact it is a surrealist ballet that he dances in this sequence of *Yolanda
and the Thief*, which incidentally has an *Arabian Nights*
theme, and the sequence certainly shows as much dancing
per se as Dali's first ballet presented in America.

The dance and circus elements are absent from the dream
sequence of *Spellbound*, which instead has the air of animated, badly done Dali oil paintings. One understood that
Mr. Dali was displeased with the photogenics of Hollywood dream art, and to an extent we can theoretically agree
and even sympathize with him. But only a megalomaniac,
which, as I recall, Dali boasts of being, could imagine that
he could get something on American film to which he would
care to sign his name. Yet the Dali sequence is better than
anything the movie city could have thought up unaided,
and in effect no doubt it had the desired element of

exoticism. One of the hardest problems of psychiatrists is to convince the patient that the crux of the matter lies deep within himself and has not been written in the heavens since time began. Yet by and large there is no question that psychiatry has vanquished astrology, tealeaf reading, and yoga in settling problems of the heart and head, and this triumph doubtless is due to its actually attacking the psychic root of modern social evil more directly than its rivals do. Religion in all its foreign and domestic, official and semi-official forms is more a solace than a remedy, more compensation than reconstruction. But not its science, patently, makes psychiatry adaptable to the screen; rather it is the photogenic character of the dream.

If a doctor can read the mind to its final depths, can penetrate past even the seventh veil indicated by the therapist in the movie of that name as the last veil that the mind, unlike Salome, is so loath to shed—if he can do this, then in a sense the intangible is rendered tangible, the ghostly takes on flesh, the unseen becomes seen, and we have an equivalent of the materialization of spirits in mediumistic séances and even a convincing demonstration of thought transference; the psychoanalyst gets to know the true content of a patient's mind as soon as he or she knows it—or sooner.

This very factor provides the cinematic charm of *Spellbound* insofar as that charm has any novelty. The young woman psychoanalyst (Ingrid Bergman), inducing her amnesiac patient (Gregory Peck) to relate his dream, puts the pieces together to make a coherent symbolic pattern.

112

This feat leads to their marriage, which previously hung dangerously in the balance. So the lady psychoanalyst becomes a super-equipped opponent of the dark forces of life that so often have been seen to interfere with the course of true love. Again the suffering individual has had a severe shock. Yet one unpleasant speculation does not occur to anyone in the film and so perhaps should not occupy a devout movie-goer; it is that some malady deeper than forgetfulness may motivate the gentleman's impersonation, a strategy that he has adopted to avoid arrest for the crime he imagines he has committed. The fact is that *Spellbound* has the same flaw so many problem movies have, that of begging the question when it comes to taking a really profound psychological view. However psychoanalytical, it stops short of true analysis in the way so many movies, however realistic, stop short of true realism.

Now that on the other hand the dream has been found so photogenic and the emotional atmosphere of psychoanalysis, with its obvious kinship to the sinister sex of monster movies, has been found so flexible as screen idiom, it might be thought that Hollywood has rapidly prepared to make up for many sins of omission in respect to psychology. But such restitution can never be accomplished so long as the final-clinch psychology dominates the mythos of movie producers and script-writers. The critical characterlessness of psychoanalytic films rests to date on their assumption that the psychic crisis is exceptional, outside the pattern of normal events. The psychoanalytic myth, which seems quite plastic for Hollywood mechanics, is no other than the dark deed of wanton or perverse sex—a fact that hardly needs my documentation in this particular place. Thus the same personified sex paradox, in full make-up and with unruffled coiffure, issues complacently from the psychiatrist's office on modern movie lots as issued from the minister's chamber in the old, old days: no matter what thrills the heroine's vicissitudes have afforded the gaping spectator, no matter what unmentionable perils have touched the hem of her skirt, she finds herself rescued, safe, and pure in the suitably civilized and restrained arms of her true lover. If Hollywood should deign to notice such a complaint as mine, the reply would be almost automatic and also, given modern scientific faith, foolproof: "Is it not the claim of *psychoanalysis itself* that the evil ghost, even if only the tyrant of a dream, is to be laid forever, and the patient, cured, to go home to a normal and happy sex life?" The counterargument must be that, like all generalities phrased for readers of *The Saturday Evening Post* and *Reader's Digest*, normalcy and happiness, whether considered under the spiritual aegis of astrology or psychoanalysis, are very relative conditions, earning proper skepticism in the heart of hearts of every thinking housewife. At which cue, one fears, Hollywood will merely wink and perhaps articulate, as it is wont to do in its fancy way, the truism that the public wants not truth but entertainment. Timelessly one may respond to this platitude as follows: How could the public want truth when all popular art, outside folk arts such as jazz and dancing, makes the true synonymous with the dull? One of my present pur-

114

poses is to reveal a weightier entertainment value in films than Hollywood itself is aware of. And in this respect such analyses as those in the magic-lantern metamorphoses in this book are in competition with the *Spellbounds* that have been and the *Spellbounds* to come. If I aim, however, at orientating my analysis of movies to a deeper psychological truth than routine dream interpretation, it is because Hollywood's dream products (or films) are much more complex than its script-writers lead, and are led, to suppose. Indeed it is script-writer and director who should be analyzed. Not that I really mean the "should." I should say: Let them go on by all means. But let them not get too technical. Let them exploit the photogenic dream without calling in too much hired help with medical degrees.

A pioneering psychological fantasy was *The Eternal Mask*, a Swiss film made in 1934. This movie showed a mental world conceived not in casual dreams but as an integral part of the fantasy life of the protagonist. There was an intuition of the fact that the imaginative life may be something to rival real life and that illusion-filled broodings may take obsessive hold on a subject without the point's being his own ruined reputation and that of his family. The great moral step accomplished by Hollywood's recognition of the psychoanalytic technique is to have drawn a sharp line between the psychiatric clinic and the insane asylum, a line that for divers reasons has remained fatally blurred. Indeed in emancipated circles it is now fashionable and something of a liberal duty to have been, as the word informally goes, analyzed. It is somewhat like having gambled a fortune at Monte Carlo, having had tea at the White House, or having chatted with the Duke of Windsor—or on a more intense plane having had a lover who attempted suicide. Of the profound ethical challenge given man by the psychoanalytic ritual most psychiatrists themselves are meagerly aware; like five dozen other professions in the modern world psychoanalysis is the craft of a specialist who himself may be said, in the hallowed term of Thorstein Veblen, to have an occupational psychosis.

The happiest function of the psychoanalytic trend in movies would be to focus attention on the dream world *as a place;* that is, as a three-dimensional theater like the physical world held in common by everyone but individualized like artistic vision itself and holding another mental dimension, that of the fabulous and impossible. While *The Eternal Mask* is not a very satisfying achievement, its sense of the depths of the mind as a poetic realm as well as a chamber of moral struggle is cinematically tonic. The unconscious, the fantasy life, the derangement of reason—these are not human manifestations that necessarily strangle the individual or prestidigitate him out of normal society. Real dreams and fantasies may be just as well air-conditioned and just as commodious as Radio City Music Hall.

6. MAGIC-LANTERN METAMORPHOSES II

Revenge by Hollywood

Ever since people started paying nickels to witness the moving photographs of their fellow men, the legitimate theater has looked leerily, warily, enviously, at the ease with which the cinema spectacle could woo clients away from doors hallowed by the great tradition of the actor's corporeal presence and by the words of splendor floating from his mouth—from between his own lips, not from a copyrighted if verisimilitudinous duplicate of lips that till 1927 did not make themselves heard. Just as ensconced enemies of the phonograph sat in their homes swearing that Caruso and Galli-Curci and Schumann-Heink could not possibly render themselves virtuously vocal if the medium of communication was a round black disc whirling on a turntable, so devotees of the stage spectacle and its classic tradition of Shakespeare shuddered at the thought of an ersatz presence deprived of its greatest golden privilege of uttering hallowed words—even if these were only the words of J. M. Barrie or John Galsworthy. Naturally a neat hundredweight of social snobbery together with artistic Philistinism went into the boycotting of media that seemed to many well-upholstered souls the impudent gadgets of a precocious age of science and commerce. That many of those who objected were making money hand over fist with commodities far

117

less close to the spiritual life than movies or Victrolas did not occur to the nay-sayers. And for the very good reason that those who flattered themselves they controlled the economic processes also flattered themselves that they held a monopoly on the high arts of drama and opera, which they placed on the same level as the acquisition of a painting that nobody but a millionaire could buy. The story of how wrong these antiquated Philistines were, in every department of intellect and taste, is told multiply on many another sheet of paper. Here I wish to draw the reader's attention to the last vestige of the hauteur of artistic standards as held by critics of the legitimate theater and by drama-goers who believe, articulately or in silence, that no matter how rotten a stage play may be, it is more honorable to sit in a theater stall, sniff, sigh, and refuse to applaud than even to be seen in the lowly cinema.

It is perfectly true that the tradition of the prose and poetic drama is not to be compared artistically with the tradition of the movies, nor is the tradition of the foreign movies to be compared with our domestic tradition. At the same time many otherwise sophisticated souls blind themselves to the fact that they go to the theater precisely for one of the same reasons that I, for instance, go to the movies; that is, to be witness of a medium that amuses and provokes me. Of course, as I have written this sequel to *The Hollywood Hallucination* to show, I consider that my reasons for viewing and studying movies are more valid than any conceivable reasons for seeing New York stage productions. The source of this conviction is that the stage

mechanism is by no means so fertile of the illusion of complex and often hidden realities as the movie mechanism.
It is not merely that, as I explained in a previous chapter,
the movies have created a tradition of supernaturalism
out of their innate character as a means, but also that in
their mad search for novelty, the iron necessity to keep
producing and to find ideas, angles, they are much more
life-giving than efforts of dramatists to congregate enough
words in three or four acts to permit the curtain to ring
down on another Broadway hit. I should like to point out
that everything new that has come to technical presentation
in the theater in this century has come directly or indirectly
from the movies—with few exceptions. Even the German
expressionism from which derived the fantastic sets in the
advance-guard film, *The Cabinet of Dr. Caligari*, was based
on recent ideas of painting that the theater later took over,
and painted sets of a fantastic kind had already been used
by Méliès in his films, *A Trip to the Moon* (1902), *The
Palace of the Arabian Nights* (1905), and *The Conquest of
the Pole* (1912), all of which in their freedom of movement and use of visual fantasy and trickery were considerably in advance of the stage at that time. As for the Broadway devices of streamlining by fleeting incidents, revolv-
ing stages, quick-change sets, and cross sections of apartment buildings, the mobility of feeling was obviously
created by the montage of cinema.

It is likewise perfectly true that so far as serious intentions go, it is likely that a Broadway dramatist will supply
a spectacle a little more honest and closely related to life

than the same creation will be after Hollywood has meta-
morphosed it. But how important is the Broadway dramatist's honesty and closeness to life? And what kind of an
esthetic Crossley has he? How does his work compare with
the tradition of the drama? The fact is he is apt to fall
shorter of this tradition than the better Hollywood product
falls short of the standards set by the best foreign films.
These are things that need laboratory verification by the
skeptical and the wary; happily, for the benefit of the
interested, several New York cinema houses have an exclusive policy of reviving weekly both foreign and domestic
films.

One fears that many snooty observers of filmic development are innately soft-boiled and always will be. This cultural gelatinousness is a trait of the listless conservative,
whose temper is always roiled by the hint that he can be
torn away from Mozart, Shakespeare, and Rembrandt to
sully eyesight and hearing with less pure addresses to the
two faculties involved. It is the same old, faintly malodor-
ous petty-bourgeois fairy tale: the opera, the ballet, the
concert hall. . . . Even the modern esthete, since his very
mental life is based firmly and solely on his estheting,
takes special satisfaction in remaining cloistered before
the blandishments of the cinema entertainment, pastime of
hoi polloi. I affirm that the only reasons for being too good
for the movie theater and for its vibrating messages about
the modern psyche are the best in the world, and the best
in the world is the exclusive property, at this juncture of
planetary time elapse, of the exceptional and validly ac-

credited individual; anticinema grounds therefore fail to constitute an attitude of real significance. It is always possible for the sincere intellectual to read a good book or write a good article or just stay at home, safe from the attacks upon his nervous system that countless movies with their gremlins of bad taste are lying in wait to launch against him. But a passive dependence upon ideas of perfection seems hardly just to really creative standards of human activity. What material is not good enough for creative transmutation? Look at what happened to Mortimer Brewster, dramatic-critic hero of the farce melodrama, *Arsenic and Old Lace,* an exhibit that proved a natural for Hollywood and offers a rich lesson in cinema initiation. As will be seen, I use the term "initiation" with considerable deliberation.

Mortimer Brewster is one of those fine sophisticated fellows who earn their keep by occupying one of two seats on the aisle and writing up the experience later for a daily paper. As we did not need the Messrs. Crouse and Lindsay's adapted play to tell us, this mercenary habit has rendered the critic's finer sensibilities a little warped and petulant, not to say also vicious and abnormal. Let us abandon right here any conception that spectators of the play on Broadway may have of this critical fellow and of the Manhattan reviewers who generically served as prototypes for the gentle burlesque. For Hollywood's famed violence has stepped in and done everything in the movie-lot mode. The success of the farce in New York was so great that it made the play one of the chief drama baits of the season. As is well heralded, Hollywood with its delusions of grandeur has no respect for the original intentions of an author but feels that a play or novel must undergo a normal and inevitable transformation once it reaches the otherworldly precincts of a movie studio, where it becomes the ghost of its former self. It is something like an initiation rite, involving both purification and change . . . a rite through which the dramatic critic in the case of this movie is himself forced to go!

In *Arsenic and Old Lace* the sensational, which is a prime Hollywood objective, came ready-made. It was only a matter of titivating and enlarging the spectacle. But let us pause for a moment and consider the theme of this goose-pimple opera. Its very inspiration was a satire on the manners and motives of movie melodramas; it brought in as the chief villain Boris Karloff, a pathological killer who has behind him the tradition of Frankenstein's monster. One of the old maids, his aunts, remarks that after all these years he reminds her of someone—and the wisecrack is that he reminds her, as she says, of Boris Karloff, the movie actor. Hence when Raymond Massey played the rôle for the movie, he was made up—and very well too—to look like Mr. Karloff so that the sacred epithet could be preserved.

A former stage melodrama, duly movieized, provided some of the basis for *Arsenic and Old Lace,* and that was *Ladies in Retirement,* in which a lady's companion murders her mistress for her home and money in order to provide for her destitute and feeble-minded sisters. In the farce under discussion, it is the feeble-minded pair of sisters who appear as the cold-blooded murderers; moreover, here the relation of sex to murder is more plain, for the good *tantes* victimize errant old gentlemen who apply for a room or beg some food and then stuff the callers' dead bodies in the cellar. This Pollyanna pair of Lucrezia Borgias the critic has for aunts, and therefore supposedly he also has the Boris Karloff number for brother. The play occupies itself with the way he learns their concealed activities as well as the fact—which frees him from his fear of inherited insanity—that he is only an adopted member of the family, not a blood relative. Of course despite the lurid innuendoes on sex and insanity—the critic has another brother who charges up the stairs to his room under the delusion that he is Colonel Roosevelt leading his troops up San Juan Hill—the exaggeration of everything and the comic lines are supposed to turn the material into good unclean fun. The insidious tendency of the movie to turn itself into a lunatic asylum during a riot subtly enhances the authors' original purpose.

Yet I am not quite sure whether this is not a leading illustration of the dictum that Hollywood, when all is done and edited, does not know what it has on its hands . . . and I don't mean blood. Mortimer Brewster is a mourner of the dramatic art whose merciless mottoes extend to the decline of current dames no less than of current dramas as objects that woo men's love. In the movie he has written a book against the fair sex. But we observe, as the film opens, a bouncing blonde with whom he has flirted since school days and who does not take literature seriously. She reverses the verdict of his book and gets Brewster into line at City Hall for a marriage license and finally, chased by reporters, into a telephone booth, where the poor handsome fellow acts like a cornered rat with his teeth pulled. The ceremony takes place, and Mortimer rushes to his aunts' house in Brooklyn for their blessing—since he is a great favorite of theirs—before entraining for Niagara Falls. Leaving his bride at her home across the adjoining cemetery, he uncovers in his aunts' house a dead body lying in a chest, this corpse being the latest victim, whom one of the damned old dears has put out of misery before her sister, away from the house on an errand, could participate in the delicate pleasure of administering to him the poisoned elderberry wine.

I don't know how canny a pair of contrivers Messrs. Crouse and Lindsay are, but the structure of their lavender lethal machine is extremely sound, however improbable its verisimilitude. As a hoity-toity dramatic critic Brewster's two pet aversions, beyond bad plays through which his profession makes him suffer, are women and movies, through whom and which he has implicitly refused to suffer. Yet when a woman gets him, lo and behold! with the stark operation of Nemesis the movies also get him. Thus the fact that the play was bought by Hollywood was strictly analogous with the fact that in it the dramatic critic, in giving way to the lure of sex romance, becomes involved in a melodramatic mess typical of the movies. Indeed we may take it that he regards women and their practical ideas for him as institutions worthy only of movie romances, so that the over-all pattern of Nemesis is watertight: he is trapped by precisely everything his life is dedicated to escaping—even momentarily a lunatic asylum.

I by no means imply that Hollywood master minds understood the root and rudiment of all this. But I do imply and hereby assert that the mere mechanical nature of movie means, together with stereotyped studio purposes based on exploitation of these means, ordained that the original pattern of the stage farce should be brought out even more effectively than it was on Broadway. This signifies that Hollywood art has been immeasurably helped by what superficially might be called coincidence. But how can it be called coincidence when quite evidently the play was originally concocted as a burlesque of the melodramatic deeds of the movies? After a circumlocution on the stage the fictive creation has been brought around to realization through the cinema, which inspired it.

As a fearer of lunacy Brewster quite naturally may have conceived a lifetime inferiority complex that he came to take out by being uncompromisingly cruel to the drama. Some life force, however, breaks him down, and he takes the sexual step he feared: marriage. Now one doesn't quite know what may have lain at the bottom of the authors' minds, but according to the movie-script interpretation of the critic's part and what we may call Cary Grant's wholesale and talented co-operation the play poisoner is a virgin for whom marriage is also an introduction to a basic biological function—the act of procreation. The eyes tell us that Mortimer Brewster, screenized, behaves like a sixteen-year-old schoolboy on the verge of his first sex affair. In the play we may take it that the critic won't marry because he fears his children may be born idiots. With regard to this point the movie Brewster's worries are cast in a more direct and basic mold, attributable largely to Mr. Grant's choreographic execution as the bemused critic, once he has learned the full extent of affairs in the cellar. Therefore on the grounds of the mutually increased animation of Mr. Grant and the movie plot, both influenced by the magic principle of cinema action and serving to knit the movie into a semblance of nightmare and therefore of dream life, we may take a psychoanalytical view and see if we are not well justified by the bare bones of the situation.

The contretemps of Brewster's discovery that his dear old aunts are confirmed murderesses provides a halt for his honeymoon plans; thus in effect one night intervenes before his bridal night, which is duly supposed to eventuate when the mad farce is over: one night in which he sleeps alone— alas, perchance to dream! Now Brewster wishes to prove both sane *and* potent; psychologically, for someone with the inferiority complex he has developed, since impotency may have become the physical denouement of prolonged abstinence and suspicion of insanity, sanity and potency are virtually the same thing. Another dualism obtains. Let us not be squeamish; let us assume that the dead body Brewster first uncovers in the chest is a symbolic apparition of a passive genital. This is precisely what he wishes to avoid having on his honeymoon, and yet it is exactly what he feared he might have! Consequently in this dualistic symbolic pattern it is only logical that his sweet virginal aunts should be complementary to dead bodies. For in Brewster's mind the facts of *lunacy, virginity,* and *death,* the last a mask for *impotence,* are inseparable. The fright he gets and the pandemonium that follows in his efforts to keep the old girls' crimes under cover merely reflect his own feverish anxiety that his bride should not learn of his hidden incapacity. The bodies in the cellar—here the subterranean element is sexually significant—might then symbolize the number of times he has failed to consummate sex affairs. The aunts, be it noted, murder only old fellows who seem destitute and lonely—thus these dead objects might well symbolize for the critic, in imitation of his aunts' psychology, a *desirable state;* that is, death may seem preferable to lasting and lonely impotence. The further development in his criminally insane brother's appearance signifies Brewster's alternate conception of insanity as identical with potency; we recall that Frankenstein's monster is a symbol of rape, and here it may be remarked that the mechanical rigidity of the synthetic man is a sign of the implacable priapus. So, in distinction from his anxiety over his impotency, related to his aunts, he has a further anxiety: that he will be potent, a quality related to his criminal brother, who thus unites for Brewster the complementary anxiety trio of *lunacy, potency,* and *crime,* the last being the moral status of the birth of idiot children.

When the mad brother decides to do away with Brewster and—with his confederate stooge, played in a very obliging spirit by Peter Lorre, who must act disobliged—ties

Brewster in a chair prior to death by torture, a curious symbolic travesty appears, crystallizing the hypothesis that this is all nothing but the bridegroom critic's nightmare. . . . Many a time have Broadway Drydens cried aloud over their bounden duty to sit out an ailing play, however uncomfortable and sleepless they are. To make this point quite clear—that the play that Brewster must really witness and criticize is nothing but his own bridal night—a life-saving policeman intervenes on the murder scene at the crucial moment, and while Brewster sits bound and gagged and his would-be murderer chafes, the cop reads the critic a scene from a play he has written. The guardian of the law, alas, is innocent of the real foul play being enacted, for he has been told that Brewster's state is merely part of a rehearsal. But the play-reading incident saves Brewster's life.

Now what is the true identity of this hallowed deus ex machina, the play-writing cop? We must note that he represents the law. The law here is a multiply charged symbol that not only provides an extenuation for the punishment of insane murderers—the two aunts whom Brewster loves —but has elements of a divine as well as a dramatic law. As divine law the policeman's mirage gives Brewster hope for life in all its desirable senses: reason, virility, and healthy progeny. As dramatic law it releases Brewster from his trap, his mental as well as his physical trap, and the former particularly for this reason: the cop's play as read to the critic is bad, but its very badness probably suggests to his mind that his fears about himself may be a bad fiction rather than a bad fact. Indeed the play-reading policeman is a messenger announcing complete deliverance, for later his superior officers arrive on the scene and following a knockout rumpus subdue the criminals and arrange matters peaceably to Brewster's satisfaction. Everyone gets put where he belongs—and Brewster sets off on his postponed honeymoon.

I don't know if readers who may not have seen the play and/or movie realize that these shenanigans of bad sleep were supposed to provoke rending risibility pains. They did so far as I went. Although the above exposition may seem solemn in its underpinnings, the true nature of the plot is comedy. We have here an exemplar of the dogma that extravagant murder melodramas provoke laughter because of illusory fears in the actors (see the fourth chapter). So it is precisely to the degree that things that should not frighten are shown as frightening the characters that this movie has comedy status; the obvious clue is that all these normally frightening things cannot be taken seriously when exaggerated so grossly. I have pointed out that the resultant laughter must be partly hysterical because beneath the obvious causes of fear are concealed unobvious causes of more valid caliber—such as sex fears or inversely sex desires that through frustration are projected in extravagant or perverse form as in dreams.

Despite dramaturgy that resembles football tactics— Hollywood usually has as little chic as Broadway—*Arsenic and Old Lace* emerges as a flicker festival of considerable charm. It is American folk art of the highest available grade. If a while ago I invoked the fate of Brewster's dreadful experience as a warning to snobbish disparagers of the movies, I did so in rather a tight-lipped seriousness and thus in a spirit of comedy. Critical clamor against plays may be justified, literally speaking, but when unrelieved by a creative spirit, by a viewpoint that can detect the life virtues of the spectacles under inspection and that relegates their worst faults to their country cousins, the movies— this clamor not only represents at bottom ultraconservatism but tends to create what may be called "sterility complexes" in its instigators. It is in this sense that sterility-minded Mortimer Brewster is a satire on superior-minded Broadway critics. After all many of them realize that they must sometimes be kind, but this is primarily a business, not an esthetic, matter. It is when they assume the judge's cap and from the platform of esthetic judgment castigate a poor naked floppola that they suggest the masochism that was inevitably a part of Mortimer Brewster's make-up, as shown by the bound-and-gagged critic forced to listen to the policeman's play; for it is their *own* suffering that they sadistically celebrate. If main force becomes a symbol for critical duties, then a masochistic element in critical Caligulas is no farcical illusion but a sober fact. If criticism be a symbol of hatred, something is also wrong with critical loves as these flower in the dramatic columns of the *Times,* the *Herald Tribune,* and the rest . . . all of which, while it may have the proportions of satire in the Crouse-Lindsay confection, quite reasonably accounts for the stupid praise meted to Broadway dramas by critical old maids as regularly as is disbursed the murderous blame by their nephews, the Boris Atkinsons and the Howard Karloffs. . . . It would not be going too far, I think, to say that whenever a Broadway critic is a booster, he's also, by this psychoanalysis of criticism, a Brewster.

7. THE WAXWORKS OF WAR

There was no mystery or cause for speculation about the line Hollywood would take toward the war. For the movie city was, like one of the many factories made over to manufacture guns and planes and other matériel, ready with very little reconversion to start on war production. Its formulas not only had immanent precedents in the movies produced for the First World War but were also perfectly standard equipment for the shuffling of military matters with love affairs, the equation of death with life, and the painting of the pathetic idyl of the bereft and unhappy at home and among the conquered peoples abroad. For the last war was no more news to Hollywood than to the rest of the globe. But like the rest of the globe, in many areas and from the standpoint of many interests, this war meant a sign of new life, the release of latent energies and capacities. "Things," war-actuated, "expanded."

Indeed as war automatically dissolved many a dilemma of contrasting stripe and provided an obvious starting-point for new operations, it delivered Hollywood from the pressing problem of substituting some new type of melodrama for the old. True, there was the constant stand-by in the murder mystery and the Western story as well as the more recently developed horror melodrama; but Hollywood does not like to depend on its stock in trade. There must be sensations—and platitudes too. New arrivals in the heaven of stars were not in the astrological charts. With the new world atmosphere of war, even before the United States was actively and positively engaged at the end of 1941, interest in individual murder and the individual murderer, the gangster, was definitely on the skids. As a flower of exoticism the gangster had long been wilting at the edges, despite the arrival of a Brooks Brothers model in the bad-man field, Alan Ladd, who proved as surprising and enticing as a handsome soda-fountain clerk stripped of his apron and abroad on a Sunday afternoon in a made-to-measure. There were some nasty fellows of the naughty nineties who had to serve as props for old-fashioned cowboys such as John Wayne and Joel McCrea to knock over, and there was a very nice nasty fellow who finally wouldn't be knocked over because he stood up so well at the box office: Humphrey Bogart. No beauty and not a bit refined, Mr. Bogart did it with personality plus. Even by an anachronistic old maid he would be pronounced the loveliest bad man we ever had. The Sanskrit experts of Hollywood had no difficulty in finding the key to the cipher on Mr. Bogart's prewar forehead. It read: "Criminal Redeemed in the Crucible of the War for Democratic Ideals." So we get Mr. Bogart's cozily shady character as someone on whom the good people work their propaganda with eventual success; witness: *To Have and Have Not, Casablanca, Sahara,* and *All Through the Night*—in reverse order chronologically but in identical perspective in any order.

133

In the last a whole American gang converted its nocturnal energies into rounding up foreign agents. *Sahara* was a war operation itself, as neatly put together as a submarine, with Bogart leading in from the desert a platoon of Germans and his war-bitten tank. I confess this was a moment I relished because of its sheer romantic logic: the individual triumphing over the many by brains, guts, and luck. In this dramatic climax to Mr. Bogart's grueling experience, during which practically all his tank crew had been killed, there was posed the type hero of all wars from the popular viewpoint: the mere private or the subordinate officer who individually distinguishes himself in valor and so equals and conceivably transcends the static glory of a general or president.

In my previous book I pointed out that in a few pictures made about the war before the United States was a participant, such as the English-made *The Invaders*, the traditional romantic pattern of the lone wolf in triumph over multiple odds had been inverted to illustrate the need for democratic alliance against a single powerful enemy, Germany. Thus in the international sense, among the leading nations whose colonial and world-trade interests could be opposed to Germany's, it was salutary to suggest that these nations should band together according to an esthetic symbology contrary to the popular conception of individual heroism. Popular leading actors of England and America took minor parts for the sake of this moral lesson, which was that it required a sum of successively alert individuals having courage and skill to trap a single

German submarine captain who with his crew had invaded Canada.

This film belonged to the early cinema logic of the war and was essentially British in its propaganda, but it conformed perfectly with the global myth pattern of the individual murderer and the society, innocent and unprepared, which he has attacked in an organized manner in the dark. As the gangster stood in relation to normal and respectable society as a modern civilized ideal, so the criminal among nations, Germany, stood in relation to the society of nations formally dedicated to modern civilized ideals—liberty, democracy, independence, etc. Yet economico-political considerations in general automatically converted the glamour quotient of gangsterism when it came to the gangsterism of an entire nation. Everybody knows that it is tolerable in terms of popular fable to glorify the gangster, for he is a socially dissident element capable of a most limited amount of damage and to the vast majority of the public morally indecipherable. For the gangster hero's popularity is owing not only to his romantic character as an individualistic hero defiant of authority but to the *incoherence* and the apparently obscure *source* of his social rebellion . . . an incoherence and a source that the man in the audience darkly identifies with those of his own purely passive and phantasmal rebellion.

We may note that the responses of the man in the audience are calculated to have the same fluidity and ambivalence, so far as mythical symbols go, as belong likewise to the mutations of the romantic hero in popular art as he

shifts from peace to war. Thus the pantheon of movie heroism is a kind of Madame Tussaud's, superplastic in both
the temporal and materialistic senses, a waxworks capable
of melting and recomposing in an almost magical manner,
so that one is seldom quite sure of the identification tags,
which may shift about as in dreams. Of course a museum in
the strict sense is to be distinguished as *art* from what we
know as *ethics* or ideals, in contradistinction to the fact-
giving of journalism. Presumably and, one may add, with
a certain degree of common sense, ethics and ideals are in
more danger during wartime than during peacetime, since
in wartime the society of a nation is threatened and its
collective security undermined. Hence what in peacetime
is a mere rigid waxworks, the phantoms of a museum of
history, becomes curiously animated during wars—for the
simple reason that public attention is then recalled to them
in a vitalized way. It is no accident that they are mythically
composed of the substance of wax, which is easily decom-
posed by heat and capable of hasty remodeling.

II

Roughly speaking, it took about six years for Hitler to pass
from the compound image of Attila, Landru, and Napoleon
—as he was painted by the most hysterical—through the
caricatures seen in Chaplin's *The Great Dictator* and other
movie comedies to the elaborate documentary conception
of him eventually portrayed in the movie, *The Hitler Gang*.

The dissolving of heroic substance as related to museum images has its parallel in the permutation of a purely moral wax that melts and resolidifies in ethical molds. Part of the moral metamorphosis of war entailed a going from lightness and humor to the weighty and straight-faced on all levels.

In this there inheres the tactical necessity of administering the moral side of contemporary war, with especial reference to America. On this side of the Atlantic and Pacific Oceans there is a well-known historic tendency to take foreign potentates with several soupçons of laughter. Even the world figure of Napoleon, with his romantic and somber odyssey ending on St. Helena, was a subject for universal caricature, and *The Mikado* of Gilbert and Sullivan is a perfect instance of the frivolous manner in which Occidental racial philosophy holds the dignity of alien rulers, however lofty their legends. In part this tradition can be attributed to the native institution of democracy and its automatic ridicule of any sign of tyranny, so outmoded and, to us, affected, such as the vestigial European institution of kings. Yet suddenly in the very waxworks of life such figures as Hitler and Mussolini appeared as endangerers of the world democracy that had been hallucinated as heritage of the previous World War. As individual images the two men, Hitler and Mussolini, were pure waxworks in the comic sense, their physical characteristics lending themselves ideally to caricature. And since their very myth, mutual as it was, was that of dictatorship, something abhorrent and anachronistic, the most natural esthetico-historic impulse was to laugh at them. It was inevitable that this attitude, purely for reasons of common sense, had to be reorientated. A natural line therefore was to depict them as lunatics, since it seemed lunacy enough that men whose abilities seemed to have designed them to be low comedians desired to be rulers of hemispheres. So the psychiatric interpretation of Hitler began as part of the automatic program of inducing people to consider him a dangerous menace and to take the war more seriously. I am afraid that Hollywood must be accused of remissness, for Hitler was still being caricatured in films after he had overrun nearly all Europe.

To some extent this may be imputed to the natural unreality of foreign war to a country whose domestic precincts have so little actual taste of real conflict and violent physical suffering. Reason is one thing, imagination another. Americans may be said even at this maturer moment to suffer from the hemispheric neurosis, a hallucination of exemption. But the fact remained that Hitler was in command of one of the most powerful armies the world had ever seen and that, having marched far into Russia, it was having an overwhelming series of successes, and therefore it was difficult for the fact (that is, myth) that he was an absurdity, a clown and a madman, to remain intact. Chaplin, as might have been anticipated, carried the artistic conception of the Fascist delusion, democratically criticized, to its high point in *The Great Dictator* by making an elaborate puppet show of the European dictatorship setup. He placed the tradition of tyranny in the marionette theater rather than in Madame Tussaud's and thus reduced its life-size rigidity to miniature plasticity.

But Hollywood, like nature, tends toward the golden mean, which can often be identified from another standpoint as the leaden average. Not that any historic figure, however great, is ever pure gold. Wax therefore seems as ideal for the purpose of mythological criticism as it is for Hollywood. That the movies, unlike statues, photographs, and moral conservatism, literally *move* is perhaps their prime virtue. They also, when it comes sometimes to portraying ghosts, melt . . . perfectly logical, therefore, that the popular movies should melt and recast the ghosts of history. After all, the gangster is himself a vestige of Robin Hood and medievalism, since he is the knight errant of chivalry turned inside out; in *The Hollywood Hallucination* I pointed out the Robin Hood traits essential to the popular portrait of the gangster and that Hitler was a self-professed Robin Hood for poverty-stricken Germany. A normalized version of Hitler, from the viewpoint both of myth and of reason, issued finally in *The Hitler Gang,* which under the surface was an analysis of Hitler's social rôle and, in reverse order, of the birth of the gangster from the vestiges of chivalric myth. In Hitler's hands the tradition of gangsterism, roughly definable as the interest of minorities hallucinated as the interest of majorities and prosecuted in an extralegal or antilegal way, was organized on a supralegal and national scale, so that the nation became a gang. An accurate parallel to this problem is even now right at home, where there is little indecision as to what to do with the

139

Dillingers and the Dutch Schultzes, when and if legally convicted, but society can find no remedy for the illegal institution of crime. Imprisonment and death have not corrected the criminal tradition. That the German nation, which has produced so much world culture, should be *uniquely* criminal is beyond all bounds of reason—a conclusion that postwar reaction apparently has confirmed.

Hollywood remained faithful to the interpretation of Hitler as head of an international gang, and there were numerous intimations that his end would be along the same lines as a gangster's betrayal by his own gang. Incidentally I might point out that this assumption was by no means extraordinary, as the methodical realism of *The Hitler Gang* helped to emphasize. Heroes of history and art, especially tyrants, are traditionally betrayed from within— if not by their own consciences, then by their most confidential lieutenants. The fact that Hitler's own generals therefore should have plotted against him left the way open for interpreting their motives as token of some virtue, if indeed Hitler was the historic, quintessential evil tyrant. Latter-day movies such as *Hotel Berlin* sometimes frankly posed the question of whether all Germans were bad. *The Hitler Gang* was commendable for its studious portraiture of Hitler and his minions—edged with a little satire but fundamentally straightforward, like a sort of glorified *March of Time* into the private life of the Führer. In this movie Hitler himself had a very real texture, his wax being astonishingly mobile and anthropomorphic; indeed a very astute performance of the rôle, with neat injections of neurotic styling, was given by an actor of no consequence. Curiously complementary to this picture of how Hitler might have been destroyed from within was *Man Hunt*, a rather amusingly done movie of the solo and repetitious failures of a British game hunter to bring down the biggest game of all, Hitler. The gentleman cannot be discouraged in this super-African project and is dropped off a plane by parachute right into the grounds of Hitler's mountain estate, Berchtesgaden. The Briton is captured but escapes for another try. This was the genuine fairy-tale version of Hitler, a tyrant in the untouchable tradition, whose legend of immunity was not taken seriously by the democratic technician, the British game hunter, symbol of scientific objectivity. It is piquant to compare his attitude with that of Wilde, whose domesticated unicorn, Dorian, was transformed into a hunted beast of prey and, escaping, was murdered by his own conscience. The effect in *Man Hunt* was augmented by the fact that Hitler is not seen but once in the movie and then from a great distance. The grotesquerie is the outdatedness of the hunter symbol; the ingenious gentleman uses the most modern methods, including a special gun—silent in reverence for the great occasion!—and yet the game eludes him. The question remained as to whether Hitler was watched over by a supernatural fate, which preserved him, or a dual alternative would have to be accepted: the hunter merely got bad breaks, or the wrong technical theory was being applied. The wrongness of the technical theory would have resided partially in the wrongness of its successful as well as its

141

unsuccessful application. . . . Suppose a Nazi trooper had *not* arrived in time to deflect the accuracy of the hunter's long-distance shot at Hitler? Suppose Hitler *had* been killed in this movie? It would have meant swell advertising for the British sporting spirit, for the arms manufacturer, and for Britain in general, but would it have helped materially to end the war sooner, and would it not have given democracy more prestige to reserve Hitler for public trial—just as it is considered wise that the justice dealt to criminals take a courtroom form? Although actual events robbed the world of the spectacle of Hitler's trial, we see Hitler reconstructed in the Museum of Natural History as *Tyrannicus germanicus,* a neuter beast, indeed. Perhaps the real movie moral was: "Don't shoot until you see the hairs of his mustache."

III

The saga of the German army of occupation and the fate its various attenuated limbs could suffer was depicted graphically enough by two complementary films: *The Moon Is Down,* which showed the helpless albeit courageous martyrdom of a Norwegian town, and *Edge of Darkness,* which showed a similar town, assisted by British gunrunners, rising up in defeat and crushing its vanquishers in one fell engagement. Both films were done with a good deal of "nerve-gripping" melodrama and picture-postcard photography; certain sets in *The Moon Is Down*

142

were lit by studio light very much on the up if not the up and up. As a matter of fact, not only is its plot very custom-made, with the attempted seduction of a young woman of the native population by a dissolute young German officer —beginning as an idyllic love scene and ending by her stabbing him to death—but everything contributes to the blatant staginess of placing the Norwegian citizenry in the limelight of an embarrassing carnage. It should be an axiom that sometimes it is best for the camera too to look away.

We know, and with some gratitude in view of the abundant files of documentary films both casual and elaborate, that often the camera did not look away, and just as often, to make us war-conscious, propaganda documentaries unaffectedly set out to shock our sensibilities and abash our inadequate awareness of soldier suffering. There is a certain fleeting poetry in many of these grim fragments of photographed reality. And I have noted that where the film is not something merely informative and arranged to make warfare look actually pretty, like much of *The Memphis Belle*, documentary of a Flying Fortress, the impulse of the suffering soldier was to shield himself from the camera almost as automatically as from the enemy. But he has to oblige the cameraman, and he has to think of those back home who would relish seeing him in the public eye. The soldier caught deshabille, as it were, in the midst of war was not quite sure of his actor's mask—for we must remember that we all think of our masks as soon as a camera faces us. He was miserable, fatigued, sick, messy, preoccupied, perplexed, mourning . . . none of these feelings, basically, was the sort to send home. He found the cinema record, except on ceremonious and calm occasions, rather irrelevant—so much so that I think it was in *The Memphis Belle* itself that the disinclination of men to pose for a movie camera after having seen their comrades die was manifest enough for the narrator to remark on it. But at least the newsreel camera and cameraman, in artlessly having done their jobs, can be held unaccountable, esthetically speaking. But not so the devised and self-conscious fiction.

I think that the valiant Hollywood employees who gave a rather heartfelt exhibition of being Norse townsmen filing to their execution in the last scene of *The Moon Is Down* and duly being slaughtered should have been seized with some of a soldier's realistic reticence in such drastically distressing circumstances and should have tried to avert their faces from the camera. The logic is that people who do not fear publicity hold their heads up; people who are in the right die fearlessly, proudly. But to be killed like animals in a slaughterhouse, which is what happens to the Norse townsmen, is a humiliation to the whole human race. Those before the Nazi firing squad might have hung their heads in shame, of course not for themselves personally but for the uncontrolled sadism of their conquerors, also members of the human race. And therefore, even if of course the convention be that there is no camera recording the scene, they should have been sorry that the spectacle might become a sort of legend, as indeed it had to become in order to preoccupy a film. Here the movies' relation to journalism, carefully calculated by John Steinbeck, author of the original book, became an antiartistic trap.

Much is made of the fact that the Norwegians are innocent, unable to understand why they should be thus demolished wholesale, and their ignorance is evidently presumed to arouse special compassion for them. Not being politically and economically educated, they could not comprehend the implacable character of the catastrophe that befell them. This sort of ignorance, while not criminal, was still nothing of which to be proud. If a brick drops on your head and you die instantly, must you hold your head up in heaven and assert, "It was through no fault of mine that the brick fell on me"? I do not mean precisely to identify the German invasion with a natural event, but I do mean that a calamity such as befell Pompeii and perhaps Atlantis does not make tragic heroes of its victims, for the reason that tragedy consists in understanding the nature of a flaw in life and locating it somewhere in oneself. Destiny is the self—individual, human, divine. The tragedy of the war was that the military aggressors too were human. If the simple Norsemen did not comprehend why they were being mass-murdered, they should have looked, puzzled and horrified, deep into the eyes of their enemies. They should have been extremely uncomfortable and incredulous. Rational calmness—for the moment I am not considering brutish apathy—means either forgiveness or utter resignation, the first of which is the true prerogative here of the divine and the second of which comes only from acquiescence in an acknowledged act of the divine. Yet the Germans are neither divine nor worthy, it would seem, of divine forgiveness. At least this is not a point brought up by Hollywood philosophy. So far as *perplexity* goes, in regard to the meaning of mortal human injury to human, this is not an officially endorsed sentiment on a movie lot or beyond. At least Christ could raise his head and say, "Father, forgive them, for they know not what they do."

To add to the movie's false notes, the music for *The Moon Is Down*, opening with a series of blasts like those of a steam calliope, had an unbearable shrillness intermittently throughout, as though self-conscious of the mock heroism of its message and seeking to justify it. At least *Edge of Darkness*, endowed with a more ingenious presentation, possessed Norwegians who were lucky and plucky enough to evade similar self-exposure on the dubious stage of Hollywood tragedy. They slaughtered the Germans in a very honest and active street battle until the town became a cemetery of unburied bodies, both German and Norwegian. This, I think, was, like the newsreel, closer to life, even though relatively few towns had such a chance to fight back.

One other outstanding film, besides *Hotel Berlin*, I recall as having dealt exclusively with the German war scene—*The Seventh Cross*. It is unusually well done and shows the organization of terror in Germany making every common man a government agent, so that anyone who succored a German prisoner escaping from a concentration camp became a full-fledged co-criminal. The thesis of the picture is that Germany had more than a few such people, brave enough to defy, one may conclude, the newsreel inquisition into every man's movements, since people behaved as though the Gestapo had a preternatural listening device or a secret form of television in every man's home. Here is a true latter-day example of the supposed operation of magic law, raising (or lowering) mental action to the realm of superstition: "The walls have ears." If a German "betrayed the nation" by aiding a fugitive, he assumed that the rest of the German nation was ready to turn informer on him —an illusion justified not only by magic psychology but by the thickly populated world of modern times. The good sense of this screen story changed Spencer Tracy into a creditably sober actor—he who usually is so heady with ham.

It would have been wrong to suppose that the art of Hollywood would fail to picture some good Germans, even in uniform, so long as no belligerent postwar conference had officially declared them beyond the limits of the human race; at the same time there was a very small percentage of Grade B atrocity movies, with their Hunnish inverted valentines brought up to the Second World War. The most human German in uniform, according to my memory, was in *The Pied Piper:* an officer, extremely well played, who bargains with an English ex-general trapped in France that he will permit him and an assortment of kids to escape to England in a small boat if the ex-general consents to take along also the German's own little daughter. Yet for a straight portrayal of blunt Prussian unpleasantness in uniform, one of the best assuredly was that of George Coulouris in *Edge of Darkness*. Of course no such part had the flavorful style that Von Stroheim would have given it, stereotyped and stagy as the veteran German-American actor is.

IV

The golden mean was shed even among the already legendary monsters of German militarism and succeeded in giving a gilt edge to their human wax, however sculptured in horrific poses much of it was. The American soldier in war films was a wax kneaded not only for divergent postures but for a novel purpose, since millions of American youths who had never held a gun had to be trained to fight in our armies. American wax had to show steely qualities, and of course it did; everything produced in America is and must be of first quality—at least a great part of it, whether it be a rocket ship to the moon or a soap dish. If first-quality chewing gum was not to be had till after the duration, we knew that something else of supreme quality, if not of flavor, was manufactured and consumed. The waxworks of a war can only be contingent on the waxworks of society with its economic base element. When human wax was required to make steel soldiers, human wax had to do, and its conversion was successful—as much so anyway as the search for a substitute for rubber.

Films such as *Wake Island, Corregidor, Bataan,* and

148

Salute to the Marines, showing the esprit of American military forces in the early losing stage of the war in the Pacific, duly appeared and registered their message. We cannot ignore that part of that message was the urgent need for high war production in both men and matériel. *Salute to the Marines* and *Gung Ho* showed with supernewsreel intensity the rehammering of men into soldiers, while *Guadalcanal Diary*, *Destination Tokyo*, *Objective Burma*, *Thirty Seconds over Tokyo*, *They Were Expendable*, and others showed the finished military products in action. *See Here, Private Hargrove* and *This Is the Army*, with others, portrayed the humorous side of camp life, some of course being frankly in the musical-comedy mold with not a candle drip on the brims. Many a film revealed the mercurially sought objectives of soldiers and sailors on leave, perhaps the most amusing being *Johnny Doesn't Live Here Any More* because of its irresponsible fantasy.

The girls were called upon to show the wax beneath the cosmetic, and *Cry Havoc*, the women's version of *Bataan*, might have been entitled *Cry Havoc on Cold Cream*. While the story was realistic enough, barring a certain tight, tailored theatricalism, the girls obviously had difficulty both in the plot and aside from it in giving the impression they were not still, or did not want to be, in intimate contact with the glamour business . . . although supposed to be army nurses on a doomed island. When they succeeded— as in the cases of the real "Army," the commander and the sergeant—the acting noticeably improved, but the skin Crossleys fell as loudly as the bombs. The opposition of beauty and war in feminine ethics was made much of in a later film, *Keep Your Powder Dry.*

The motif of professional entertainer turned trooper, not camp entertainer, for the duration appeared in this film and in *Days of Glory,* a movie about Russian guerrillas in which the famed ballerina, Tamara Toumanova, who had done nothing of the sort in fact, pretends that she has remained in Russia and, when dancing seems bombed out for the duration, decides to stay with a guerrilla band who find her wandering in the forest after an attack on her train. But it is all really as safe, you feel, as backstage at the ballet—with one exception when Toumanova is telling a guerrilla adolescent about the glamour of the theater and, poised to take the first steps of a dance, sees the figure of a German soldier creeping down the steps of the hideout. Strangely enough, Joan Blondell, in her rôle as the ex-strip-tease artiste in *Cry Havoc,* is about to relieve dormitory tension on Bataan by going into her number when an equally pressing interruption occurs. The more obvious similarity is that the ladies never get to perform. Aside from the virtue of theatrical surprise in both cases, the device occurred each time probably because the rhythm of the story would have been spoiled by a complete performance, even though the orchestra, representing wartime art out of gun range, was waiting to assist the obliging artistes. I could not help wishing, when I saw *Follow the Boys,* a saga of troop entertainment that covered the entire map of the visible screen, that every now and then air-raid practice had halted the performances, most desirably when the Andrews sisters appeared. For me this trio is far more listenable than seeable. Two of them look as two of the three witches in *Macbeth* must have looked when they could still pretend they were girls.

Considering all these films, it seems to me that those about the making of a soldier and the subsequent test of his material rate higher in interest than any other type. The heat required was for metal, not for wax or human flesh, and the human units were not taken from museums but from life—from the rich and poor, the educated and uneducated, the gross and the refined. . . . And all had to go into one mold, a military uniform. After all, Madame Tussaud's museum had not become a mere anachronism, a costume house in which the costumes were not for rent. Every war has its candidates for the Hall of Fame, every war its symbolic and medallic Purple Heart, its image of the wax that survives the flame and goes on the imperishable record for posterity. Hence there were films such as *The Purple Heart*, this one named for the reward won by soldiers, whose courage in this case does not fail even at the door of death, well after they have had time to study that door's threatening pattern. In late years some of the most convincing acting in Hollywood has been by young men in the rôles of military novices, though an amusing if rather caricatured portrait of an old-timer was given by Wallace Beery in *Salute to the Marines*. This group-acting achievement, I think, was due to the fact that these young men, indulging in their waxen make-believe but virtually heroes as yet only in the Madame Tussaud sense, could measure in their

151

imagination the spiritual cost of offering to sacrifice their lives if and/or when called upon for *actual fighting*. Many were so young that, granted they were ambitious actors, they could intuit an odd parallel to their Hollywood hazing in the less familiar and less desirable training of a soldier preparing to go to the front. The very quality of their faces —here again the newsreel effect partially enters, because the actor's life is being literally portrayed—showed a melting mixed strangely with a hardening, something not so violent or high-pitched as molten metal but as ambiguous as cooling and heating wax. . . . A very beautiful symbolic episode of this sort was provided in *Gung Ho*.

V

This movie recounted a special mission by the marines, involving much danger and a specific, most vigorous training program, participation in the mission being determined by volunteering. The volunteers on whom the story centers are introduced when they give their reasons for coming forward; they all have believable enough reasons. Then, just as though it were a *March of Time* program, we watch the training of the young marines, which whips them up to a peak of fitness and razor-edge spirit. Finally, the training program completed, the nature of their task, hitherto kept secret, is revealed; they are to take an island held by the Japanese and thus will secure a foothold for a major military landing force. This revelation occurs almost at the moment of their departure; the next morning—walking miracles of military equipment, so oddly do they resemble Frankenstein's monster with all they carry!—they file into the alien bellies of two submarines.

Psychologically the donning of all their personal equipment is the climax of their long preparation; the next logical move is its use against the enemy. Therefore the days-long submarine journey is an unexpected delay in the rhythm and preconceived shape of their project, and this hiatus of inaction is especially jarring because of the peculiar nature of its environment, the submarine. None of the marines has ever been inside a submarine before; the submarine crew is an entirely different outfit. This inexplicable wait before the moment of action, for which they are all prepared like tightly wound springs, causes a spiritual reaction characterized by a literal as well as a symbolic *divesting*, necessitated by the close and heated quarters of the submarine. Their training has prepared them for a totally different adventure of war, which they have conceived mentally in a single arc, at the climax of which will be *the battle* and its hoped-for denouement, *victory*.

In the case of some of the men their disappointment is evident by exhibitions of temper, and there is one outburst of hysteria. Of course a not uncommon phenomenon is present, that of before-the-battle nerves. Every officer is expected to cope with it. But in this particular situation it is fraught, as a mere phenomenon, with peculiar and suggestive poetry. For as we see the naked, perspiring flesh of these youths, softened by the coincidental presence of their

153

identification tags necklacing their chests, their military mold is visibly relaxed, as though the heat of the closed submarine caused to melt the less resistant metal of war that has become part of their bodies even as it has forced them to remove the rigid encrustation of war, their unmelting military paraphernalia. The spirit of war seemed to have reduced them to one substance, of which a gun, in its cold metal and hot bullet, was only a single outer limb; they had mythically conceived themselves as fire-throwing instruments, cold as steel, and not subjects for the attack of a mere peacetime heat, which, as in the city, they could wish only to flee from. The sea, by which doubtless some of them formerly had sought refuge, was in their present situation extremely close but technically quite unavailable, since the sides of a submarine separated them from it. Their fate is now to sit tight—and simmer.

This reconstruction of a natural surface, camera-recorded, is not a mere analysis unconfirmed by organized textures and important signs. Besides the feeling of melting discomfort the faces of the young marines bore a curious and curiously mutual quality, the direct result of the actors' feeling for this imaginary situation. The situation was expressed in their faces as if it were true. But its truth in the sense of its subjective character was partly spiritual, not merely objective in the sense of physical event and physical images.

The spiritual content of this imaginary situation was so powerfully real that it wrote its subtle and wordless message on their faces irrespectively of any acting business or

154

the precise meaning of the lines they had to say. It was pure mood, pure atmosphere, but uniquely of this situation. Hence it transcended any literal representation and entered the realm of poetry or symbolic statement. The wax of war received an unexpected transmutation through the submarine's subsurface position, watertight compartment, and pervasive heat, and the consequent dramatic divestment of the warrior's rôle—his mask, costume, and gesture.

The psychological reversal was from spring-taut aggressiveness to helpless passivity. Trained to a high pitch of competence as fighting machines, the marines were unexpectedly plunged into the disintegrating depths of a submarine, which was not a theater of action for them but a theater of inaction, since it was serving as a mere transport. The sign of reaction on their faces was one of passive appeal with a profound worry just below the surface. The sublevel of their aquatic vehicle brought to their own surfaces a sublevel of themselves, there being no mask of war to hide it. They were returned to a state of childhood, and for these boys it was naturally to that state when, depending on their mother's benevolence, they were accustomed to ask bounty and loving protection from her. So their faces assumed that mask of innocent and pure appeal that little boys wear specifically to attract and compel the good will of their mothers. There is something infinitely calculating and hypocritical about this automatic mask . . . a form of playing possum. Its purpose acts through an image of passivity, almost of divine indifference, which strives merely to seem *to be* rather than to seem to *want* or *demand*;

for the unconscious wisdom of the little boy intuits that nothing can appeal to his mother more strongly than his passive image, on whose materiality he has felt her most lavish caresses, given eagerly *without his asking* when he was a baby and now to appear, according to his desire, in response to hinted requests for spending money or un-speaking desire for permission to go out and play . . . or merely to invite a remembered deep kiss, which now she is too sensible to give him. . . . But why this hallucination of the mother? It is not merely because the submarine is a kind of womb, which the marine unconsciously associ-ates with the body of his mother, although this too can be supposed, but more directly because from the summit of a manly independence, which he has felt when armed with all the weapons of war, he has been dashed to the earth of a helpless kind of inertia—which, however, is a sort of echo, in that it retains the impress of recent violence, of recent design to kill. . . . The mirage of himself as the killer, now completely disarmed and in the belly of a submarine, renders the mirage of others as killers. After all, the enemy fleet may detect the submarines, and if so the ma-rines may die ignobly, helpless, with no personal way to fight back. The impulse is to pray for the mercy of divine Providence—but this impulse is not well developed in our society, despite the religious ceremonies held before going into battle, and is relatively incongruous in the heated and untimely cooled blood of a young soldier. But the impulse to appeal to something is very strong; hence by the meta-phoric bridge of the submarine as a womb they reach their

mothers and through their mothers an image of overhanging nature, to which, as the blue sky, warm sunshine, and
invigorating air, from which they are now farther away
than ever, they make a humble appeal, automatically dictated by the type of innocent guile they practiced on the
maternal being—their spontaneous charade of being
Mamma's precious boy to whom nothing can be denied.
. . . Add a fugitive touch of grimness, a barely discernible
patina of cynical protest, and you have the mutual expression on the faces of the young marines waiting in the
submarine for the command to go into action on land. But
this cynical protest, this aggressiveness about to burst the
little boy's angelic mask, is only his manly, individual,
conscious nature asserting itself as of old, when he prepared the initial stroke of the little boy's war against his
mother, the war to *make* her do his will that was an inevitable part of his human growth. From the waxworks of
the womb to the waxworks of war is a straight biological
line, to which as scientists we must perforce add even that
rotten child of German history, Hitler.

VI

Oddly enough the title of *A Walk in the Sun* implies the op-
pressiveness of heat, calculably tending to melt the soldier's wax. But here operated possibly the most profound
law of human paradox to be found in modern behavior,
something the movie faithfully reflected. The reasons for

157

this phenomenal verisimilitude are significant but not far to seek. Following the first military landing at Salerno in Italy, most of the platoon commissioned to take a certain farmhouse come through wilted but essentially solid. A sergeant, unexpectedly promoted by the incapacitation of his superior, eventually collapses from battle fatigue. But he is the symbolic exception, the hideous example, the one who breaks under the strain supported by all the others. Each man of course sees objectified in the sergeant's collapse the logical consummation of his own ordinary suppressed fears for his stamina.

A homespun philosopher, a tall laconic fellow said to take long solitary walks, remarks of the broken sergeant that "he's built a foxhole in his head and will never crawl out of it." This is picturesque and accurate and states symbolically the transcendent situation into which all the men are automatically tempted but that is resisted by crawling out of the actual foxhole when the time comes. Suddenly the afflicted sergeant lies face down on the ground and sobs. The scene of the narrative leaves him, and we never know his fate, although it is implicit that nature has cursed him. *A Walk in the Sun* has a well-rounded assortment of plain Americans—nearly all, incidentally, former clerks—unexpectedly turned into soldiers and doing an unpleasant job. As the byword in the platoon goes: "It's a stinking situation." Yet there is nothing to do but get out of it as quickly as possible. The path by which to do this is naturally to obey orders—to defeat the enemy rather than capitulate to him.

Many movies expressed this all too self-evident soldiers' moral. *A Walk in the Sun* accomplished it by the most realistic and internal of methods—by revealing the moral relations among the men, their feuds and friendships, their verbal reactions, and their private judgment of the facts. It is a long movie, which as a mere extended anecdote puts great strain on one's attentiveness. Here the notable kinetic variety of the movies was restricted to a small, very unpanoramic area. According to one interchange among the men there is not even conclusive proof that they are in Italy. So where are they? Their situation takes its character from the military action: to kill the enemy and arrive at a certain isolated objective, where, if successful, they must remain till receiving further orders. All life is reduced to obedience, fighting, and an environment limited technically to immediate scenes. This contact with nature is well expressed by several men, one of whom, a farmer, insists that the dirt he passes and repasses through his hands is "no good, it's old, tired dirt." At least this man has some direct, specialized contact with nature through the soil of the planet. And the same man, doubtless mindful of food rations, can't get out of his head the image of a big red apple, which seems eventually to be some sort of image of the planet itself and implicitly is associated with a woman as well.

The foxhole in the head, the sexual apple, these are figments of symbolic thought, concentrated samples of the wandering, fanciful conversation of all the members of the platoon, trudging along in the sun or nervously waiting, prone, for the order to fire. It is extraordinary to note that precisely in this military situation of tension, a tension of life and death involving extreme physical activity, ordinary men become most philosophical. And yet after a moment's consideration one concedes it as a perfectly natural phenomenon. They are close to death. But unlike the men brought to a complete physical impasse in the submarine, these relaxed and unrelaxed soldiers are at direct grips with death; it lurks everywhere, behind every cloud, every bush, every turn in the road—even, illusorily, in the very heart of the sun, from which an attacking plane seems to swoop down. The irony is that they feel free, untrapped, just because they can *walk in the sun,* because they exist in the actual open space of war, where they constitute a fighting organism keyed to its utmost and constantly expending itself in action. And yet a particular kind of boredom afflicts the men of this platoon in the Salerno operation, a philosophic boredom. War is not simply constant action in the fighting sense; its decisiveness in terms of victory and defeat, life and death, is perpetually postponed in an irritating manner. As many writers and philosophers have told us, war is anything but a pitched battle. Still, the men are in it. But how are they really *in?* They are in it precisely by being able to stand outside it and contemplate it even while in the act of firing or crawling on their bellies during an engagement. When marching, when exposed to attack at any moment, their next word may be buried in their mouths by a bullet in their sides.

A truism it is that under modern conditions the common

man has too little time in which normally to perfect himself in thought, and modern conditions are such that leisure becomes a symbol of neurotic search for amusement, for escape and diversion from the monotony and insipidity of physical work. Yet the crisis of life and death in the midst of war automatically involves the reflective mode of thought, first by the conceivably brief time left in which to think things out, second by the magic transformation of peaceful environment into warlike environment. Previously for these men the natural scene implied an opening out into the world, a link with the eternal peace and plenty of nature, at least symbolically, but now nature is actually but a background for the act of killing and destruction and hence is alienated. This transformation of scene infinitely narrows the world; as an eccentric fellow tearfully complains in *A Walk in the Sun,* "You don't ever get to *see* anything of the war." But this situation of being in the midst of something without being able to see it in its entirety merely reproduces the commonplace predicament of men who live in the midst of peace without being able to see it in its entirety; namely, without understanding their own lives, rural or urban—without being truly philosophical. So *A Walk in the Sun* revealed an important and ironical truth: war actually offers men a decisive though elliptical opportunity to evaluate life and themselves; it is a situation coercive toward philosophizing.

The casual conversation of soldiers in this movie, however, is not per se the most vital evidence that in the swift crucible of war ordinary men have an irresistible impulse

Magic and Myth of the Movies

to make deferred decisions and evaluate life in general terms. Conversation is but the word counterpart of their nervous rhythm and physical behavior, their vocality and the peculiar pulsation dominating every mental and physical movement in the theater of war. In the curriculum of march, rest, maneuver, and fighting action it is *the lull,* the time out while reconnaissance is taking place, that illuminates the heart of the soldier's situation. Most impressive it is that *A Walk in the Sun* uniquely reveals the degree to which a group of five soldiers, relaxing on back and elbows, can draw together as a unit, a kind of thinking, complex animal with five voices, replying to each other as in a litany; the tangential quality of the remarks, the oblique, fanciful way in which each remark is taken up by another speaker, this process creates a form completely defining the kind of human community this fortuitous little group is. Here is no usual bull session, not merely because the circumstances are crucial, but also because the men are thrown together without instinctively mutual interests; their common interest stands at two poles, their status as human beings alive today and the military action in which they are engaged, and thus provides an absolute leap from the most general unity to the most particular unity without any intervention. Always, everywhere, in one sense man faces his philosophic destiny whether he likes it or not. He faces it because as the thinking animal he also faces death.

A very remarkable fact is that the actors delegated to impersonate these soldiers furnish the most generally brilliant acting of the American movies in recent times, a contribution to the style mentioned above. Only one of them was a star of any magnitude in his profession. Probably some will never again achieve rôles so important. But the fact is that a group spirit present in this picture is cryingly absent from the usual cinema product. For one thing the reality of the situation, the overhanging forces of life and death, automatically drew the actors together as it drew many an actual group of fighters in the war. I submit that this could not have happened in a movie whose purpose was not, as here, specifically the group level of war's experience. That discredited spirit of democracy served to give each actor here the impression that he was in what any multipersonal artistic endeavor is, a collective enterprise. On the other hand, the Hollywood rule is, "Everyone out for how bright he can shine, and the devil take the shadows of the hindmost." As a matter of fact it would have been impossible for the actors to achieve such a unity had not the basis for it existed in actual life.

Why did all the actors feel so much at home in their rôles? The answer to this depends directly on the answer to another question: Why did it seem so natural to these soldiers, in the fiction being displayed, to lie so negligently together and open their minds to each other—to philosophize, so to speak, out of the blue? It seems to me this would not seem so natural, as pre-eminently it did, had not a parallel situation already existed in peacetime, a situation of which their present one is a mere extension and concentration. Briefly, the lull during an operation is not only analogous with those moments back home when they would rest and loll and vent casual observations on life but also a concrete symbol of their whole life situation as it exists in their spiritual depths. The casualness of their own front-porch philosophizing is, even as later in the theater of war, merely a deceptive coating for an illimitable area of tension in their depths. In some sense life and the future are as much in question during peace as during war. In the reflective mood of idle leisure, the extreme possibility of death is balanced by the extreme possibilities of life. Cynically, while on the march at Salerno, these men mention opportunities; that is, career opportunities. Are they so much further away from these now than they were at home? Their coarse philosophic irony is token that they realize the future at this moment is not so different, from one viewpoint, from what it used to be.

What can we conclude from this admirable lesson of the cinema but that a kind of philosophic paranoia, the persecution of men by thought, taunts them with unrealized, unrealizable ambitions—thought that cannot, as with pure philosophy, exist for its own sake but is only a symbolic substitute for action and material reality? War represents for the average peacetime citizen the diametric opposite of everything he has visualized as desirable in the material universe. At the same time he is a member of that unofficial peacetime army composed largely of unorganized individuals who conduct a permanent struggle to earn money and outdo their competitors. Soldiers sense some of the inhumanity likewise involved in peacetime struggle, an inhumanity comprised mostly of machinelike labor, merciless push, and dull fatigue connected with a limp twilight of the mind.

So the lulls in the midst of battle literally correspond with those lulls back home wherein they could momentarily relax in the competitive struggle and exchange with other men, dreamily or intensely, their most fanciful hopes, fugitive fears, common ambitions, or winged opinions. The necessity to be released from the tension of fear—fear of failure, of hunger, of shabbiness, of the contempt of more prosperous men—becomes more imperative when faced by an imminent death, a final cessation of human endeavor. So the old peacetime ritual is revived in an anonymous little gulley beneath trees that these spectators will never see again, and the human voices grow strangely impersonal, paradoxically tender; the men are lost together in the profound spiritual depths of this moment wrested from grim and exhausting effort, a moment of intensified peace more restful than any such moment formerly experienced . . . for now, both morally and physically, this moment is called upon to prepare them for what neither religion nor philosophic experience has yet prepared them—the supreme effort and mortal risk around the bend in the road.

VII

Of those films that visualized the more or less macabre results of war, like the problem of rehabilitating the mentally shot soldier, and those that have revealed the sadness of homes deserted by fathers, husbands, and sweethearts, such as *The Impatient Years, Since You Went Away, I'll Be Seeing You,* etc., etc., the best that can be said of them is that they all assumed with admirable optimism the survival of the human heart. In actual performance, from scene to scene, actor to actor, stunt to stunt—Monty Woolley is forced in one to drive away the domestic blues by standing on all fours and waggling his behind for several minutes—these films are spiritually more mutilated than the average film during peacetime. *Since You Went Away,* wearing a bouquet of orchidaceous players including Shirley Temple, was like a miraculously prolonged Christmas greeting from the family to father and hubby at the front, with the tears still wet on it. When one considers the reality of war and postwar problems and then turns to regard them as ritually conceived by Hollywood, one observes that the land of moving pictures has inverted the larger truth of things. In the average sentimental movie plot the war has simplified life for the individual by ignorantly oversimplifying it. There is facile eloquence to the thesis that the absolutist pressures of war—military conscription, rationing, speed-up labor, precipitated acts of all kinds—give people a stronger, more urgent pattern by which to live. Even if the ethical problems of human beings were gauged by a low popular standard, it would be foolish to think that in any ultimate sense, wartime haste and precipitation, as time-tested, are truly a moral tonic.

In silver-shadowing a popular novel, *Marriage Is a Private Affair,* even Hollywood showed it could be aware that on the contrary, in the cases of some individuals whose natures take time to find their mold, the human wax is too liquescent for war psychology. As the young woman who finally chose a soldier to marry, the husband later being denied return to the front because he is an expert lens-maker, Lana Turner may have been unduly excited by the exigency of wartime marriage; her family complex is only more handicapped by the subtle urge of the military clock to push reality ahead. She dislikes her mother's frivolous marital promiscuity and secretly fears the same ungainly fate for herself—as repellent, she believes, as fat on the waistline. But this yen for monogamy—maybe in the more realistic sense this is what *creates* her vacillation neurosis and causes her to be haunted even on an idyllic honey-moon by her mother's example. If we put aside any specu-lation about a possible Electra complex—she meets her father, whom she has not seen for many years, on her bridal day—the fear for the integrity of the monogamous pattern may be dictated in *form* by her observation of her mother's fluid domestic arrangements, but its *essence* may be the simple fear of division from her husband by death in battle; he stays at home, and yet he is away from her many an evening. Miss Turner's young woman, full of natural life and attractiveness, obviously has some deep-lying diffi-culty, but its symptomology seems strictly contemporary. Finally the husband is allowed to go back to war; her anxiety may have been increased all along of course by the thought that he was eager to leave her side for the sake of his country. When he is somewhere in the Pacific, she makes her irrevocable decision: it is *he*—not any of his rivals, with one of whom she has had a serious flirtation—whom she truly loves. Thus she had to wait for their postmarriage actual separation by war in order to make up her mind. To inform him of her about-face (she has started divorce proceedings prior to his departure), a melodramatic hookup by telephone to a Pacific island base is arranged. To tell him that she really loves him even while he is far away seems part of the reality of her decision. Thus, substituting in the twentieth century for taboo forms of behavior observed by wives in savage eras and communities when the men were away fighting, the telephone becomes a means of a similar unification through space. The monistic element in monogamy may thus be the same element as that in vocal communication over a great distance . . . a magic spiritual element, an ideal unity, existing today as many centuries ago it did in a differing form; the same element makes a photograph of a man substitute for his actual presence—two things, the man and his image, equaling his single reality. Strangely enough the young wife does not really get to hear her husband's voice or he hers, since they have to exchange their endearments by courtesy of a central operator. This may indicate that she can really love him only through some elliptical identification of him with a third person, an intermediary, perhaps her father, whom she has now joined after a long absence from him that was broken only by their meeting at her wedding and who is in the room with her as she telephones.

Furthermore the young wife's erotically wayward

mother, the Billie Burke genre, may symbolize not sexual fickleness but that fickleness of fate that might in the wife's imagination guide a Japanese bullet to her husband's heart; thus by analogy she fears the playful and irresponsible moves of the moral life . . . which would be no more than a precise application of rules of taboo that have an immemorial tradition. In all fairness to the analysis, however, we must register the fact that some of the young wife's consternation at her impulses toward men other than her husband, even after the marriage ceremony, is due to strictly contemporary taboos. With the growth of an age of reason it is logical to suppose that such errant impulses are only normal and may be harmlessly overcome or disposed of, but our barbarous middle-class system imposes a mythology whose anachronism breeds unfortunate results in psychological states. Postmarital sexual impulses outside the domestic area are supposed moral stigmata. The real point is that if the confused young woman is really as mercurial as her mother, no number of telephone messages to the Pacific will curtail her eventual activities at this end of the line. . . . So another movie myth evaporates before our eyes.

The supernaturalist atmosphere, subtly dominating silent and dramatic farewells in movie-lot life, and the precipitation of real life during wartime are aptly caught up together in *The Clock,* fable of a young small-town chap who comes to New York on a two-day furlough before sailing for parts unknown, picks up a girl in Pennsylvania Station, and promptly falls in love with her. The couple's

169

crucial moment is at night in one of the murkier dells of Riverside Drive, where they have found a nook lit discreetly by a lamp at the path crossing and where they divulge to one another their mutual feelings. Judy Garland and Robert Walker do the scene very well with a minimum of trimmings; obvious and sentimental as it is, it was very hard to do well. Soundproofed poetical invention rose to its full height when the couple remarked on the illusion of isolation provided not only by the park, its outlying darkness, and the view of the night sky but by the silence. . . . But the silence, as the girl observes, is not really silence, being full of the night sounds that congregate from automobiles, subways, fire engines, and steamships even as she speaks. But the Reverential Hush triumphs! As we listen, the city's aimless cacophony is magically converted into one of those heavenly choruses to which I referred in my first chapter, a soaring harmony of voices like an articulate music of the spheres that lays bare each young heart and draws them to press against one another. . . . So Hollywood avails itself of a perfect example of the thesis that the fever and haste of war breed moments of pause and spiritual elevation magically snatched from the propulsive context of life and, as it were, hung on the walls of time like a religious print. . . .

In *I'll Be Seeing You* screen oversimplification reaches its most hobbling stage. That a man must be mentally or physically maimed to simplify his moral problems in our time would seem a rather high price to pay for moral contentment and individual happiness. Hollywood's box-office

170

mythology did not dare assume that the problems of post-war would be only a deepened continuation of the problems of the late peace—even though this was something that every serious newspaper columnist admitted—because movie art a priori has never acknowledged the existence of socio-psychological or socio-economic problems excepting in the rarest of instances, with a couple of which I will deal in my penultimate chapter.

VIII

The season of 1944-45 was important for the sudden outcropping of psychological murder films—at least one of them, *The Woman in the Window,* being as well done as *Double Indemnity*—and this upsurge could be accounted for, I feel, by the inevitable albeit subconscious interest aroused in the public by the conception of war as murder and, following this line of thought, the conception of murder as psychological; that is, motivated by a kind of kink, a madness, a disease—perhaps not in order to feel that the psychological element is what identifies war with murder but rather what dissociates the two; hence it would have been the public tendency to justify the war morally simply because it was an accomplished fact, a thing to which one was morally committed simply because it existed. This might well be the reactionary heritage of having conceived Hitler as an insane warmonger.

It may be noted that the conception of psychological

murder is legally orientated to murder by someone more or less irresponsible for his act and therefore eligible for extenuation of his punishment both in kind and degree. So, even though superficially the war, considered from the subjective viewpoint of the warriors, is not acknowledged as mass murder, it seems possible that in the minds of public, script-writers, and script-editors alike, a simultaneous process of association took place. On the one hand, in the new set of movies there was interest in establishing murder as the act of an ordinary citizen, not of a gangster, a group, or a nation; on the other, in emphasizing the psychological rather than the moral motivation of the crime, its mechanical compulsion rather than its ethical responsibility, public and professional interest would seem to have reflected a concern to establish an extenuating legal status for the act of killing. . . . But was not Hollywood—and perhaps we the audience—caught in a peculiar trap here? For it is not many steps backward from the psychopathologically excused murderer to Frankenstein's monster and other extrahuman and extramoral killers as well as, according to one theory, Hitler himself. That the American soldier was in danger of becoming extrahuman to the extent that he could be de-socialized, unmarried, and de-economized to one degree or another on his return from the battle front—this extent of extrahumanization was self-evident, and the problem it created was known as of yore by the phrase: rehabilitation of the returned soldier. A Frankenstein's monster is held a fabled creature, but on a modified scale does he not ghoulishly reappear among us as the physically, mentally, or socially deformed ex-soldier?

These are very disagreeable matters, I realize, but that Hollywood products are only fiction does not mean that the life they in some sense reflect is likewise fiction. In *The Woman in the Window* it turned out that the supposed murder by the sex-motivated criminology professor was a dream—and therefore according to naïve Hollywood logic unreal, a fiction by double indemnity. Being such, it was implied, it could never land the really nice professor in the criminal section of a Madame Tussaud's on our contemporary Coney Island. But the fact is that in making the professor's crime occur *in his dream* its psychological reality, its mental precipitation, this alone, is established. A dream is symptomatic of unconscious psychological precipitation; indeed the prophetic dream is a common tradition, the ancient form of the wish-fulfillment or fear-fulfillment dream of Freud's system. Mental anticipation of a self-planned probable or possible act or event—whether death of a husband on the firing line, murder of a sex rival, anxious bridal night, or vision of a holy person—this anticipation is symbolic precipitation achieved through impatience or fear. In the criminology professor's case, since the murder takes place as the direct consequence of an indiscreet sex adventure, the dreamer is dominated by both desire and fear. To save his own life the professor has to stab to death a man who seizes his throat in a deadly grip when he catches him having drinks with the assailant's girl friend in her apartment. Now let us suppose that in the waxworks of war that I have interpreted in this chapter there be substituted for this criminology professor—who is, one will note, an ethical expert—an American military strategist who dreams that he has to kill a Japanese assailant who tries to stab him in the back. Dreams often invert literal facts. The strategic dreamer here, having stabbed his Japanese enemy in the back, as the professor his sex enemy, would have awakened to fear that his enemy might stab him in the back. . . . Would that, well before December 7, 1941, we had had such a strategist guilty of mental precipitation in dreams! We would have forgiven him his crime as we forgive the professor his. But, alas! we would not have accepted his dream brand of politics with sympathy as quick as that with which we accept the professor's dream brand of sex.

8. MAGIC-LANTERN METAMORPHOSES III

Double into Quadruple Indemnity

In the misty, before-dawn streets of a city a roadster races, barely missing other vehicles but apparently not pursued, therefore bent on some destination. It pulls up before an office building, and the tall, rather hunched figure of a man alights and rings the night bell. One arm seems to be stiff as the elderly, chatty custodian takes him up in the elevator. He stalks onto the mezzanine of the spacious quarters of a life-insurance firm, seeks an inner office, and falling awkwardly into a chair, removes his coat, worn cloak fashion, and reveals a dark, wet hole—blood—in the shoulder of his jacket. Breathing heavily and sweating, he reaches for a dictaphone, starts the mechanism, and settles back, gasping, to begin his message. It is a confession of murder . . . addressed to the head claim adjuster of the firm for which he is a salesman.

This is the bravura and effective manner in which the bravura and effective *Double Indemnity* opens, a story that emerges from film hands as a thing considerably different from the novel by James Cain on which it was based. However tight and attention-holding the telling—and it is that—there are momentary interims when one wonders why the culprit, who has murdered a man with the man's wife as accomplice in order to collect his life insurance,

175

should be confessing in this manner when he might be attempting a getaway over the near-by border. The cinema specialists would hardly create the device merely in order to be mechanically effective. There is a most interesting reason for it, however, when all the elements of this melo-melo are correlated.

From top to bottom and from side to side the pattern is one of dualism, both intentional and unintentional. Indeed what would Hollywood do without its supplementary automatism? Thus the title, *Double Indemnity*, has a basic symbolism. Murdering the gentleman in question without being aware that he has been the object of previous solicitude entails payment of a sum to his widow, who, as it happens, is to share it with her lover and co-criminal, the insurance agent. But Neff, the agent, quite familiar with the double-indemnity clause, has planned a doubly lucrative death, since, according to the statistics of mortality, falling off a train is a most out-of-the-way accident. Both the lady, Phyllis Didriksen, and her colleague, Neff, might be supposed subject to mere greed—well and good. But considering the saturative dualism in the movie, too much in the way of ambiguous motivation is present to make such a simple premise seem valid. We must skeptically investigate the possible claim of Hollywood and common sense in this respect.

To start back even before the insurance agent happens upon Phyllis, with her exposed legs and her anklet, one hot afternoon when he calls about accident insurance on the Didriksen car—and finds the master of the house absent—

176

it is plain that Neff's relation with the claim adjuster, Keyes, contains the dualism of subtle business hostility and personal friendship. Keyes's job is to determine if insurance claims are valid; in other words, he is the guardian angel of occasions when Neff's policy sales have their most unfortunate and anticlimactic aspect; that is, when their logic of possibility, death or accident, becomes a factual certainty and the firm groans and has to pay up. Thus Keyes stands by, always alert, as an internal corrective, from the firm's viewpoint, for fraudulent representations of deaths and accidents. Keyes in Neff's eyes is ever present to validate the myth of his daily sales talks, which is that human wisdom has provided a method of safeguarding against certain consequences of accident or death. On the other hand, Keyes is also waiting to *invalidate* this myth by sometimes assuming and on notable occasions proving its falsity. If a client of Neff's burns down his own truck and wants to collect, he is willy-nilly realizing the *logic* of Neff's sales talk, but Keyes in rooting out the fraud mocks the ideal logic, the mythological charm, of Neff's sales talk by calling attention to the unpleasantness involved in its consequences—not to the mere fact of destruction but to the causation of destruction as in the case of the burned truck. The would-be beneficiary is no ideal victim of fate but a low cheater of insurance firms.

Let us examine more thoroughly the reasons why the invalidation of insurance claims might bother a policy salesman. As we know, the insurance company is a profit-making organization, and the logical basis of its profit is that in the great percentage of cases the emotional logic of the sales talk—the scientific possibility of the insured party's death or accident to property or self converted into emotional probability—is false. It is on this type of falsity that a salesman's earnings are based, for, as is well known, he has to overcome the psychological aversion from the emotional probability of death as the nucleus of resistance in his prospective client. It is the client's ordinary prejudice against formal psychological consent to the possibility of his death that spoils many a policy sale. The salesman's persuasiveness overcomes this prejudice, only perhaps to be followed later with a claim for accident indemnity that the claim adjuster believes invalid. So claim validation stands as an ethical corrective to possible fraudulent consequences flowing from the policy sale.

We are well aware that insurance firms are not torn asunder by such an ethically obscure and rather abstract sort of dichotomy. But here we are involved with a particular salesman and a particular claim adjuster, the structure of whose personal relationship is an extension, partly symbolic and partly material, of the moral elements contained in their business relationship and its overtones of human ethics. In view of the plot itself, we have to assume a special sensitivity of conscience on Neff's part, a special recognition of Keyes's claims on him, both business and personal. His climactic confession into the dictaphone is a convincing symptom of this situation. Moreover, as Keyes's last speech, uttered over the wounded and trapped Neff, effectively clinches, Keyes takes a personal, neo-paternal interest in Neff, a concern to whose warmth Neff most belatedly and ironically responds by confessing the murder; in doing this, however, he proves that Keyes has cleverly penetrated the fraud concocted by himself and Phyllis and so gives the claim adjuster his deserved triumph as an expert. But on the face of it why should Neff, who seems a rather typical hard-boiled sort, appear as the self-immolative instrument of tragic irony? Some obscure fate must dominate him, one related to but by no means wholly defined by a desire to redeem his conventional honesty before the firm and its claim adjuster. In seeking out the nature of this fate I mean to indicate the more or less unconscious rightness of the author's and movie-maker's instinct in supplying a double symmetry, business and personal, for the relations between Keyes and Neff.

At a crucial point of the tension preceding the carefully planned crime Keyes offers Neff a job as claim adjuster, and after Neff responds with an uninterested negative and Keyes gives Neff's self-esteem a pep talk, Phyllis interrupts by phoning to say the moment has come for the crime; her husband is making a train trip. Neff calls her Margie and successfully disguises the meaning of the conversation. But the blunt Keyes scoffs at this Margie and rather directly blames women and carousing for Neff's indifference to the honor offered him—since at first he would have to take a reduction in salary. "I'll bet she drinks from the bottle!" Keyes exclaims of Margie. Neff's habitual treatment of Keyes's friendly feelings, which are obvious enough beneath the claim adjuster's hard-shelled exterior, is laconic and grinning, touched, moreover, with quaint irony by an often repeated and, I think, symbolic incident.

Keyes is always smoking cigars but is just as consistently without matches with which to light them. With an ironic little grin Neff ritually pulls out a matchbox, strikes a match, and lights Keyes's cigar. This may have been a bit of routine invention by busy studio scribes, or they may have borrowed it in characteristic blind haste—but blind haste may be most intuitive. From the mellow tenets of psychology we know that very small habits of this sort become rituals through the deliberate, even if veiled-from-self cultivation of the person who receives the favor. A master at his job and a poised individual, having made his moral peace with life, Keyes, extremely well played by Edward G. Robinson, may especially enjoy this tiny bit of moral dependence on Neff, whom he likes and whose liking he solicits. Emotional liking—there is no evidence that Keyes is married or has women—may be the only thing lacking to his daily satisfactions. Neff is not responsive, but in his good-natured yielding to the ritual of providing Keyes with a light he is submitting to an etiquette of friendliness that he performs in no other way. On the surface it is an empty form, and it may be as a mere symbolic form that Keyes accepts it—just as a lady secretly in love with the doorman of her hotel may derive a subtle, withal empty, satisfaction from his touch as he hands her into a cab.

It seems to me that the presence of the little ritual between Neff and Keyes is no accident and that its graphic nature is highly suggestive. Keyes has reason to be envious of Neff in those very sexual relations at which he scoffs, for Keyes is short and homely, and Neff is tall, younger, attractive, and obviously lusty. But if Keyes is always completely well balanced, Neff is subtly unbalanced; and we take for granted that Keyes, explicitly a psychologist, cannot help noting albeit subconsciously the accentuated signs of nervousness in Neff during the period when the crime is planned and after it occurs. But the very fact that the alertly intuitive Keyes, with his interior "little man" who informs him whenever a claim is fraudulent, does not register the pertinence of Neff's tense manner during the Didriksen case may indicate that *he has already interpreted the cause of Neff's habitual manner and the basis of his own interest in it*. Therefore added tension in Neff would not be especially striking to Keyes.

Neff's personality has undoubtedly been doped out by the friendly psychologist Keyes as sexually promiscuous, uncomfortably so, entailing the sort of irresponsibility and lack of serious intention that makes a man drink too much, carouse too hard, and eventually fall down on his job. Therefore Keyes's offer of another job seems an effort to reorientate Neff psychologically to a position where he does not have to make himself so persuasive with people; it is in order to impersonalize him and make him a more objective judge of people that Keyes wants him to become the impersonal, objective, and justice-minded claim adjuster. According to this assumption, it is plausible that, subtly envious of Neff's success with women and having an incoherent affection for him, Keyes aims basically with the job offer at a specific reorientation of Neff's attitude toward women—a curbing of sexual promiscuity by the suggestion of the curbed promiscuity of his sales personality. So the pattern of Keyes's interest in Neff divines and repeats that of the very extension of Neff's salesmanship, which leads to his doom, for Neff virtually sells Mrs. Didriksen a sex policy on himself at the moment he literally sells her a death policy on her husband. Now if the primary relations between the men, Neff and Keyes, have this sexual underpattern, the nature of the match-striking ritual has its sexual interpretation. Neff is demonstrating to Keyes his successful sexual "spark" and *symbolically* communicating this capacity, which Keyes lacks and of which he is envious no less than suspicious.

The congruence of the sexual motivation of the crime with this pattern is self-evident. Since it turns out, however, that Phyllis asserts she was never in love with Neff but was coldly and cruelly using him all the time, we must analyze the limitations of the involved sexual motives. This is the story's climax: since the insurance company, inspired by Keyes's supposed though actually mistaken identification of Phyllis' accomplice, refuses to recognize the claim, Neff —under much tension—turns tail and thinks only of saving his own hide; one night he and Phyllis meet secretly in her darkened house, each planning the other's murder as the only way out. After he mockingly betrays his own purpose, Phyllis quietly plugs him with a revolver shot but does not fire again when she has wounded him in the shoulder, because, although she confesses her love has been insincere, "something stops her." They move into each other's arms, yet Neff does not kiss her upraised lips; he has taken the revolver from her hand, and now he puts it to her side, pulling the trigger. She falls dead. Neff then goes on his mad ride to the insurance company's office and confesses fully and pictorially into Keyes's dictaphone.

Here the version of a sexual motive for a criminal act is so cynical, and Barbara Stanwyck in the rôle of Phyllis is so unrelieved by any frill of nice femininity, that the wiseacres of Hollywood have provided the movie with a subplot, a romance between Phyllis' stepdaughter and a misunderstood youth, which turns out to be the real thing. Yet the muscle tone of this highly diverting fable of modern sex does not yield to the drug of romance thus cutely administered while apparently the story wasn't looking. Phyllis' sexuality and Neff's are obviously more genuine and convincing than the other pair's so far as modern mores go. Insofar as personal sincerity is concerned, it is only a most unsophisticated version of it that, now or in the previous history of the human race, is not considered subject to possible self-deception and the objective dangers of moral and legal conventions. The indemnity involved in this movie is not only double but quadruple. For the lovers start out on a declaration that is not only life insurance for Didriksen (money) but life insurance for Mrs. Didriksen's adulterous affair with the insurance salesman. It is true that the original inspiration for the crime, emanating from Phyllis, occurs in the form of opportunism; she sees the salesman is smitten with her, and the idea bursts into bloom.

But this does not mean that she herself is not sexually moved. Indeed, although apparently the motivation of the money-making crime is only mechanically sexual, the true objective being the selfish one of money, why may it not be just the reverse? The crime against her despised husband's life may function for Phyllis as the logical mechanism to involve her in a purely sensual, and this time honest, sex affair. The inducing of Neff to commit the crime to win her would then be merely a vulgarly morbid method of binding him to her, since she might threaten exposure if he ever wanted to leave her. Thus the crime may be Phyllis' own accident insurance against Neff's insincerity or the possible eventuality of his sometime desertion.

Certainly this is sex without conventional idealism, and in baring so morally base a mechanism, so calculating a form of sexual psychology, Hollywood has provided a chunk of truth hard for sentimental patrons of the movies to digest. But really sentimental or at least militantly sentimental movie-goers are growing scarcer, I believe, all the time. Of course they exist in large numbers in the great outlying wastes, but Hollywood has plenty of antidotes for such a dose of sex poison as this one. Neff himself, his motivation, is of course the crux of the plot and its controlling mechanism. It is Neff who mediates between the highly explicit form of sex in Phyllis and the highly implicit form in Keyes and thus balances these forces of the plot.

As yet we have not looked directly at Neff, played with a certain grotesque aptitude by Fred MacMurray. If the

184

movie makes one thing obvious, it is the genuineness of Phyllis' attraction for him. So in a sense he is rooked into the crime. And yet, when it seems that the only way to clear himself of the whole mess is to rid her of life, he unhesitatingly sets out to murder her. He is abetted in this objective by the information from her stepdaughter that her marriage to Didriksen may have occurred because Phyllis had hastened the former Mrs. Didriksen's death when she was her nurse. This motivates Neff's desire to murder her; he is completely disillusioned with her, and lust, under the pressure of fear, turns into hatred. But the point is that both Phyllis and Neff are psychologically licked and capitulate to the shrewd maneuvering of Keyes. Yet there is small basis for assuming that they would be panicked by mere threats from Keyes. Why are they?

As a matter of fact, if Phyllis had had time in which to push her suit against the firm and if she had kept the superb nerve she had all along, Keyes, having wrongly picked the stepdaughter's sweetheart as Phyllis' accomplice, would have been baffled in court. It is true that if her sweetheart had been involved, the stepdaughter would have talked; but even if she had, not only would she have sworn an alibi for her boy friend, but there was no iota of evidence to prove that he or any other man colluded with Phyllis or even that there was a murder. Yet both Neff and Phyllis, adult, experienced, and hard-boiled, are thrown utterly off balance. Why? Evidently they do not trust each other. And why do they not trust each other? Because, I hazard, both know that one of them does not get or give satisfaction in sexual relations. Regardless of the ambiguity of Phyllis' motivations, I believe the over-all pattern of the story makes it inevitable that Neff is the sexually handicapped party and wishes to be done with the affair irrespective of the crime factor.

In the course of their plotting Phyllis has surreptitiously visited Neff several times in his apartment. We must not forget that Neff is the master hand in the affair. Provided he has a clear sexual conscience, he has every reason to be confident of ultimate success. Indeed, given assurance of sexual prowess, both subjectively and objectively effective, he is the sort of man to be misled by overconfidence rather than lack of confidence. It is too absurd to believe that the stepdaughter's hysteria stirs his conscience and unmans him. At the same time it may be true that the rumor of Phyllis' previous technique with Didriksen's wife may convince him that she intends deserting him if not killing him. She would do so only if she did not care for him. But Neff on the surface has every reason to believe he is the type of man to make her care. He has little cause to calculate that she intends the same fate for him as for Didriksen, especially because a dead Neff would considerably complicate her claim for the indemnity. Even if Neff imagines he will be humiliated later by Phyllis' desertion, he is certainly much overestimating such a humiliation in view of the fact that he is counting on half the money with which to console himself—*unless* this sexual slap in the face should be the climax of previous less crucial humiliations, casual ones that Keyes is always hinting at even though blindly in his little lectures to Neff. The general psychological situation is such that Neff may have placed some supreme hope on Phyllis as a sexual partner who would inspire him to get and give satisfaction—a hope that is crushed.

Moreover, when Neff first meets Phyllis and hears her daring, scarcely veiled suggestion, he may grasp at the deed as a way of finally ridding himself of Keyes, *who presides over his life as the hidden judge of his sexual claims as well as the insurance claims of his clients.* Neff, let us assume, wants permanent insurance against Keyes's subtle inquisition into the ostensible claims of his sexual life; to murder a man for his wife appeals to Neff therefore as an ideal method of refuting Keyes's moralism and defying him as a sexual claim adjuster. If we do not accept this pattern, there is no stable foundation for Neff's panic, capitulation, and irrational murder of Phyllis—nor, to sum it up, for his voluntary confession of guilt rather than an immediate attempt at a getaway over the near-by border into Mexico. Yet all tallies perfectly if we accept the present supposition.

The elevator operator reports blood on the floor of the car after Neff has entered the office, and as a result Neff has barely completed his confession into the dictaphone when Keyes appears. Previously Keyes has vouched for Neff to the insurance company and prevented the salesman's being put under surveillance in the case. At the last Neff wants to vindicate Keyes and his professional reputation, for in doing this he is vindicating Keyes's over-all conception of fraud—including the technical fraud in invalid *sexual* claims as well as the technical fraud in invalid *insurance* claims.

Neff asks Keyes for a chance at a getaway and staggers out, after Keyes, realizing that Neff has lost much blood, says he can't get as far as the door on his own feet. Neff slumps in the outer doorway and, as Keyes overtakes him and kneels beside him, fumbles for a cigarette; he has no match. This time it is Keyes who has the match—the answer, the symbolic instrument of power. He strikes it for the supine Neff, now convicted of his double fraud. Trying to grin, puffing on the cigarette, Neff makes a remark to the effect that no longer will they see each other daily across the desk. Keyes replies that Neff has been, to him, "closer than that." I don't know what other evidence is needed to show that Keyes himself is obscurely aware that he symbolizes Neff's sexual conscience and that the plot demonstrates that the double-indemnity clause in the insurance policy symbolizes Neff's last desperate and doomed effort to prove the latent efficacy of his *sexual salesmanship*.

The lugubrious face of the movie is provided by the fact that to the Phyllises and Neffs of this world there seems available no other form of compensation for sexual inadequacy but money. Despite its barbarously Zolaesque quality—and a little because of it—this movie is one of the most psychologically cogent ever to emerge from the developing studios of Hollywood—presenting, as it does so ingeniously, the insurance company's judgment of sexual problems. Neff's pathological illusion is one of the diseases of American culture: that salesmanship can be an esthetic value. The larger truth may be that, analogously to those who adopt and cultivate a war psychology, Neff desperately sells himself the idea of murderous violence as an aid to moral enthusiasm—in his case an enthusiasm for sex.

9. SCHIZOPHRENIA À LA MODE

I

The most important representations of schizophrenia in contemporary art, the comedies of Pirandello, are intellectual counterparts to certain comedic tendencies in the movies, the latter appearing as devices to create laughter rather than as concepts of character involved in the drama of modern personality. Yet the movies do not altogether fail to give serious attention to the problems of personality —if by "serious" is meant merely what is done with a perfectly straight face. Besides the Dr. Jekyll and Mr. Hyde type of thriller there has been Garbo's performance some years ago in a piece adapted from Pirandello's *As You Desire Me,* as well as in her more recent films, *Ninotchka* and *Two-faced Woman.* All these movies illustrated this star's own schizoid traits as a human type, considered apart from the particular rôles she was obliged to act. On a trivial and superficial plane Hollywood is engaged in a permanent experiment with its feminine stars, in giving a schizophrenic tone to their personalities by casting them in diverse successive rôles and hair-dos, which may entail changes in them as basic human types for the delectation of movie customers; as yet, however, no Pirandellian dilemmas have resulted in the studio dressing rooms, perhaps for the good reason that a star does not shrink from making any sacrifice to revive his or her prestige at the box office.

That schizophrenia should be the tone given the efforts of a movie actor at versatility of character is one of the sad destinies of Hollywood. In any case the split personality has no prestige in the movies as thematic material. However, among the stock devices of Hollywood's characterization of human beings are inadvertent—secreted—uses of the schizophrenic motif of much wider meaning than the clumsily handled and stark schizophrenic theses of Garbo's *Two-faced Woman* or Crawford's *A Woman's Face,* although both these films have their own underlying interest.

Below the general heading of the retarded mental reflex, the schizophrenic phenomena I have in mind possess three separate characters: momentary loss of identity, Hugh Herbert acknowledging himself rather than the other person when being introduced; the durational loss of the meaning of what one is doing, creating a split between mental activity and physical activity, Jean Arthur letting Joel McCrea make love to her while she talks of things unrelated to their present physical behavior; and what might be termed the "retarded mental reflex simple," technically known as the "double-take" and used in countless comedies and comedy dramas as integral material or ready relief for tense situations. Formula: girl happy as a lark and chattering like a magpie because she's in love; informant casually remarks that her boy friend has a wife. "Really? Isn't that nice!" she chatters on, and then: *"Huh?"* . . . Laughter.

The comedian Hugh Herbert has made the retarded mental reflex *simple* a steppingstone to fame, but it is not merely a comic device with him. He and to a lesser extent

191

Bob Hope have integrated it into their screen personalities so that one would feel them different characters without it. An analysis of Herbert's fussbudget, burlesque personality reveals a strange hybrid; he is a combination of the most hallowed popular legend of schizophrenia, the absent-minded professor, and the mere figurehead in a business firm, perhaps the president himself, who gives hundreds of meaningless orders and fidgets around while others do the brainwork and get things accomplished. Of course this does not allow for the variation that this same lunatic fussbudget may turn the trick to the mortification of the brain trust, but this is a wrinkle for Mr. Herbert and, although itself a stock situation, must be considered apart from the basic split in the personality pattern; anyway it is usually put to the service of a young fellow trying to get places with some crackpot business scheme. In fact if Mr. Herbert were such a young fellow, his split would be mended.

Let us consider the cultural meaning of the absent-minded professor's state—its meaning apart from the mere ludicrous accident that betrays his state. Of course he is dreaming. His head is in the clouds; he is thinking of some profound and academic problem removed in import from his immediate surroundings. Significantly the movies are by no means beneath converting even the absent-minded professor into a genius. But that is the happily irresponsible faculty of the movies, wherein anything can become a state of genius. It is the essence of the romantic comedy as opposed to the serious comedy of Pirandello; what in the latter is a fatal fault may become in Hollywood a fatal virtue. In Herbert's personality pattern an over-all motif is to be divined, linking the fuss-budget head of the firm to the absent-minded professor. This is a Utopian brand of psychology peculiar to America.

As I just implied, in the American movie the clown needs only a romantic plot to become a genius. A cardinal feature of the American business dream is the crackpot inventor as the matrix of success, the business genius as the author of a wild get-rich-quick scheme that will eventually work. Hugh Herbert is the apparently futilely vibrating incarnation of this mythic matrix. He may be the most ridiculous man in the world, the source of a million laughs, but according to this Utopian psychology he is innately capable of giving birth to the unique idea that will make him rich and powerful, that will bestow on him the privilege of fooling around on yachts and ranches and in night clubs as well as in the office. Indeed his present universally indulged situation may be but the result of some fabulous coup de grâce he put over as a young twirp.

All of this naturally is integral with the democratic system as we in America know it, under whose psychological aegis the fool (the poor man) may become wise (the rich man). In fact the democratic system sophisticatedly provides for the possibility that the fool is merely a clever man in disguise for his own purposes, this being perfectly consistent with the metamorphosis of the absent-minded professor into a man with practical ideas; in a recent movie made from a successful Broadway play a college professor suddenly turns into a police detective hero merely through

193

force of circumstances. As cultural group symbol Hugh Herbert and his many Hollywood colleagues in the Society of the Retarded Reflexives represent among other things the amusing aspect of the failure of the ideal of business success; they are the satiric commentary on, for instance, the typical and dominantly American notion of expert efficiency. Hugh Herbert and such a charmingly naïve little lady as Jean Arthur are, so to speak, expertly inefficient. We must not overlook the fact that their inexpertness manifestly accomplishes something—something more than the large salaries they earn as actors. Beneath our amusement and laughter at their awkwardness or absurdity is our sympathy, not only because, speaking collectively, we may identify our own defects with theirs but because we divine the sense of their behavior.

The broad social moral to be drawn from such artistic phenomena is that cultural *Lebensraum* for the mentally inefficient actually exists in our world. I have hinted at the reason: the American superstition, or call it what you will, that out of fooling around will come the effectual and unique spurt of genius. At bottom this is assuredly no unsound idea, and in their way the movies know this. The biographical tributes of the cinema to such men as Bell, Pasteur, Ehrlich, and Edison, who contributed discoveries and inventions to human progress, recognize the existence of those who have a definite and serious motive in fooling around. On the other hand, the implication of the comedic use of fooling around, with its psychopathic connotations, is that the cultural undercurrent of the schizophrenic motif inevitably affects the average personality with which we all somehow identify ourselves. Thus Jean Arthur and Hugh Herbert are in their screen personalities far more typical than Bell and Madame Curie, whose serious experiments in fooling around were very exceptional. In deciding, then, what is the social accomplishment represented by the expert *in*efficiency of the comic actors the artistic phenomenon must be related to the simple concepts of material economy and the correspondence of that economy in social psychology.

An economy of quantity exists in basic literary devices inversely related to schizophrenic phenomena. The pun and the double-entendre represent an economy of scarcity together with a psychology of plenty; one thing is made to stand for, that is, do the work of, two; thus in the mental process two ideas or images come together for the sake of producing an effect that is actually a third image, a dialectical result containing elements of both, since it is the synthesis of a thesis and an antithesis. It is a qualitative enrichment through the ingenious use of available quantities of material. The contrary economic extreme of the pun and the double-entendre, however, is the retarded mental reflex, since in this an image registers in more than the time it should normally take to register, which is a split second, so that it actually has to hit twice, take up *two* working units of the mental energy, before producing a *single* result. It is the exact inverse of the pun, which hits *once* and produces *two* results.

When Jean Arthur's resistance to Joel McCrea's physical

195

advances gradually breaks down to the accompaniment of a mild dialogue unrelated to the couple's immediate concern, it is the *inverse* of the double-entendre, since its duration is directly counterposed to the duration of the dialogue —mostly Miss Arthur's monologue; and hence a split occurs between the parts, which in the double-entendre accomplish a double purpose simultaneously. Instead of saying one thing and meaning two the inverse double-entendre *says one thing and does not mean it*, at least at the moment when it's said. Both the retarded mental reflex and Miss Arthur's device are inverse in the way that witlessness is the inverse of wit. What does this kind of witlessness accomplish?

In the case of Miss Arthur's progressive, though not entire surrender to Mr. McCrea's caresses it accomplishes a moral sanction for a desire that cannot be morally realized on the conscious, or single, level. Two moral levels exist in the young lady, one desiring not to be caressed, one desiring to be caressed; the upper level is that of propriety, which adjudges it indelicate to be made love to by a young man on the steps of one's apartment building in view of the passers-by. The accomplishment of what I may call the inverse double-entendre—mental activity covering up for physical activity—is the basic one of mental economy. But according to my verbal analysis this is an inexpert economy, one of *waste* rather than *saving;* the words accomplish nothing for themselves, they merely negate the meaning of the physical behavior of the speaker.

But if we consider the economy not from the verbal but

from the literally material aspect, then what? We find an economy of plenty, since the physical passion is in plenitude on both sides, excepting that one side (the girl) is faking and postponing. One point must be amended: Miss Arthur's monologue of irrelevancies negates Mr. McCrea's physical behavior and her partial acquiescence, but it provides, at first, the pantomimic pattern for her behavior, because every time his hands make a new foray on her person, her hands disengage them. It soon becomes apparent, nevertheless, that she has foreseen her ultimate acquiescence in the physical pattern; she will let him kiss her in the midst of some verbal irrelevancy and then take up her words again once their lips have parted. Her defense mechanism has been in operation, perhaps, just to take care of this kiss. Thus, insofar as she is covering up for an act in which two people participate (a kiss), her monologue momentarily exemplifies *a double-entendre in the realm of the material.*

What have we underlying Miss Arthur's inexpertness, her inversion of the clever economy of the double-entendre as a purely verbal form? We have a transference of the double-entendre from the qualitative state of psychological economy (verbal symbols) to the quantitative state of material economy (life). Miss Arthur and Mr. McCrea are primarily two people with but a single thought. Their psychology is profitably afflicted with a scarcity economy, since Miss Arthur as one partner is not intelligent enough to recognize that when two people can profit by a single thought (kissing), it is mere mental waste to impose a second thought, even though the double thought serves an ultimate single end. The profit is in the compensative device enabling physical organisms to achieve an ultimate material end (the kiss) at the immediate expense of spirit—indeed an expense of spirit in a waste of shame.

Perhaps it is somewhat more difficult to determine what Hugh Herbert's pun inverse accomplishes, what economic value the retarded mental reflex has. This phenomenon of psychology has more subtly widespread roots than the inverse double-entendre, although the latter is no doubt commoner. For one thing the pun inverse covers up for the absence of physical activity rather than its presence. For example, it is a symbol of the unkept appointment of business or pleasure—which is to say it is not always the pointed thing that draws a spontaneous laugh in movie houses. But to take Mr. Herbert's stock character, if the retarded mental reflex has a prominent place in an individual's psychology, it becomes an obvious means for excusing that individual from responsibility for mental commitments, as it is also a means for excusing the professor's absent-mindedness. It is per se an idiosyncrasy that renders its possessor helpless. Mr. Herbert is thus a burlesque of the business executive who deliberately drops appointments from his calendar on the basis that he has a plethora of appointments, a plethora that, if explanations are in order, must be sponsored by his secretary and perhaps in turn by a hectically busy existence in the office. Hence again we meet the material economy of plenty, here more than enough and thus automatically productive of a psychology of plenty based on an embarrassment of riches; the implication in the case of the business executive is that a redundance of business appointments indicates a corresponding redundance of business profits. So Mr. Herbert's axiomatic retardation of mental reflex is the redundance to absurdity of the big business executive's double embarrassment of profits and appointments.

A definite myth of American business emerges from our investigation of a movie comedian's personality—the Utopian dream of preoccupation with the pursuits of genius. All business men, even quite successful ones, idea men included, like to give the impression of being preoccupied whether they are or not. Indeed this impression, substantiable or not, is itself an automatic reflex of the business world, just business common sense. Not only does it excuse a man from contacts he doesn't relish and that waste his time, but it also gives the impression that he is perhaps involved with large and mysterious mental occupations, that he may be deep in the Promethean effort to attain a sure-fire way of becoming a millionaire merely by hatching a little idea. Hugh Herbert's fussbudget burlesque with its constant verbal and psychological fumbling is a perfect way of pointing the existence of this myth, covering up an empty mental shell with the illusory wings of an eagle, in the American business world. Between the moment in which an image should normally register on Mr. Herbert's brain and the moment in which it belatedly and ludicrously does register lies the matrix of the inspirations of genius according to Utopian psychology. That absent-mindedness is not absence of mind but preoccupation of mind is essential to this myth. So the legend of the absent-minded professor is patently necessary to Mr. Herbert's personality pattern as typical and symbolic.

This thought confronts us with a certain flat contradiction between the two subjects of our investigation. Unlike the inverse double-entendre of Miss Arthur, the inverse pun of the retarded mental reflexive covers up for any number of meaningless actions, actions not at all like the simple cause-effect mechanism of desire and activation in regard to love—actions whose moral justification is purely hypothetical. Mr. Herbert's actions, an empty mimicry of such a mechanism as Miss Arthur's and Mr. McCrea's, accomplish nothing in their own organic pattern but mean merely to cover up for a vacuity of real purpose. Yet this vacuity is one of ostensible purpose only if we consider its general background in society. As I have said, it is the comic version of fooling around with a purpose, letting the mind as well as the hands work freely. It is fooling around with an *ulterior* purpose, the telephone being the ulterior purpose of Bell's constant speculation and his toying with gadgets. Thus the material economy of scarcity implied in Mr. Herbert's funny business is supposed, in the imaginative mood its art invokes, to be merely apparent, not necessarily actual. In this respect then his pattern is identifiable with that of the supposed crackpot inventor such as Bell or S. F. B. Morse. Now we may observe that the inverse pun of the retarded mental reflex signifies a transference parallel to that accomplished by the inverse double-entendre, which covers up for two persons with but a single thought, such as Miss Arthur and Mr. McCrea in love. The retarded mental reflex covers up *for two thoughts with but a single person.*

. . . It covers up *transparently,* and this transparency of course is what is laughable. Such a harmless lunatic as Mr. Herbert's mythic character is merely, by virtue of the r.m.r., a pretender to the consideration that everyone realizes should theoretically be awarded to crackpot inventors. In the present hierarchy he is a wayside station on the road to the absent-minded professor with his concern with purely academic problems, who in turn is a wayside station on the road to the inventor genius, who may have a practical idea by which humanity will profit. What is the essential ludicrousness of Mr. Herbert's character? It is the comic effect of a person embarrassed by a redundance of thoughts, one thought explicit and one thought, the retarded one, implicit—a scheme itself reversible in a comically short time. The image addressed to Mr. Herbert's attention must wait —as the unexpected caller must wait in the reception room to see a businessman till he is free—until there is mental room for it.

The most pointed aspect of Mr. Herbert's mentally retarded personality is its pace; this is an element of the clowning required for caricature drawing. This pace, which is haste, makes the waste of time that the inverse pun takes to operate—the double talk of the psyche that brings automatic laughter in movie houses. It is a variation of the bromide that haste makes waste. Yet Mr. Herbert's haste is obviously the characteristic of an anxiety neurosis, not identified as such by the average member of the audience but nevertheless recognized by all as a burlesque of those whose ambitions at being clever or efficient exceed their talent or aptness.

At the same time the inevitable tendency of the spectator, toward comedy no less than tragedy, is identification and generalization of fiction with himself. It is axiomatic that we love those we laugh at because we feel superior toward them, we being more competent than they. But in the higher symbolic sense, on a transcendent plane, we generalize not only the comic actor's behavior with ours but his behavior with the serious ideas and myths that can be connected with it. In this way we become comedians along with him. We laugh at and love the myth that the retarded mental reflex, so common to ordinary mental preoccupation, is really an ambiguous symbol and may cover up not only useless and therefore foolish dreaming but may also represent an activity instinct with power—the Utopian dream of the mind thinking up money-making schemes, inventing a highly useful instrument, or discovering an important secret of nature. We laugh because, after all, we know it is an empty illusion that abstract thought, idea-planning, inevitably breeds action and power, profit and success. Suppose that Mr. Herbert's vacuity of substance essentially afflicts nearly all of us or more significantly that his comical neurosis symbolizes the insufficient time that many of us have in which to do what we wish. The r.m.r. may also stand for the retarded *moral* reflex. . . .

Mr. Herbert's mentally retarded clown is therefore the

exhaust valve for the popular tension created by expectation that one's dreaming will logically, faithfully translate itself into one's doing. There is also irony in the substratum of superstition that the word failing to register as it should on Mr. Herbert's brain is the knock of opportunity in disguise. This echo of another hallowed bromide helps explain our eagerness, once we are used to his device, in waiting for the reflex to occur—an eternity of suspense!

II

Having gone so far beneath the surface of these two artistic phenomena of the movies and related them to American mythology as well as to a couple of basic literary devices, we might as well go further and discover where they lead in a less specific and mythological sense; that is, what basic significance do the retarded mental reflex and the inverse double-entendre have with relation to normal rather than abnormal psychology, to psychology per se rather than Utopian psychology. What meaning do they have when they are not occasions for laughs, when they are not myth symbols?

The striking thing about both Miss Arthur's and Mr. Herbert's devices is that they are cover-ups, one for a substance of purpose, the other for a vacuity of purpose, unless we recognize conversely the myth of preoccupation of which Mr. Herbert is a burlesque. They both entail, however, wasted mental and physical action, and Miss Arthur's is demonstrably economic only because to begin with there is an economy of plenty in the material realm; she and Mr. McCrea physically love each other. In the case of the American business myth of mental preoccupation, extending into its extreme form of the fooling around of the genius, there is a positive redundance of plenty, so that when attention is demanded for something outside the subjective interest of the one preoccupied, the economy of plenty is automatically displaced, yielding at once to an economy of scarcity and tending to make the subject seem foolishly inattentive to what is going on around him. This criticism of mental inattention to immediate surroundings is based on the assumption that there is or should be an identity of interest between what is internal and external, or at least that the personal economy should be such that its flexibility is competent to take care of all normal contingencies coming from the outside in. Such a person is regarded as alert, poised, capable, and so on.

Now such a normal state of affairs in the individual can only be the result of the systematization of his life and is owing to his own knowledge and control of this systematization, his rhythmic sense of timing enabling him to anticipate all interruptions, casual business, even aggressive taxis in the street, so that he is never caught short, ruffled, embarrassed in any way, or run over. Schizophrenia or split personality conversely can be only the habitualized symptom of a contradiction or of an absence of rhythmic co-ordination between the external concerns and the internal concerns of an individual. If we were to symbolize it quantitatively or personally, it is not two persons inside an individual but one person inside and another outside. The one outside is always the one of whom a demand is made from outside; it is the one who calls forth recognition from the external world; the one inside is he who decides whether or how much he desires to respond to this recognition. This normal pattern can be easily applied to both Miss Arthur's young lady and Mr. Herbert's fussbudget; the latter is in a perpetual dither of indecision about a basic moral choice between the inside and the outside. But how normal can their patterns be made through analysis?

The sum of recognitions from outside is the total economic value of the human organism in the environment in which it lives. In the purely practical sense a man is only an outside; he is of value to himself and to others only as he is a manifest and animated surface—as he lives and speaks and moves. Inside him exists the guide and judge of a man's actions, the one who determines the precise shape of his social pattern—so far as he can determine it, according to the given materials and the degree of his freedom of choice —and who decides among the given possibilities what attentions he will respond to, what recognitions he will woo.

Now it comes about in the human organism that sometimes a definite growth of internal interest occurs that has no immediate or adequate use on the outside and hence is stored up inside without atrophying or losing its inherent impulse toward externalizing itself. The individual under such circumstances sets up a symbolic economy within, which is an economy of plenty because the subject matter corresponds to the form; the mind is systematically engaged within to the exclusion of any external economy. This is a description of mental preoccupation, whether the impulse toward externalization be pronounced or very weak. How does the schizophrenic element introduce itself into such an individual? Let us take the apparently crude and inadequate, if classic example of the little boy caught redhanded in the jam closet.

He is guilty of theft. But this conviction of guilt is based on an economic law by no means of the little boy's own making. After all, the jam is in the family, there is plenty of jam, and he is in a continual state of desire for it. His answer to his mother's stern accusation, itself a redundancy, may be: "I haven't taken any jam, Mamma!" The obvious explanation is that the negative denotes his wish to escape punishment. But the mechanism of his denial is certainly more complex than this. His automatic denial of a manifest reality has a deep moral basis and is of a schizophrenic kind. Why? Because the attention of his mother at this moment is highly unwelcome to his intense preoccupation with jam, which perhaps only at this time is externalizing itself, for it may be his first offense. His outer person suddenly becomes a projected symbol merely of an inner preoccupation: jam-eating. The instant his mother enters the jam closet, the jam-eater (*he who is preoccupied*) retires into the little boy and becomes transformed instantly into the one preoccupied with the *thought* of jam-eating, for in his precipitate desire to avoid punishment he swiftly returns to his state of mere guilty thought. So when he is required to speak, he answers with the truth. The "I" of his statement has not been eating jam; he has only been *thinking* about it. Especially now is his answer negative because this "I" is quite reconciled—the jam having been consumed—to the scarcity economy supposed to prevail in the jam closet. After all, the policewoman who enforces that economy is present.

The retarded mental reflex and the inverse double-entendre are both involved in the above analysis. His mother says: "You've been eating jam." His sudden wild desire not to recognize the jam image causes it to fail to register properly so that automatically he replies, "No, Mamma, I haven't!" What prevents the registry of the image is its concomitant element of the thief of the jam (himself). He obeys an internal economy of plenty, for the jam is in his stomach; but he denies it verbally, although Exhibit A is on his hands. If Mr. McCrea in his love scene with Miss Arthur had suddenly said: "Don't you see I'm making love to you? Be human!" Miss Arthur would, just as automatically as the little boy, have denied her guilt, her complicity as sufferer of these attentions, because the whole object of her verbalistics is to conceal the *fact* of his attentions. Hence she might have replied: "You are not!"—that is, *I'm* not, even if *you* are. She would have shunned participation in the theoretic social contract that the inside must always agree with the outside. Insofar as she submitted to his caresses outside, she denied it inside; insofar as she desired his caresses inside, she denied their actuality outside. "The girl sitting by you," she might as

207

well have said, "may be about to kiss you, sir, but not the girl sitting in me!"

Hence the verbal symbolization of schizophrenic motifs indicates a moral barrier in the individual against participation in an implicit agreement existing between the inside and the outside of his consciousness, the outside always being integral with an implicit social relationship. Remember that the submarined marines were both vertically submerged and inclosed . . . hence their schizophrenia. There occurs a direct or implicit verbal denial (the inverse double-entendre) or a postponed verbal assent (the retarded mental reflex). Verbal response is the objective recognition of an attention; verbal response *symbolic of schizophrenia* is the objective recognition of an *unwelcome* attention—unwelcome because it interferes with a subjective state or demands a moral assent the subject is not prepared to give.

How can we say that Mr. McCrea's attentions to Miss Arthur are unwelcome when we know quite well they are very welcome? The investigator himself tends to fall into the trap of the schizophrenic structure. But the problem is not difficult. Mr. McCrea's attentions are not unwelcome, but for some reason Miss Arthur wants it to appear that they are not entirely or superficially welcome . . . perhaps not welcome, as I have hinted above, in the peculiarly public situation in which they find themselves, sitting on the steps of her apartment building. Here let us abandon my former metaphor of the two vertical psychological levels in Miss Arthur and consider her horizontally as an inside and an outside. We must not forget that the movie in which this scene occurs was laid in Washington during wartime. The chief comedy situations revolve on the scarcity economy resultant from the housing situation in that city; the parlor of Miss Arthur's building has been converted into a dormitory for businessmen, and she herself for patriotic reasons has decided to share her small apartment with an elderly male visitor to Washington who has in turn taken in young Mr. McCrea.

The element of prudery in Miss Arthur's conservative character is emphasized by the deficiency of *Lebensraum* for love-making, not even an indoor public parlor being available. Yet there is a contrary tradition in business life, that of extending the home into the office rather than vice versa. Private secretary or stenographer may take dictation, according to the myth, while sitting on her employer's knee or submitting to his arm about her waist. The public place where Miss Arthur and her suitor sit is therefore, to her conventional mind, not so much a *parlor* as a *bedroom*, for she thinks in terms of the extremes that strained conditions in Washington suggest; every evening before reaching her couch for the night she has to walk past a roomful of sleeping men. Mr. McCrea has sprung his love-making on her—he is officially only her apartment sharer, and she doesn't know him well enough to let him make love to her in a misplaced bedroom. Hence, although in one sense there is an economy of plenty (erotic emotion on both sides), beyond the immediate social periphery (two persons) there is a scarcity economy of living space for the hundreds of thousands who inhabit Washington; therefore, together, Miss Arthur and Mr. McCrea, regardless of their complicated personal relations, form a private "inside" in relation to a large public "outside," and in this particular situation there is literally not enough space for all of them because of the over-all economy governing social relations. The inside that is the private residence, the site where the individual entertains his close friends, has been forced into the open on the steps outside. There is actually enough room for two people in this spot, as in the other situation there is enough jam for a little boy, but a certain economy in time and space supervenes in each case to limit the internal economy of plenty—boy alone in a jam closet, lovers alone in a room—and make the economy one of scarcity. Both lovers and little boy become thieves of the plenty to which subjectively they basically entitle themselves. So when Miss Arthur, in speaking about remote subjects while Mr. McCrea is caressing her, is doing so not only for her benefit and his but also for the benefit of passers-by; to them, as the little boy to his mother, she asserts, "Not guilty!" Alas! the lovers, a single personality symbolized by the kiss, are falsely split by the schizophrenia of society. As incorruptibly *one* as Shakespeare's phoenix and turtle, our lovers of the Washington steps do not have to be confronted with death to experience the need to flee "in a mutual flame from hence."

10. MAGIC-LANTERN
METAMORPHOSES IV

Mildred Pierce; or, Doubting the Evidence
of the Senses

There have been critics of my method of interpreting
movies who claimed that the movie I reconstructed on an
analytical basis bore little resemblance to the actual Hollywood product; the more literate if less acute have implied
that my criticism was but a superoptical rationalization of
visible reality. I don't mean to apologize by justifying
myself on the basis of "Granted, so what?" On the contrary, I want to carry my theory of meaning as essence
rather than as form to the point where the senses themselves
are in question, in just as much question as though we were
dealing with magic psychology rather than rational or
scientific psychology. I am prompted to do this by the appearance of a most extraordinary movie, *Mildred Pierce*,
which followed one in similar mood, *Double Indemnity*.
Moreover, at this point I am certain of this: as I went to
some length to explain in my previous book when analyzing Orson Welles's *Citizen Kane*, the psychological method
known as the reconstruction of the crime is esthetically akin
not only to my method of interpretation but to the artistic
composition of the film product itself. Therefore in a curious psychological-moral sense the Hollywood movie is a
variety of crime, and the evidence of the senses—that is,

the whole sum of the separate camera shots—does not portray the whole truth of the story. In regard to a film such as *Mildred Pierce*, a murder mystery, it fails to portray truth not only as essence but as fact, as *formal datum*; that is, fails—until the end—to identify the puller of the trigger on the murder weapon. I know of course that this very omission is the object of the entertainment, but that is not precisely the issue I mean.

As I said in respect to Welles's picture, the unique power of the movie camera, being an impersonal eye of nature, the "Universal Spectator," is to create an illusion of omniscience. But this illusion leads to a compromised situation when a murder mystery is in view. The individual spectator in a movie theater keeps subconsciously asking, "What is the matter with the Universal Spectator that he is not on hand when murders occur?" The only logic would seem that one is being deliberately, with implicit consent, tricked for the sake of entertainment, as in card tricks and games. Thus film mysteries have the basic psychology of platform magic, sleight-of-eye magic. For the spectator to see so much and yet to miss the link in the visual chain that explains everything! This is the tantalizing tension created pre-eminently on the screen, where vision is primarily optical and where sometimes it is not mainly through the detective hero that the mystery is solved, the murderer revealed. In *Citizen Kane* the professional detective's intelligence was subtly displaced with that of an amateur newspaper man, whose efforts signally fail; it is Mr. Welles's notably ingenious device to have had on hand a Sherlock

Holmes disguised as the Universal Spectator (the "man who sees all"; that is, God), carrying into the depths of human mystery a flashlight that is the camera eye. We remember that only the camera in *Citizen Kane*, climbing over the masses of expensive bric-a-brac left behind by Kane at his death, reveals to us the word "Rosebud" on the boy's sled being burned in the huge furnace; in this way the answer is given us to the reporter's search for the significance of the last word uttered by the dying Kane, while this answer is shielded from the human beings in the movie. It is a convention of prenaturalistic fiction, deriving from a belief in an omniscient God, for the author to make a direct commentary on an event—a commentary of which persons in the story are not necessarily aware, do not themselves make. As to *Citizen Kane*, only we and the narrator are aware—we, who thus take the place of God, Who is more knowing than mere humans. In substance the meaning of the solution of *Citizen Kane* is the psychological platitude that a man may be frustrated all his life because he cannot recapture a boyhood experience. The Sherlock Holmes for whom the camera is a substitute is really Freud, the God of the human darkness, who thus becomes the sign for the narrator. But movie-makers are almost never so literate as Mr. Welles, and as to *Double Indemnity* and *Mildred Pierce* we have to deal with a myth consciousness less aware, less specifically universal, than that of Mr. Welles. At the same time we must note that because the movie theater is a darkness, a kind of sleep in which we dream, the psychoanalytical view of movies would seem

213

to have been shared in some automatic fashion by many movie-makers, themselves influenced by the character of their medium and by knowledge of the theater ritual.

Mildred Pierce opens almost immediately with a series of revolver shots that crash into a full-length mirror; we then see a man at whom the shots have apparently been aimed collapse and fall prone, his form illuminated by the flickering of a hearth fire. He rolls over on his back, apparently dead, but manages to mutter one word, "Mildred," before expiring. I hope it disconcerts no one to say that this beginning is artistic and entirely integral with the design of the film and that, as for the sordidness against which several noble Manhattan reviewers cried out from the depths of their intransigent ethics, this middle-class baseness is far closer to life as it is lived than the Hollywood products the same critics have seen fit to condemn not so finally or not at all.

To start with, I want to draw the parallel between the shots fired into the mirror and the sequence of camera shots in which we see the outside of the house, the woman's figure (or was it two figures, separately?) leaving it, her ride in the auto, her walk on the bridge, her impulse to leap over —these optical shots are psychically almost as staccato as the revolver shots themselves and just as incomplete of meaning, so that we are as unfamiliar with their exact motivation as with the motivation of the murder and the identity of the murderer—even though we are tempted to suspect the murderer is the woman on the bridge, especially when we learn her name is Mildred.

But naturally, being familiar with the convention of mystery stories that appearances deceive and circumstantial evidence is not all, we are wary; indeed we feel that somehow we had better not assume that Mildred Pierce Berargon has just killed the man we duly learn is her second husband. On the other hand, as the story progresses, it is possible to perceive a rather familiar pattern, the revenge of an outraged, doting mother on the man—her second husband—who has ruined her efforts to make her daughter by her first husband happy. We are tempted to assume this logically almost from the beginning, when it appears that the head of the local homicide squad believes he has trapped the murderer, Mildred's first husband, Pierce, who has been picked up. We cannot be sure Mildred is innocent, however, because we have seen her on the scene of the crime at its occurrence. Moreover, we have seen her later try to pin the circumstantial evidence on a third man, someone instrumental in her financial ruin, by locking him in the murder house. Whom is she trying to protect, herself or her first husband, who deserted her? The story is unfolded from this point on by Mildred's narrative to the police inspector, as to which we are ignorant whether or not it will end as her confession of the murder.

For the most part *Mildred Pierce* as film narrative is a brilliant job. Yet this judgment does not consider the acting. What of Mildred? It would seem that much of the essential credibility of the story depends on the actress who takes this rôle. There is poetic justice in the fact that the Hollywood award for the best acting performance of the year went to

Joan Crawford for this part. For she possesses a quality peculiarly suited to this movie—or I should say to movies in general and this one in particular. Here we must pause to praise Hollywood's faculty for developing types suited for camera expression.

First of all Miss Crawford is one of those seasoned Hollywood girls who started out with the lucrative determination to please and do nothing but please. She has always been, and remains to the last glimpse, a fashion plate. At the appointed time the color of her hair changed from brunette to blond, and now it is back again. She was plump; she became svelte. She followed the trend of highly artificial eyebrows (à la Garbo) to natural brows (à la Garbo); she is at least as photogenic as anyone who ever faced a camera. Her face is nothing but obliging planes and angles, as stark as a talented abstractionist painting. Place her head skillfully somewhere in the film frame, and her head and coiffure, with or without hat, automatically make a composition. Despite the deficit in Miss Crawford's emotional wardrobe, her face is without neither sympathy nor interesting quality. It is ideal for the screen because her acting style is devoid of the calisthenic element that other actresses, Bette Davis, for example, have continually to guard against—the element that makes their features gyrate. The esthetic etiquette of the screen only gradually developed facial manners that exiled the grimace, invariably caught as it was by the lynx-eyed camera; for this reason we are apt to laugh at otherwise serious scenes in movies made ten or twenty years ago.

It is odd to compare Miss Crawford with her antithesis in screen history, Lillian Gish, whose face was like a pool perpetually rippled by her feelings, welling up ceaselessly, quixotically, from inside her troubled breast. But then Miss Gish's face was unusually delicate and girlish; Miss Crawford's face is not at all so. Miss Gish's face could portray refinement of feeling, however stereotyped. Miss Crawford's face cannot. The latter is one whose photogenic quality is much superior in repose. This is not to say that it expresses nothing, that it is a stupid blank; rather it is a semimobile mask designed for certain purposes. Chief of these is what I may term the dramatic poker face, the suppression of feeling to the point where it restricts itself to a certain static dilation of the iris, a tension of the lids, and an arrested movement of the corners of the mouth. This expression has its infantile prototype in the heroic refusal to weep, something that achieves control in maturity. Miss Crawford is a natural mistress of this type of expression and exploits it phenomenally in the present movie. The most effective moment of this kind is just after her critical quarrel with her daughter, Veda, when the girl slaps her mother's face. A close-up of Miss Crawford shows her prototypic poker face full to the brim with its suppressed emotion. There is something stark, animal-like, and haunted in this expression, and within its limits it is highly authentic, its suitability to the camera being peerless. The special suitability in this movie is that the expression seeks *to deceive,* to present the incommunicative mask of Mildred Pierce to the police inspector and yet another deceptive mask, if one

217

more communicative, of another Mildred to the Universal Spectator: Mildred Pierce is a woman who has really suffered and, like the ideal accused woman at a trial, wins sympathy whether guilty or innocent. At the same time she is keeping secret two different facets of herself. The one known to herself she is keeping from the police inspector; the one unknown to herself as a conscious fact she is—technically at least—keeping from us and from her own intelligence.

Observe the paradox: whereas the instrument of the Universal Spectator as an intelligence is the camera eye, we as agents or vessels of this intelligence are necessarily conspirators in the convention of the art work being unreeled before us, the convention of the trick work *that is the murder mystery*. So in Mildred's device we may grasp the basic talisman of the mystery work itself; for the irrational or symbolic mystery of *the human soul* the murder mystery substitutes the rational or mechanical mystery of *incompletely available facts*. Briefly the detective mystery deals with the science of facts rather than with the behavior of the soul. At the same time, just because the mystery story may deal with murder, the greatest of human crimes, we hover perpetually around a historic problem of the human soul, the basic question of guilt and innocence in human consciousness. Therefore the important thing in an artistic spectacle is not the substitution of one method of the search for knowledge for another—science for intuition—but the apocryphal confusion that results from this very substitution, which can never be wholly successful where any problem of real human interest is involved. This substitution comprises a specific problem of interest; that is, the resistance of human beings, the audience, to what science in general and the police detective in particular calls "the facts." The woman, Mildred Pierce, wants to conceal the facts while revealing her tragedy as a woman. But even so she herself is ignorant of the true motivation of her tragedy, its concealed mechanism, its inner facts.

We are familiar with detective mysteries in which, during the unraveling of the murder, a number of family skeletons are incidentally exposed to view apart from the corpse destined to be another skeleton. Consequently a crime in which an entire family and its friends are involved is but a climactic point in the history of that family—or it might better be said an anticlimactic point, the point of the general breakdown of a system of deception that nature will no longer tolerate. The true climax is the revelation of the family skeletons. In a few revolver shots the family genius for social integrity may at last belatedly express itself. It is so in *Mildred Pierce,* which is the reason it is better than ninety-nine out of a hundred Hollywood movies.

Indeed does not the very term "family skeleton" imply death—even, we might reason, a variety of murder crime? For the instincts themselves may be imprisoned, disfigured, and murdered because of a wide range of pressures resulting in moral substitutions and repressions of a radical kind over many decades. But the skeletonic pattern, because of natural law, never disappears. It is always in the closet. One of the most diverting aspects of *Mildred Pierce* is that it takes place in a variety of buildings, each of which represents some motif of desire in the characters—a middle-class suburban cottage, a luxurious beach house, a series of restaurants, a roadside night club, a great family mansion, and finally the police station itself. Each has dangling in its closet the phantom of its peculiar skeleton of aborted desire.

Mildred Pierce's daughter, Veda, hates the family's suburban cottage because she is glamour-minded, and her mother bakes pies for the neighbors and selects childish dresses for her. Eventually nothing but the Berargon family mansion will suit her, and to gain this ideal for Veda and to effect their reunion Mildred marries the gigolo remnant of the Berargon glory who has been courting her and taking money from her. But this fellow is no good—is himself a healthy variety of family skeleton, nurtured on the beaches of California—and he becomes involved with Veda, who falls in love with him. This precipitates Veda's dream world of glamourous love to its debacle, for in a crisis, after Mildred has surprised her new husband and her daughter making love, the man spurns Veda and mocks her hopes of getting him to marry her after divorcing Mildred. At the end of Mildred's narrative the family net ritually cast by the police yields Veda, caught while about to escape by plane, and through a ruse the girl is induced to betray her guilt; it is *she* who pulled the trigger of the revolver that killed Berargon, and Mildred has merely decided to shield her. Finis—with the conventional fadeout of Mildred leaving the grandiose hall of justice, by the side of her first husband, to seek a new life.

This tag ending is so much a convention that nobody pays any attention to it excepting those who feel duty-bound to give it another lash of the whip. Yet it too is integral with the previous proceedings. What indeed is the meaning of the tour de force of the happy ending? It is psychologically symmetrical in the way that waking from a dream, however tragic and fatal in itself, is a happy ending; for we wake up, even if screaming, into the reassuring world of rational, daylight consciousness. In the tragedy *Oedipus* —that phenomenal rattling of perhaps the first skeleton in the human closet—it is intimated that many men dream of copulating with their mothers, but that it is only a dream. As we know, it was more than a dream to Oedipus, and therefore his story could not merit a happy ending. So the unhappy ending for a dream is merely its realization in life. The unhappy ending that Freud visualized was the creation of a complex of which the dreamer was the victim; that is to say, the Greek tragedy was a logical and cathartic dream, whereas the actual dream of unfulfilled Oedipuses is but a symptom of maladjustment to life in that they have not succeeded in getting their original sexual impulse toward their mothers out of their systems and have not sublimated it. The ending of a dream of incest is always happy to the extent that the dreamer awakens to a rational, conscious state of innocence; it is the tag ending of his conscious logic, saying implicitly, "I can re-enter the physical world of reality guiltless."

So what do Joan Crawford as Mildred Pierce and her leading man as her first husband, Pierce, become as they drift away from us into the majestic dawn with a new hope in life? They become symbols of the Universal Spectator who is likewise the average movie patron, someone whose viewpoint has participated in the making of the movie; because no matter how many skeletons have been rattled in the audience's own closets, no identification has really taken place between the spectator's skeletons and those of Mildred and her husband. Consequently the movie has been a kind of dream, with the same dissociation by the spectator of the rational, conscious responsibility from the human motives in the movie that the dreamer has from the actions of his dream. Note that the actions of dreams are but the repressed motives of life. Dreams, we are to assume, take place out of this world, just as, so to speak, movies take place in Hollywood. And Hollywood is happy in the way that awakening from a disturbing dream is optimistic; there is always an anticipation of redemption— not that sort of redemption that would take place on the plane of material or conscious guilt but that sort marking the pseudoredemption of the dark of dream by the light of reason.

Such a picture as *Mildred Pierce* is unreal, therefore a kind of dream to the spectator, because, although he himself may have felt impulses of a murderous or otherwise criminal kind and although his life perchance bears striking resemblance to Mildred's, he has never actually committed any crimes; nothing like that has ever happened in

222

his family. So we may perceive the essential difference between Hollywood dream art and genuine art; in the former the spectator is convinced of the reality of an unhappy story only by turning it into unreality through a happy ending, a new beginning on the same plane as the original beginning—what is represented in popular psychology as another chance. But in genuine art the spectator is convinced of the reality only by complete symbolic identification with it, by a symbolic assumption of the sinner's guilt and a symbolic redemption from this guilt by catharsis, the self-admission of psychological guilt.

A common pattern of guilt in detective mysteries is to involve the family unit and especially to expiate the family guilt by having one member actually commit the crime and thus, being found guilty of it, to cleanse the family of guilt in the eyes of the world and in their own eyes. *Mildred Pierce* exactly follows this pattern. The girl, Veda, supplies the skeleton in the closet who is also the scapegoat. Yet, understanding this, the most important question as to the substance of *Mildred Pierce* remains. What is the movie really about in the sense of the specific human problems involved?

I have analyzed the integral contingency of the special problem of human intelligence in this movie, the presence of concealed human motives as opposed to the available facts or science, and I have shown how the dream, Hollywood cinema technique, and the detective story are all in one esthetic order—they strategically conceal the facts. But latent in the meaning of the movie, *Mildred Pierce*, lie the fundamental motives of human character that make the persons of the story authentic beings, just as latent in the dream is the basic scheme of meaning that illuminates its incoherent logic. The technique of revealing how the crime was committed, and why, is a special movie problem parallel to the same problem in detective fiction—that of ingenious presentation, an art of legerdemain perfectly suited to the pure optics of cinema. When the movie is over, we have all the facts; we have a scientific report of all the relevant events, with all the visible motives neatly catalogued both in the optical eye and in the eye of the mind. But as I implied at the beginning, the circus art of the movies and the circus art of the detective story are in direct alignment in that in each case we must suspect the visible evidence in a double sense. Not only must we penetrate past the circumstantial evidence of the senses in respect to the appearances of the murder act and the murderer's identity, but we must suspect even that supplementary portion that is supposed to complete the evidence of the senses and to satisfy as to the meaning of the story's action. For the meaning is *not* really complete or satisfying.

We are inevitably forced to ask: *What is meaning?* In the form of the detective story meaning is purely rational and mechanical; the wheels of justice grind until the person of the criminal is turned up from the maze of the world. However, as we well know, the identity of the criminal and the establishment of his motive constitute the most superficial conception of the meaning of a crime. Take either Oedipus or Raskolnikoff. We, in the rôle of the Universal Spectator, know their identity from the beginning —in the former's case because the story is legendary. The point of each of their stories is the quality of their guilt, its claim to forgiveness, and even the question of a fundamental innocence. That is to say, no story of crime is meaningful unless it brings into question the very nature of guilt itself. What is the responsibility of the criminal? This problem of course is far from the intentions of Hollywood in *Mildred Pierce*. But the movie's plot is complex enough and its human relations have enough verisimilitude to state a reality of human guilt and, by *sabotaging* it through the form of an ingenious mystery story, to raise the question of crime responsibility by supplying a bogus answer. The bogus answer is the happy or dream ending of *Mildred Pierce*.

Who is the dreamer in this movie? From whose point of view do the events unfold themselves? From Mildred's. She is the dreamer, the one with the guilt complex. To the world she presents only the poker face of her emotions. Yes, she is a Hollywood girl whose face won't talk when it comes to confessing Hollywood's shortcomings in art! But she cannot fool us, because the evidence of the senses can be disbelieved to the extent of interpreting them. We can say to her: "Come out from behind that dream make-up, Joan. We know that *you* know that it was *you*, not Veda, who fundamentally if not actually pulled the trigger of the death weapon."

What is the meaning of Mildred's relations with her daughter? At her most impressionable stage of life Veda sees her father leave her mother for another woman and her mother content to bake pies and slave as a waitress in order to keep her and her sister in good clothes and give them dance and music lessons. Now the instinctive contempt that a sensitive girl would have for a mother willing to live without sexual love and to lower herself socially for the sake of her children—this automatic contempt in Veda's lively and egotistic nature should have been recognized by Mildred early in the game and proper measures taken to set Veda straight on the issues. But Mildred is not a bright woman except in one sense, the business sense. Her rather excessive passion for her daughter cannot be explained save by the Electra complex; that is, Mildred imagines herself as Veda, in love with her own father, Mildred's husband, as *Mildred* was in love with *her* father. The passionate desire to give Veda everything, to see her grow up happy and successful in every way, is an ordinary case of displacement; paradoxically Mildred wants to give her every charm and chance to accomplish that which *she* was prevented from accomplishing, union with her father. But the desertion of Mildred by Pierce, Veda's father, lends extra neurotic energy to Mildred's aim, and it is not till late that she realizes she must supply Veda with another "father" to complete her own (Mildred's) incest pattern. This she does by marrying Berargon; sure enough, this brings Veda and Berargon together, and Mildred duly surprises them in an incestuous embrace. But in the shock of the moment Mildred wakes up, so to speak, from her complex and objectifies her own guilt as a daughter, identifies

Veda as her own past, and changes at this moment into the outraged mother that her own mother would have been had she caught her (Mildred) in the arms of her own father. At least this is the theory, which events of the movie somewhat modify. Logically it is Mildred therefore as a betrayed mother and wife who would have killed her husband, Berargon, and not Veda, who actually commits the murder according to the movie. If Mildred seeks to protect Veda, it is because Veda is a form of herself and for some reason has taken on her incest crime. Since it is implausible to believe that Veda would really have had the nerve to commit such a crime, the whole movie may be accepted as Mildred's dream of guilt, from which she exonerates herself, in conspiracy with Hollywood, by walking out of the hall of justice a free woman; that is, under the conditions previously defined, *by waking up into an optimistic, daylight reality*. In this way every dreamer exonerates himself of dream guilt. A Hollywood guilt dream, of course, is paradoxically done à la Ziegfeld.

Even if we do not accept the dream convention per se and on the contrary visualize Veda as actually committing the crime, a logic still obtains in the linkage of the conventional happy-ending fadeout with the psychology of the Universal Spectator, the audience whose mental eye the eye of the camera is faithfully imitating by tacking on this bromide of movie esthetics. A family's reputation suffers publicly when one of its members commits a crime, but such a criminal becomes the prototypic scapegoat of sin. Inwardly the family is cleansed; their cumulative evils have burst out, and the wound will heal. Moreover, such a crime and its conviction are a sort of public penance, a saving grace in the eyes of the world. This is social logic. The esthetic error of Hollywood therefore is that the camera's eye is on Mildred at the fadeout rather than on Veda. Any genuine conception of tragedy must focus itself on the scapegoat, the criminal whose guilt with respect to personal responsibility is ambiguous. In the end, we may recall, Oedipus rebelled against the judgment of Theban law while wandering in exile and at his death received a special apotheosis into the arms of the gods. How guilty is someone who, in a moment of passion, pulls the trigger of a handy revolver? A subtly hidden weakness of *Mildred Pierce* is that a clever defense in court would even let Veda go free. The movie ends before we can know if this happens. Tragic irony derives only from the punishment of the guilty one, who wears a strange, invisible crown of innocence. Neither Mildred nor Veda is guilty enough to strike from the depths of human emotion any powerful reaction. This is merely because of Hollywood's lack of realism. Indeed in this case I should say that the lack of artistry lies much less in the form than in the substance. Both Mildred and Veda are too shallow as human beings to be conscious of their guilt rôles, and only consciousness of the ambiguous logic of guilt can give a character the majestic stature of true crime.

Symbolic of their shallowness—and here Hollywood must be praised for its substance—is the concentration of Mildred and Veda on the manner in which they are housed.

Everything seems to devolve on the luxury of living quarters, of which the luxurious restaurant chain that Mildred creates is a direct symbol. When one's interest is in walls and what lies within them, then the skeleton in the closet is the leading character. So finally we are constrained to accept the hypothesis that although the most interesting and psychologically valid aspect of *Mildred Pierce* is its psychoanalytical form, the logic of the Electra complex, the true nature of the debacle is the collapse of Mildred's business success, the stealing away of her interest in the restaurant chain she has built. Since her husband himself has conspired in this dirty trick, Mildred has a double reason for killing him. Realistically therefore it is much more logical for her to have fired the murder weapon. Even so, as things were, it is appropriately enough the kitchen closet in which the skeleton of Veda's crime is left to rattle, for Mildred will probably start over again baking pies and, being given the classic other chance of the happy ending, build another restaurant chain. Thus the chain of Hollywood esthetics also remains unbroken. In another decade or so we shall probably see the same awkward commercial tragedy re-enacted in the movie mode of the time. And meanwhile the Hollywood dream of exoneration from all varieties of guilt goes on unchecked by anything—except perhaps by studio strikes.

11. MIRAGE OF THE SUNKEN BATHTUB

Not long ago, at a New York repertory theater specializing in Russian films and those of a proletarian nature, there appeared a most illuminating double bill consisting of Hollywood's most generous contribution to the propaganda cause of the underprivileged classes. The more important item was the version of John Steinbeck's novel about Okies, *The Grapes of Wrath*, and the lesser was a straightforward propaganda offering, which took for its title a casual phrase from one of President Roosevelt's speeches—*One Third of a Nation*, denoting the percentage of the inadequately housed in the United States.

The Grapes of Wrath was directed by Hollywood's best director, John Ford, and thus was supplied not only with the latest style gadgets for speaking cinematically—the year was 1940—but with those effective emphases in dramatic and pictorial speech for which Mr. Ford's work is noted. The feeling for the flattish, desolated landscape from which the Joad family is unwillingly uprooted by circumstance is beautifully rendered by the camera, especially when the truck, overloaded with all the family possesses, including too many of themselves, starts out on its cross-country trek and in each successive shot seems to lose some of its visual detail, so that when it hits the main highway, it is no more than, like some dark ship at sea, an untethered entity of abstract design, moving small under the huge sky. In these shots the lens is not too fine. There is a sort of newsreel coarseness about the blacks and whites and their contiguous edges that makes one feel the frayed margins of everything—the boards of the ramshackle house that the Joads leave, exactly like that in the less serious *Tobacco Road*, the weeds, the clothes and belongings of the Joad family, and their very lives. These first scenes, just after Tommy Joad is released from prison on parole, are almost flawless in their feeling for the quality of the Joads and the spot of nature where they have existed.

As the truck of fortune approaches the land of milk and honey where the Okies expect to find work and happiness, California, the gradual transformation of the quality of the natural scene, the figures of the Joads, and the pattern of the story create an odd logic. That history provides a striking parallel to the Joad migration was doubtless present in Mr. Steinbeck's mind when he devised his original highly wordy fable. Despite its evident merits the novel is no better than second-rate literature, but the poetic and ironic analogy of the Okies' saga with that of the families who settled pioneer America and also of those who abandoned their homes and traveled to California during the Gold Rush is quite valid and, protracted as it is, imparts to the film a simple, eloquent arabesque, unhappily weakened at its climax.

Some families fattened in the ambiguously golden land of California; many did not. As the capitalistic structure gained in significance and strength, those who had struck gold and knew how to capitalize on it became the sons of heaven; the many and the less clever remained definitely sons of earth. The Okies of course are the sons of the earth inherited from those who may have deliberately abandoned their share of it generations before in the flight for the pot at the end of the rainbow. Yet in our time the poor whites, unable to make enough grow from the land in order to exist themselves and frowned on even by nature, have been lured to California by what might better be termed the will-o'-the-wisp of the promise of jobs and there have become itinerant workers, whose only subsequent blessing was the war industry. At the time of which the novel speaks, fruit-growers and other industrialists in California distributed thousands of leaflets offering work when only hundreds of jobs were available. The trick of the ranchers was to lessen the wages for fruit picking through the plethora of labor. The Joads learn this ruse only when it is too late for them to turn back. Hence they eventually run into a strike at a big peach farm and innocently are led to the slaughter as strikebreakers.

The Grapes of Wrath, like novels of Zola with a similar intention, falls automatically into the naturalistic pattern, and Mr. Ford's direction has borne this admirably in mind. As *The Informer* originally proved, he is the best casting director in Hollywood, and in casting the Joads he was phenomenally successful. Although a bit too pretty of feature, Henry Fonda's big-boned face and tall, spare limbs make him an excellent Tommy, and Jane Darwell's massive face with its finely expressive eyes is striking enough in its

232

homeliness to make Ma Joad an apt and memorable image, comparable to what we think of at the words "Mother Earth." In particular Grandpa Joad, who stages a sit-down strike at the last moment before leaving home, is marvelously acted, and the subsequent scenes of his death and that of Grandma Joad, at different stages of the journey, are very well handled. The elderly Joads prove too frail to withstand the violence of the uprooting. Along with their deaths goes some of the film's naturalistic feeling. Not that incident and episode in this part of the story are not well realized. The incident of the two spick-and-span gas-station attendants who wonder that human beings can live, as the Okies do, like animals . . . the awkward and self-conscious charity of the roadside diner's proprietor, his waitress, and the lunching truck drivers toward the foodless plight of the Joads—so typical of hard-boiled American sentiment and here not in the least exaggerated . . . the scenes in the unbearably sordid workers' camps . . . all this is depicted with unusual artistry, but these isolated scenes seem smartly efficient somehow, a part of the gathering narrative art of the cinema, which gains ground with the truck as it speeds toward California, the land of Goldwyn and colleagues. We may note here that this state is the site of the biggest industry in American art, the very material of the present book; thus a symbolic appropriateness attaches to the fact that as streets, roads, and countryside become neater and cleaner as the wheels of the Joad truck turn, the movie craft shows its stuff and reveals a surface increasingly city-planned. After all, fruit and

233

movies have made California what it is today. I am not precisely complaining about the course of Mr. Steinbeck's
story; rather I am showing that it can boast of more than
a simple truthfulness.

As the fortunes of the Joads, once in California, con-
tinue black despite the sun-drenched scenery, and as
Tommy, backed by his friend, the "red" ex-preacher, gets
mixed up in a ruckus with the private guards on the peach
farm and kills one of them, the miseries of this family and
of the other workers are almost too bitter for the spectator
to bear. One feels like leaving the theater, obliterating such
rock-bottom suffering from the sight. Of course one stays,
for, as expected, the pressure is eventually relieved, and
suddenly one is shown the Joad truck lumbering underneath a decorative wooden arch whose sign reads, in smaller
letters below the camp name, "Department of Agriculture."
Like magic a pleasant white-trousered man appears before
the truck and informs the Joads that premises within are
available to them at a dollar a week; his description of sanitation facilities makes the new ground the family has struck
seem like a golden fairyland indeed and hence hard to believe. One's impulse is to think, "Only a camouflaged trap
—another blow!" But it is all bona fide, true, for the simple
reason that the government, with one of the various national
agencies that were created during the depression period,
has manifested itself to salvage the apparently hopeless
cause of the Joads. The little man in white pants is a deus
ex machina, and at this point we are faced squarely with
the true definition of the Joad burden. It is an affliction of

the spirit proceeding from a specifically material foundation; that is, its remedy logically lies entirely in the material realm. True, the government does not provide work for the Joads, whose name is all that makes them individuals, for they number, of course, hundreds of thousands and actually, if we accept the phrase quoted above, compose one-third of the nation. Yet the fact is that the Okie class is on the lowest of the economic levels, and their spiritual unhappiness originates from lacking a great part of the time even the minimum for proper subsistence. It happens therefore that the chief focus in both pictures, *The Grapes of Wrath* and *One Third of a Nation,* is on the housing problem, the former applying to the country and the latter to the city, where old-law tenements make firetraps. The latter film is amateurishly done and somewhat naïve, but the artistic factor in no way alters the common economic physiognomy underlying both fables.

In *One Third of a Nation* the landlord class, whose economic interests are responsible for the maintenance of outmoded and dilapidated buildings, is proved to have its humane and class-conscious members by the example of the hero, who, coincidentally enough, falls in love with a young dweller in one of his unsound tenements. The plot in which he moves is as much a claptrap as his building a firetrap. There is no comparison in regard to seriousness of conception between Mr. Steinbeck's book and the bromidic fable of the other piece, but the correspondence of their patterns is not to be overlooked.

Doubtless the solution of an important part of human

235

unhappiness on earth is the proper housing and feeding of its fulsome populations. But in the portrayals of art we not only view the human spirit in the sort of travail occasioned by inadequate solution of this vital problem but are privileged to discern the nature of what brings about the lessening of the anxiety as to mere animal existence and to note, moreover, the opinion of artistic creations as to the mechanism of this lessening, which permits human beings rest and peaceful blossoming of spirit as well as of body. At a moment when we were still engulfed in hideous war, the strategies of peacetime toward this special solution could not seem of paramount eloquence. But since it is a permanent problem, which the appearance of war only complicates and which at this postwar moment looms in international proportions, its structure may be regarded as highly fundamental.

If we turn for a moment to an illustration in movie art of a somewhat different kind of poverty and its attendant joylessness I think that a certain sharp illumination will delineate the features of the Joad misfortunes. In the French filmic version of Gorki's *The Lower Depths* poverty coexists with a direct equivalent of *spiritual hopelessness*; in other words the old, outused, and criminal outcast take refuge in obscure dormitories at the mercy of a hard landlord, whose figure to them is that of implacable fate. Eventually in the French film the landlord is mobbed to death by his tenants, enraged by his personal abuse of a girl rather than by any conception of his economic crime. The characters here, who range from actors and philosophers

236

to thieves, are all possessed with a feeling of fatal resignation to their lot, a kind of stupor from which only the younger and more active emerge to make a gesture toward reinstatement in normally comfortable and respectable society. Despair is the spiritual keynote of these unfortunates —despair and the outlet of lunacy. But in the American film the Okies as represented by the Joads are an optimistic, energetic lot—they are honest workers, whereas Gorki's characters are ex-workers, past professionals, and petty criminals; in fact in having among them poet, philosopher, and actor they are a group testifying to the frustrated ideals of humankind, not only to the frustrated ideal of jobs for all but to every aborted ideal of culture, art, and humane society. They are the dregs of a society that has ultimately failed on all levels, whereas the Joads in essence are merely *economic* dregs, although we cannot overlook that, realistically as they are portrayed, they can hardly, considering the level of culture in the American rural working class as a whole, be considered average, for they are in spiritual tone slightly above the average. Still their economic identity is the determining factor, and they visualize work as a means of obtaining their highest objective in life, a certain standard of animal comfort; that is, all the gadgets of the modern home, chiefly the sanitary ones. Their humanity, one might even say their human culture, is made directly equivalent to this economic aspiration, whereas, if the Joads of the world should grow so prosperous that each family owned that celestial object, a radio, the question of what in all their materialistic bliss they listened to would be, to put it succinctly, a peach of an entirely different color.

When Ma Joad reaches the Department of Agriculture's camp and its sanitary delights, her pleasure is given a status corresponding to the emotion of an embrace or, in the higher brackets of human culture, that of poetic love; and one receives consequently a sense of her spiritual elevation. But as an ideal, viewed from a broader perspective than that of this film, a decent home with all its modern appointments and conveniences cannot evoke any emotional trace, however contingent, of sublimity. If we wish to appreciate this sublimity, we have to descend to the cultural level of the Joads, whose human animal dignity at this moment is presumed to have the muted roseate colors of something like a religious experience . . . as though conceivably Ma Joad had discovered in the spiritual atmosphere of the camp a vision of one of those sunken bathtubs seen in the movies. In the case of *The Lower Depths* there is no question of the perspective, no necessity to reorientate one's culture. Here the human spirit is being tried in an isolation area that has the unalterable stigma of fate; most tenants of the dormitory have reached the end of the line and have faced a kind of self-evaluation that could never occur to a genuine Joad, who measures himself by his animal well-being—a well-being relative only, here today and gone tomorrow, but always nevertheless just beyond the horizon.

It is difficult not to detect in the pathetic fate metaphysic of the Joad family a viable element of the same cheap optimism, the same tawdry conception of happiness and fate,

that dominates fifth-rate art in all its multiplicity as well
as the majority of Hollywood products. True enough, if we
look at the real Joads, which means looking at all the
underprivileged, we applaud their courage and what in
great part is their basic human decency. *The Lower Depths*
has its rural equivalent in the spiritual malaise of the Jeeter
Lesters and their families, who are ground into the dirt and
never rise. But we must note that *Tobacco Road* is comedy,
not tragicomedy; the latently lively animalism of the Lester
family is an antic that provided endless fascination for
audiences economically more fortunate than they. This play
and movie formed that grotesque thing, an economic circus
in which poverty was clown. But at least *Tobacco Road* had
more mood than does *The Grapes of Wrath*, which rather
naturally is less spiritually a tragedy on the screen than
in the novel.

I am only vaguely familiar with Mr. Steinbeck's original
treatment, but, as I said, plot and truck in the movie take
their synchronous progress toward the end of the story
while things in general become neater, more efficient, and
artier. For one thing, whereas the effective scenes in the
first workers' camp and then on the peach farm are supposedly in the open and, with one or two exceptions, photographed in actual daylight, the scenes in the sanitary
government camp, while some are in the open and in daylight, have a studio sort of air. As a matter of fact, this is
inevitable for the good reason that the camp itself has
precisely that sort of air, being a relatively makeshift ar-
rangement, containing homes neither permanent nor quite

real, since each family throws up its tent on a flat wooden foundation for an indefinite time. New jobs may soon take the tenants elsewhere, not adjacent to such a camp; and indeed this is the way the picture ends, after Tommy has abandoned his family to join the organized effort of workers to improve their living conditions.

The plot, too, in the last quarter of the picture, takes on an increasingly conventional air, its final important scene being the highly arranged interview between Tommy and his mother. One night Tommy in his tent is awakened to see two police officers taking down the license number of his truck, signifying that the authorities are hot on his trail as a man-killer. He cannot be arrested on suspicion because it is the legal regulation of the camp that no arrests can take place without a warrant. A flaw in the plot's strength is that Tommy's flight is more or less compelled and not, as he rationalizes the fact to his mother during their interview, the direct result of his desire to join the fight for better labor conditions. He is abandoning her in her struggle to keep her family together because, he says, he believes it vitally important that help be given those who are called "reds" whenever they attempt to organize workers. This is a conversion of the familiar situation in which the young stalwart leaves the farm in order to make his fortune, sometimes for a selfish reason, sometimes to save the farmstead. From the broad, historic arc of the pioneer trek the movie is now, willy-nilly, reduced to the more particular conventions of a more recent art. Truly this is a relatively significant and realistic version of a familiar situation, but the mellow sentiment, the display of emotion between mother and son, centered squarely as it is in the dramatic and camera focus, has a quality of banality despite the modernity and realism of the fable. Moreover, the commission of crime as an unforeseen contingency of fighting for a just cause, which commission has befallen Tommy, has a patina that testifies to a rather too honorable old age as well as too old an honorableness. A weakness in logic rather than in artistic invention is that, although Tommy's rough and rapid proletarian education brings him to the conclusion that he must regard a police badge as the sign of an enemy, the government-sponsored camp is deemed sacred ground on which no one with a badge may enter without permission or a full-blown warrant. But, according to the actual experience of the working class, there are no such charmed areas—as it has perpetual cause to remember. The makers of the film, and possibly Mr. Steinbeck, chose to forget, in giving an incidental impression, that a warrant is simply something that exists at the will of a judge of law, and a judge is arbitrary interpreter of the legal letter. This myth character of the camp corresponds to the historic legend of California as a land of golden opportunity as well as to the democratic myth of free expression in art, of which Hollywood takes peculiar advantage in this film.

Cops truly enough are made out an ornery and vicious lot in *The Grapes of Wrath*, but the point is that the worst of these officers of the law are deputies engaged by private interests, in other words only a little removed from being in substance uniformed gangsters or domestic storm troopers. Not only this fact conveys that these cops are not quite American. We are also given occasion to remember that whereas America may be a land of democracy, one must be realistic enough to understand that all individuals in it are not equally democratic. Hence grounds of political reasoning appear, and on these we recall the late President's attack on the economic royalists, those among the big capitalists who opposed his economic reforms. Suddenly the economic pattern of the film can be orientated to the propaganda viewpoint of liberal, reformist democracy as conceived by the historic New Deal government of the United States. Whence did the taxes come that enabled the government to build such camps for workers as the Joads found in California? Largely, and whether they liked it or not, from those very fruitgrowers who most viciously tried to break the strikes of fruit pickers.

The camp to which finally the Joads come as the first realization of their ideal goal is therefore merely a modest and tentative version of a housing project and a literal extension of the ideology of home relief. Quite unlike their comrades in morality, those of *Tobacco Road* as well as of *The Lower Depths*, the Joads have cleanliness for an ideal, with all that ideal implies with respect to material means. Earth is naturally dirty, and without considerable means nothing in our modern and especially our urban civilization can be properly clean. A similar discontentment afflicts the heroine of the other film, *One Third of a Nation*, which grapples forthrightly though clumsily with the housing situation in big cities. This young woman complains not only of the messiness of her domestic surroundings but especially of the fact that she has to undress before her father. . . .

Taking the longer view of the Joads' worldly ambition to be comfortably clean and well fed and housed, we must go beyond the formal conclusion of the film, with its note of grim hope for the struggle of the working classes, and speculate that perhaps a whole vulgar morality dangles at the end of the Joads' ideal, beyond their own limited sight but prevalent in modern society—I mean the primitive conception of moral cleanliness that originated in the scene of this country in the puritan moral code. For there is no trace of tragic catharsis in the experience of the Joads, nothing of transcendent beauty or power, unless it be that fugitive mirage of the sunken bathtub; they intuit nothing fatal in their misfortunes, which are just bad luck. Only Tommy, fortuitously tutored by the radical-minded ex-preacher, sees the ominous silhouette of the system over-hanging them and finally seeks on principle to oppose it. In this movie an ambiguous morality, requiring stern justifi-cation of itself, is again identified with crime. *Ideological* compulsion here supplants *psychological* compulsion. But the film, like the novel, leaves off where more imaginative and serious fiction sagas of militant action in behalf of labor begin.

Perhaps it may seem gratuitous or exaggerated to say that the Joads can do no better, at best, than develop the vulgar, materialistic complacency of the middle class. But, as Ma Joad pathetically replies to Tommy's metaphors about how the many can exist in the one and the one in the many, she doesn't understand, because for all her solid virtues Ma can understand nothing but the most modest fundamentals of instinctive human decency. Well, perhaps the Joads *should* be taken more symbolically than their naturalistic mold seems to warrant; after all, they are proletarian symbols, not just people. But perhaps our two perspectives on them can be reconciled if we return to the point that as time and truck advance in the movie, cinema technique becomes more efficient.

The fact is, we are under no obligation to conceive the idea of moral cleanliness as limited to the narrowly puritanical. Modern psychology, through the technique of psychoanalysis, has given us a conception of moral cleanliness dominated not by vulgar material issues and a primitive notion of sexual decency but by a conception that relates to the modern scientific ideal of efficiency, of maintaining the normal working order of the personality in its subjective existence and its social relations—the same ideal that may have haunted the young woman who could not make up her mind if she really loved her soldier husband and who was assisted, when she did make up her mind, by a modern instrument of efficiency, the telephone. The psychic knot of psychoanalysis, which sometimes is an obstacle to the spiritual and material happiness of an individual, is nothing but an obdurate piece of dirt whose exculpation must be effected by a precise analysis of its structure—just as certain spots on clothing can be removed only by specific chemical antidotes or as dust in a watch

244

can be located only through microscopic cleaning. By parallel logic the ideally normal life of the Joads can be achieved only by dislodging the handicaps of their economic existence, by curing the economic disease of unemployment.

The apocalyptically sanitary camp thus becomes a wayside station in this social variety of psychoanalysis, a clean home being the basis for animal contentment; in the movie's scheme the camp symbolizes such a cure, since the life of the Joads dramatically changes its spiritual complexion once they are settled in it; it receives there, so to speak, a Hollywood make-up. On California ground the lives of the Okies become photogenic, and the fresh optimism attached to their saga illustrates the release of the popular spirit toward those horizons that ornate movie interiors in their super-Sears-Roebuck reality offer to the American public as every man's dream and every man's possible privilege. Perhaps the sophisticated reader will sigh lightly here and say to himself, "Yes . . . yes . . . just another popular delusion that Hollywood is here ritually, if more subtly than usual, insinuating as its routine moral propaganda."

But, as I have said, *The Grapes of Wrath* does more than just this; it makes deliberate feints at taking the economico-political dilemma by its horns. With this in mind we must deny the possible implication that economic unhappiness, of which the Okies are so convincing and eloquent a symbol, can be psychoanalyzed out of existence by devices of a type like the New Deal reform program of lending a helping hand in major crises. Yes, Tommy Joad goes out to fight the workers' fight, but we have no guarantee in this fable that he can understand the true principles in this fight any better than his mother can understand the nature of his poetic metaphors. In these very metaphors one gets a whiff of the most unfortunate sort of mass metaphysics, a metaphysics that can exist so easily on paper—for instance, in our own Constitution or in Lincoln's Gettysburg Address— and with so much difficulty in material fact. The movie holds its own refutation as to Tom's idealistic capacity for real labor education. The fallacy of his essentially verbal logic in telling his mother that he will be with her always, since he will always be in the fight to determine their common destiny as workers—this very fallacy lay in the fatal handbill the Joads had found, stating that 300 workers were wanted and inducing every one of 10,000 who found the same bill to imagine himself as one of the 300. Indeed, does the outdated legend that 400 people rule New York society limit the entries in the Social Register any more than it limits the aspirations of thousands of social climbers to enter the sacred realm of high society or be entertained by Elsa Maxwell? So long as material definitions do not limit mind, any Okie outhouse may, in terms of pure expectation, equal the sanitary quarters of a movie star.

The "we the people" slogan raised by Ma Joad in the very last moments of the film is pure Hollywood, pure metaphysics, for it represents only the snobbery for the lower classes that upper-class interests seek to popularize. The only sense in which it has any *effectiveness*, any significant application, is that in which we can conceive Ma Joad climbing down from the truck when the camera stops turning and getting her pay envelope from the studio cashier. As a result of Steinbeck's book the lot of some of the real Joads was eased by legislation. It is therefore to be deemed fortunate that the freedom of the press still exists to some practical end, however qualified. Moreover, with the opening up of war industries in California the resident Okies came to have enough extra cash, no doubt, to take in the movies. Perhaps *The Grapes of Wrath* is being kept well under cover in California now, but if any of the Joads were ever privileged to see themselves, how pitifully far and plain those days must have seemed to them when their wartime salaries brought them hot and cold running water and a bathtub, even if not the latest model.

12. SCENARIO FOR A COMEDY OF CRITICAL HALLUCINATION

Rather than bring this book to a close by a conventional summation, in which I should draw certain general conclusions, I want to consider what has gone before as a sort of movie plot, chapter by chapter as though scene by scene, for I think it is, compatibly with my basic critical conception of the movies, a comedy of hallucination. Let whatever elements it holds of pathos and poetry—of solemn dignity and stern ethics—come through as they may.

In the first chapter or scene the voice of the movie actor is introduced as a disjunct element, something that may be objectified and detached from his personality according to the view taken of him. I suggested closing one's eyes and trying to consider what the voice of the actor alone may tell. That voices in real life are significant indices to personality is of course to be taken for granted. What is brought on the stage of the book in this first chapter is the voice as an independent actor, an element that, as with all Hollywood components, refuses to be completely absorbed into the artistic mesh and creates a little theater of its own.

Foremost as an example of the dominant voice is Frank Sinatra, who as a visible personality seems separated from his vocal personality, at least so far as traditional conventions go. Evidently this phenomenon among singers gains new significance on the screen because of the illusory quality of the moving photograph, and it strongly emphasizes the point illustrated—vocal being as a symptom of split personality.

Playing opposite Sinatra comes, as a climax, Lauren Bacall, whose synthetic personality—created by the Hollywood myth out of feminine material seemingly better suited for torch singing—is indelibly scored with the fact that for her singing voice a very mannish voice was dubbed in. So what may be called the ventriloquistic myth of the movies —music is also miraculously ventriloquized by Hollywood —finds expression in two movie sensations, Bacall and Sinatra, who thus make a strange analogy with a couple whose physical rather than whose aural bodies are synthetic —Frankenstein's monster and his bride. So Lauren and Frank take the leads in the comedy of regional, racial, transoceanic, and Barrymoresque vocalization that comprises the auditory archives of postsilent Hollywood. As character voices those of John and Ethel Barrymore, Orson Welles, Charles Laughton, George Sanders, and so on, among the born English-speaking, and those of Garbo, Dietrich, Bergman, Lamarr, Bergner, Boyer, and so on, among the foreign English-speaking, make up the supporting cast that creates the milieu for a voice neurosis among actors, the voice being a musical instrument that may boldly state its independence from or superiority to its Hollywood job and the actor's own artistic destiny—something often definitely lower than his ambitions (leading example: Orson Welles). As a result the element of voice attains, in sheer sound perspective, a type of supernaturalism . . . as though produced by a heavenly chorus of actors un-

249

willingly corrupting themselves with mundane expression. . . .

In the second scene the thread of the plot is devoted to the more or less muted labyrinth of the clown, with its ancestry of the primitive medicine man—whose latter-day movie expressions are Hope, Skelton, Benny, et al.—and the court fool, supremely personified by Charlie Chaplin, who synthesizes the *Pagliacci* legend with the vestiges of chivalry. As the fool, Chaplin has shown up, in *City Lights*, the state to which the king, his ancient patron, has come in the person of the modern capitalist—vulgar, materialistic, and perverted, the apotheosis of Sancho Panza himself. The comedy of affection and enmity staged between Charlie and his fickle patron is essentially the comedy of the king and his fool, at one moment the consoler and friend of the king's bosom, at another the object of his good-natured cuffs. The modern element in the tramp-capitalist relationship is its sinister intimation of a split personality in the capitalist, induced by dipsomania, which may lead in turn to dementia praecox and the impulse to kill. . . . A leading team of comedians, the three Marx brothers, enters as the ideal combination of movie comedy, even suggesting a single organism, so symphonic is their miming; that the most lyrical of them, the harp-playing Harpo, is voiceless is curiously pertinent. The leading lady and the leading man reappear—now in the hallucination of two comedy stars, Danny Kaye and Betty Hutton, who stand at the head of their hierarchies.

Both Kaye and Hutton are singers—one might say acro-

batic singers no less than singing acrobats. In each the keynote of violence sounds loud and funnily. The male
comedian in his first movie, *Up in Arms*, establishes for his
comic fellowship the precept that its foolery, during a war,
belongs on the entertainment side of the footlights in the
army camps and that as of old the current destiny of the
clown is to relax and divert the warrior, whose business is
serious rather than comic. In parallel, Miss Hutton supplies
a warlike version of love, one of her greatest stunts being
the song in which sex is identified with murder and in which,
by practically knocking herself out, she suggests a neat,
economical way for a gentleman to reduce a reluctant
lady to submission.

The vocal acrobatics of these two comedians, as well as
their facial gyrations, invoke the mirage of two apparently
disjunct elements: the classic masks of Greek tragedy and
comedy—one with the corners of its opened mouth turned
down, the other with them turned up—as well as the visage
of the jungle beast uttering its hunger cry, the beast's cry
being, according to one theory, the origin of human
laughter. The element of violence and the ambiguity of the
facial expressions—containing happy and unhappy qualities—permit a synthesis of motives on the part of Hutton
and Kaye as well as of others. This is the savage appetite
for adulation that so many popular entertainers possess,
their faces sometimes conveying the impression they are
ready to devour the camera. So on the comedy level, though
relatively high, artistically, in Hollywood, the hero and
the heroine become savage masks of tragicomedy uttering

wild yells in pursuit of their art. Indeed they *are* hunters of a type, seeking the trophies of public fame, and as comedians are lordly to the extent that they succeed in trapping the elusive beast, success.

The third scene contains a retold Hollywood fable, itself refabricated from Wilde's original, *The Picture of Dorian Gray*. Here the hero is a narcissist and therefore a symbol of the movie hero as he conceives himself professionally, since for the movie actor the silver screen is a veritable mirror indeed. All movie actors, to themselves, are two images, the screen image and the bathroom-mirror image. Hence in *The Picture of Dorian Gray* this duality is quadrupled, for the theme itself is one of a double image, a man and his portrait. The author, Wilde, is represented in this part of my comedy as the typical movie actor who, so to speak, falls in love with himself or with some physical ideal of himself such as his own made-up image and yet, because of social realities, cannot exalt this cachet of the imagination by openly loving those like himself.

Wilde conceived Dorian Gray as the symbol of ideal pagan love, which he could not pursue amidst the alien precincts of modern British society with its accruant vulgarity and sexual conservatism. The classic pagan ideal of love between men, Socrates being the Platonic exemplar, could not be understood by this society or survive as a social object if presented as such. Hence Wilde's fable has a curious realism; it is his plot for the fate of a man who fell in love with ideal women, the heroines of Shakespeare, and fell out of love forever when the actress who performed

252

them proved herself after all a commonplace, real woman. Wilde exalted the principle of make-believe in accordance with his program for the symbolism of an esthetic heritage from Greece: love between men. The author himself fell victim to Dorian's personality plot, for as Dorian degraded himself after his disillusionment with the actress, Sibyl Vane, so, the evidence of life indicates, Wilde did similarly.

My current hero, Dorian, maintains the extremities of high and low, king and fool, by being at once a beautiful aristocrat—almost hermaphroditic in personality, therefore monstrous—and a strange sort of animal, such as the fabled unicorn, which Wilde hunted in modern England, an alien place. Like the financier in *City Lights,* Dorian has an alter ego, horrible rather than comic but equally redundant, which he fears and yet indulges. To English culture Wilde imported Dorian as an idea, a mere literary symbol, but he also sought him in actual society and—according to modern legend—succeeded in finding him in the person of Lord Alfred Douglas. Be this as it may, before his death Wilde was treated, by his own testimony, as a beast, for he went to prison; and both he and Douglas have admitted what may be termed a beastly degree of self-corruption. This same corruption appears visibly on the face and figure of the portrait, which grows old in Wilde's story as the hero remains fabulously young.

Hollywood made the gross mistake of conceiving Dorian's light-o'-love, Sibyl Vane, as a beer-hall singer, thus bourgeoisifying the whole fable. But in this there is aptness to the extent that the shocking naturalism of the

Albright brothers, who painted the portrait of the corrupted Dorian shown in the movie, is a vulgarization of the decayed aristocracy natural to Wilde's image. Indeed if the Hollywood Dorian is an effeminate version of the classic matinée-idol type of Hollywood, he is later, in the portrait, a fresh version of the libidinal monsters of the Hollywood gallery of synthetic men, the Frankenstein's monsters, vampires, and animalized humans such as the Leopard Man and the Wolf Man. By a strange process of conversion the Hollywoodizing of Wilde's legend of an anachronistic unicorn retains its truth by modeling itself on the Jekyll-Hyde pattern and thus reaches the banal vulgarism that the desires of the body are ugly and those of the soul beautiful and that the body may drag the soul into the mud. Wilde perversely insisted that the body remain beautiful, and till the end, in the movie-lot *Dorian* too, the body stays beautiful and the soul grows ugly.

Likewise overt in this cinema fable is the recurrent pattern of the hunter and hunted in my comedy, for love, even as lust, is always the hunter and is sometimes, like Frankenstein's monster and the rest of the lupine fraternity, both *hunter* and *hunted*. So we leave our hero as, according to Hollywood convention, beauty turned beast and destroyed . . . a situation beyond comedy technique. Yet can we avoid connecting him with Danny Kaye, who has as much a fixation on the movie camera as Dorian has on his portrait or mirror image? It would seem that the comic element enters when the image of the mirror becomes the *public physiognomy;* that is, when the actor's personality is il-

lusorily reproduced in terms of his individual admirers—
in a sense the actor always has his audience in view as well
as vice versa. The basic temperamental difference between
Dorian's complex and Danny's is that of the physical beauty
of the subject. Dorian, being very beautiful, pleases by being a perfectly passive image and founds his personality
and actions on this idea; in an odd sense he anticipates the
precipitated passivity of the young marines stymied in the
submarine, on whom the illusion of passivity with the
beauty that wins benevolence is forced by sudden circumstance. On the other hand, Danny, anything but aristocratic
in outlook, must work hard to please and thus is active and
proletarian; he must attract great numbers of people by
calling forth in himself a vision not of unearthly beauty but
of unearthly fun.

In the fourth chapter the mise-en-scène changes to a
panorama of general origins of the nature of movie illusion.
Perennially we have man into beast, beauty into ugliness,
Bacall-into-Hutton-into-Sibyl Vane; the knight into the fool,
the fool into the knight; the vision into the voice, the voice
into the vision. . . . How can these illusions prove so
effective? They are so like fairy tales—like magic.

Well, they are magic in a sense. Cinema trickery, in its
illusions of ghosts, its treatment of all manner of supernatural phenomena, could not be so potent did it not contain
an ancient imaginative heritage, that of sympathetic magic
—magic by imitation or contagion. The most rudimentary
camera trick, for instance, that of appearing and disappearing persons, which occurs in the wink of an eye, is a visuali-

zation of the correspondence between matter and spirit that was a cardinal tenet in the beliefs of primordial savages. Of course that we see through the trick automatically, since it is a convention of means, does not make it less convincing; and the fact that it doesn't make it less so proves that the essence of magic power is illusion and not reality, art and not life.

In two outstanding supernatural films a Hollywood product, *Turnabout*, and a Warsaw product, *The Dybbuk*, there are respectively a comic and a tragic version of the same supernatural phenomenon—the possession of a woman's body by a man's spirit, in which the woman speaks with the man's voice. In the American comedy she speaks literally with the man's voice—an effect achieved by cinema magic—just as the lady's husband, since they have exchanged personalities, speaks with her voice, whereas in the foreign tragedy the voice of the woman is used, hoarse and in travail, for that of the man speaking in her. Thus the comedy illusion is properly mechanical and the tragic illusion properly intrinsic or realistic, the latter containing so basic an imaginative premise that its support requires a rigid logic of realism.

In the cases of highly false acting personalities such as Veronica Lake, created half by the beauty parlor and half by stupidity, a kind of supernature seems to be operating through devising a mannequin, a feminine symbol, a female Dorian, who is not a real woman but who imitates being one and, through beauty, maintains the illusion of reality. . . . This supernatural sort of artifice is evident whether

Miss Lake plays ordinary rôles or those in which, as in *I Married a Witch,* she is also outside of nature.

Around the edges of this vista of Hollywood's supernatural landscape—its hell, purgatory, and paradise of another world—are its various efforts at ghost stories, all of them representing religious vestiges of the tribe or manipulations of conventional ghosts that answer to the call of Ouija boards. More direct is such a piece as *The Song of Bernadette,* in which a supposedly genuine supernatural vision occurs to a peasant girl, whose faith in it, by working miracles, brings her to sainthood. Here the comedy of Hollywood hallucination becomes part and parcel of a general or lay texture of the supernatural and allies it with various kinds of secular sacredness, such as the hushed atmospheres of hospitals and psychiatrists' offices, as well as the hushed atmospheres of churches and movie studios when the signal comes to shoot the scene. In general this pseudoreligious hush is tantamount to the silence of the movie theater itself, where the esthetic hush prevails and the myth of the Spectator is enthroned in silence. At a time when the formal and precise gestures and intonations of actors are exempt from the hurried pace and nervous, uncertain rhythms of actual society, accentuated as these are during a war, the pace of art becomes virtually a supernatural pace, and we find something preternaturally exempt in art, as though it were an absolute like Divine Being amidst the relativities and ephemeralities that compose mortality. Even in a commonplace scene of farewell between a man and a woman the time that is taken for the prearranged action—only make-

believe—seems outside of time and thus, by logical extension, outside of nature. This atmosphere was emphasized
by Jennifer Jones, the young actress who played Bernadette,
for in her purely personal leisure as the girl who had had
a vision of the Virgin she seemed to take all the time in
the world to act in order to win the Motion Picture Academy
Award for 1943, as indeed she did. So for leading lady
we now have someone who makes a modern professional
comedy of acting a serious supernatural rôle and who therefore raises our heroine comedienne above the level of the
Hollywood Huttons, Arthurs, Russells, and Loys.

In the cases of the chief psychoanalytical films discussed
the spiritual level of the heroine is thoroughly rationalized,
and on the one hand she becomes a helpless victim of her
own unconscious mental struggle and on the other becomes
quite the contrary, a competent young woman. Miss Ingrid
Bergman is perhaps the most competent young woman on
the screen. In *Spellbound* she decides the destiny of the
man she loves by her skill in psychoanalysis; playing opposite her, Gregory Peck is almost as helpless as Ann Todd,
who enacts the young pianist victim in *The Seventh Veil*.
But Mr. Peck is the type of hero who appeals at once to the
instinct of maternally minded women as well as to the
female susceptibility to stalwart masculinity, a paradox
rather neatly turned by the fact that Mr. Peck, having suffered the ordeal of being shot down in a plane, has been
temporarily unmanned. Thus, like Bernadette, the psychoanalytic Miss Bergman is a divinatory female but one
pre-eminently on the practical side, a sibyl rather than a

258

saint; yet she, like Bernadette, is likewise an instrument of the curative powers of truth. Their mutual connection with visions—one with her lover's dream, the other with the Virgin's image—is significant as premonitory of the more complete and coherent dream pattern of which Mildred Pierce is the *center* rather than the observer or manipulator.

The scene of the fifth chapter contains the hero as a sort of male Bernadette, someone likewise with a vision of a virgin, and by this token even first cousin to Dorian, who at least kept his youth, his mirror image, virginal in actual appearance. This is Mortimer Brewster, the woman-shy dramatic critic, who reverences the maiden nature of his two eccentric aunts as reflections of his own virginity. He is a virgin or at least abstemious because, since there is insanity in his family, he dare not marry. As a result he develops an impotence neurosis, and when a former play-mate, a blonde, traps him into a quick ceremony, he goes off the beam and behaves like a nutty adolescent. The plot begins when he discovers his dear old aunts are murder-esses, with a string of victims whom they have buried in the cellar. This event unleashes all his prebridal-night fears, and the reality of the situation—into which his criminally insane brother intrudes, threatening his very life—becomes a symbolic nightmare of sexual crime, the twin crimes of impotence and potency; for he is as much afraid of his virility, which may produce idiot children, as he is of his lack of it, which he fears will wreck his marriage. The dead bodies of his aunts' victims represent impotence and vir-ginity, sexual deadness and aridity, whereas the murderous criminal—his own brother supposedly—represents an obnoxious potency.

That the hero appears here as a dramatic critic is most significant, for if his breed is notoriously harsh toward bad plays, it regards Hollywood products as existing in a hinterland of rottenness that is strictly taboo. Yet because of this critic's sex neurosis marriage comes to him suddenly and overwhelmingly in the form of movie-lot ecstasy, and when he is further entrapped in a murder tangle with his own relatives, the machinery of fate has operated to victimize him with the lowest elements of the movies—popular romantic love and the murder melodrama, the latter given pointed form by his brother's striking resemblance to Boris Karloff, the original Frankenstein's monster. After incredible pandemonium the critic comes out unscathed, gets his aunts committed to an asylum and his brother collared by the police, and learns to boot that he is not a blood relative to the others but only an adopted member of their family. Again the alter ego has raised its terrible head, but our hero vanquishes it—chimera or reality!—and sets off on his delayed honeymoon.

The war movie, in the scene of the sixth chapter, introduces the hero of this comedy as the warrior on our side and the warrior on the other side—thus in the dual rôle of hero-villain. Hitler inevitably appears as the archenemy, a mercurial resident of a Madame Tussaud's, at first caricatured and then gradually becoming a sort of documentary character, a man like ourselves and yet, like Dorian, Danny Kaye, and Mortimer Brewster, one with some kind of hallucination neurosis. In going through Chaplin's caricaturing, which made him a marionette and a Punch-and-Judy scapegoat, through various glimpses and intimations of him as tabooed god or king to the common-sense version of him seen in *The Hitler Gang*, wherein he appears as a European gangster betrayed by his own confederates, the Hollywood Hitler possesses the supernatural quality of metamorphosis. All other German soldiers, with a few exceptions showing them as men like us, are mere subordinate mundane or mediocre reflections of the Hitler archetype.

Opposed to this insane individualist, as the artistic and popular census had Hitler, is the group of normal, right-thinking men, among whom naturally are Hollywood actors. Hence in this scene for the purposes of war propaganda the hero divides himself magically and indefinitely into several, as in the British-made *The Invaders*, wherein the conquering hero's part had to be filled by several characters played by famous male leads in order that finally the single German enemy, a very undistinguished actor, should be subdued.

The hero as the warrior on our side becomes, as might have been anticipated, infinite, since according to democratic canons free competition exists on the fighting lines as well as in the economic world. A mere private may transcend a general in glory and win coveted decorations as a result. Many Hollywood endeavors have exposed the hero of the ranks as he does his tasks on land or sea and in the air and as he deliberately, in calm mind, sacrifices his life rather than reveal military secrets. Needless to say, although with several exceptions, this hero has had a distinguished Hollywood player's name on his movie identification tag. And if he is on the contrary an outstanding player in the supporting cast of the film, he has had an opportunity to compare his initiation into the strange rigors of war with his initiation into the strange rigors of acting, both of which, the former in a charade version, he is undergoing simultaneously. For this reason, I believe, some of the best acting in the last four years has come from young fellows just trying their Hollywood legs and possibly anticipating army induction at any moment.

This special situation has resulted not only in eloquent playing but even in the creation of a sort of style, as was strikingly evinced in *Gung Ho*. In this movie a group of volunteers, all men in their teens or early twenties, are given a rigid training program for a special mission. The great tension created in rising to the peak of training perfection is suddenly let down at the moment they learn the nature of their task—that of taking a Pacific island from the Japs—and they are led docilely into the belly of a submarine where they must do nothing for a three-day journey. Down there in the heat and closeness, where they have to wear next to nothing and still sweat, they feel trapped, degraded, generally stymied . . . having anticipated being plunged into heroic action. Moreover, they have been specially trained as offensive fighters, but now they must nest passively in a submarine's belly, always the possible prey to enemy ships. The resultant feeling of anxiety and helplessness recalls a childhood state when they were dependent chiefly on their mother and when their instinctive technique for getting something out of her, some favor or form of protection, was to present themselves as passive angelic images, simulating the infants they used to be, on whom she would lavish gratuitous caresses. This peculiar expression prints itself on the face of every young man in the submarine; thus an unconscious group device of acting style is achieved. Since few, if any, are inclined to pray, their instinct is to evoke a benevolent image of power that will protect them; virtually this is Nature herself, appearing in the intimated form of the mother and in a special religious sense as an image of the Madonna. Consequently at this most solemn point of the comedy the supernatural hush that appeared in the previous scene revives in the submarine's belly as an unconscious appeal to the higher powers of nature; that is, as the most common variety of silent prayer.

Parallel to the submerged war hero of *Gung Ho* there enters the lens of the comedy a hero quite aware of his position on the map and distinctly orientated to the terra firma of military operations, the walker in the sun. This man is a collective personality, virtually a group of intimate responses in the litany of war on our side. In the lulls between actions, moments sometimes coming without notice, this man finds his true spiritual self—a peacetime fellow for whom the rigors and crises of war merely repeat on a life-and-death level the struggle for material welfare back home. The hypertension of the monotonous march, the enforced inaction before the order to start firing, merely accelerates the peacetime pulse; it is a condensed version of all the anxieties previously experienced in terms of the mental reflection devoted to them. Time out to think—this is the arbitrary opportunity repeatedly offered the soldier hero. He seems now the most genuine version of reality to have emerged from the wings onto the scenes of the comedy. He has the accent of real life. He is at home on the battle-field of war because essentially he recognizes it as a super-realization of the battlefield of peace; that is, alienation from the realm of fulfilled ambition is his natural state—the state of stubborn heroism by which we recognize him, as though his muted litany were as conspicuously present on him as the Purple Heart or the Oak-Leaf Cluster.

While absent in such movies as *Gung Ho* and *A Walk in the Sun*, our heroine, who remains typically at home, re-vives as the young woman precipitated into marriage; Lana Turner portrays the recidivate type, Judy Garland the two-day furlough conquest. Judy is a sort of Bernadette who has a vision of a holy bridegroom, the soldier on leave, and in the company of his bodily presence experiences the tremors of a sacred and eternal silence stolen from the auditory terrors, even in secluded Riverside Drive, of a New York night. Yet Lana too, whom we observe being tested with her bridegroom and without him, must commune silently and secludedly with herself in order to choose be-tween the ghosts of her former loves, all of whose mirages troop before her, and the beatific vision of John Hodiak on a Pacific island.

In this scene, however, there is a presage of sinister

things to come, for a popular rival of the war film became the psychological murder story. According to popular thinking this could be interpreted as the tendency of American citizens to be interested in the psychological aspects of crime, since a great public question was the then undetermined war guilt of the German nation. The link of war to murder and the question of its guilt was Hitler himself, who, popularly portrayed as a madman, a kind of monster, would seem to have been legally exonerated by the same token—as the dear aunts of Brewster are exonerated by being committed to an asylum rather than a death chamber. What should be the punishment of the German people if they in turn have been rendered mad by an insane leader? There is no asylum, at least on this planet, big enough for them. Moreover, within the exclusive region of the subconscious it may occur to some that the act of war is a mass murder, regardless of the question of right and wrong with respect to the premises of such murder. Furthermore, so far as the films go, the pathological murderer is an individual, the popular reception of whose mania may express the preference of the American people that war guilt be lodged with crazy individuals, not with a whole people. One outstanding film of this type, here appearing as another vision of the Virgin, *The Woman in the Window,* attempts to gloze some of its harshness by making the whole murder sequence and its consequences a dream; but a dream is what establishes precisely the psychological value of a murder and thus its intrinsic guilt, just as supernaturalism established the psychological value of Bernadette's vision and thus its

265

intrinsic virtue. Perhaps the dream device is a neat expression of subconscious guilt on the part of the war arbiters themselves, for the guilty man is a criminology professor. . . .

Our hero is now zigzagging madly between being a mask of Hitler and a façade for the ethical experts who determine the punishment of the German nation. Within his personality we may discern the mechanical springs of Frankenstein and the spiritual springs of Charlie Chaplin, Dorian Gray, Danny Kaye, a dramatic critic, the young men in the submarine, and the bridegroom soldier . . . assuredly a candidate for a glorified Madame Tussaud's!

Yet his personality is not yet exhausted. The eighth scene shows him as portrayed by Fred MacMurray, a stalwart young man who represents the American salesman and the sexual ambitions of his private life. In an unusually brilliant Hollywood opus, *Double Indemnity*, this devious fellow concocts a scheme with a hard honey, who happens to have an unwanted husband, to murder her husband and collect the life insurance . . . a consequence niftily arranged for by young MacMurray himself, for he sells life insurance. It is odd and apt that Edward G. Robinson, who played the criminology professor in the previous scene, should now be the salesman's opponent; Robinson is the insurance company's claim adjuster and also the paternal critic of MacMurray's loose amours . . . so again our hero has an alter ego. The plan of the story ordains that after the murder is successfully executed and covered up, the guilty pair are psychologically outmaneuvered by the claim

adjuster, go to pieces, and try to murder one another . . .
but some underlying pattern must exist to explain the anticlimactic disaster that befalls the couple's plans to collect
the insurance money.

It would seem that again we have some kind of impotence
neurosis or at least strong anxiety feelings about sex on
the part of the apparently lusty insurance salesman, so
obviously attracted to the lady played by Barbara Stanwyck. Neff, the salesman, is habitually kidded by Keyes,
the claim adjuster, about his sex entanglements, the implication being that they are cheap and debauching. Neff may
have good reason to make them ephemeral and to be
ashamed of his cheapness as well as of the mechanism—
perhaps his lack of virility—that makes them cheap. Yet
he may be inspired on seeing a woman who appeals strongly
to him and in particular a woman who asks him to commit
murder to prove his love for her, for in the violence of this
act he may hope, through virtue of sympathetic magic, to
add violence, that is, complete effectuality, to his sex behavior. That the postmurder insurance-collection plan collapses may indicate a simultaneous collapse of postmurder
intercourse with the widowed lady, Phyllis. Lovers come to
hate each other specifically because of the failure of one or
both to get or give enough pleasure, this being a vicious
and murderous plot of the sex life.

If as a matter of fact we do not accept the premises of
Neff's sexual neurosis, its disaster in his project with Phyllis, and his fear of Keyes, his would-be mentor, as a dis-
coverer of sexual as well as insurance frauds, then the

movie mimicry has no coherence. For after murdering Phyllis the wounded Neff makes haste not across the border into near-by Mexico but to Keyes's own office, where he makes a full confession into the dictaphone, this confession being the device for telling the story. Hence in showing up the mechanism of the hero's guilt as murderer, commonly extenuating facts are revealed, and Neff, emerging as a victim, seems sympathetic. Now villain and hero in our comedy are reversed. The villain becomes a hero, virtually an ethical expert, provided he is guilty only through dream (Robinson in *The Woman in the Window*), whereas the hero who stains himself with individual murder for a purely selfish reason (MacMurray in *Double Indemnity*) may be forgiven by this same expert if enough extenuation or psychological compulsiveness is involved. The claim adjuster for the insurance firm is a symbol—only in this comedy of my invention of course—for the congress of ethical experts who have tentatively decided Germany's war guilt. Indeed it seems not unrealistic to point out that the stated aims of the Big Three, the United States, Great Britain, and the Soviet Union, presiding at the world ethical congress, are insurance against future wars and, in cases of international quarrels, performance of the function of claim adjustment. . . . In this case is not Neff, the insurance salesman, a symbol of the average young man who is both bridegroom (the average husband) and murderer (the average soldier)? And is not the claim adjuster, even as was the spiritual immigration officer in *Outward Bound,* the supreme ethical expert, now with an alternate religious and political character, who will forgive him for his mundane failures and faults, especially that of killing, and who will provide, above all, the ethic for his future deeds? The hero and the image of the forgiving God here supplant the heroine and the image of the Virgin. Our heroine has evinced one new trait; as Neff's conspirator she loses all her passivity and comes out boldly for a psychological war of her own.

The ninth scene is a comedy anticlimax, revealing the lower, less vicious brackets of the split-personality neurosis, symbolized by such familiar American myths as the absent-minded professor and his cultural antithesis, the business executive, who is under such terrific pressure that he too falls victim to the retarded mental reflex. Here the ironic comedy obtains through the connection between the standard buffoonery of Hugh Herbert's lunatic fussbudget and the myth of preoccupation, which lies above that of the absent-minded professor—that of the otherworldly-absorbed inventive genius, whom Hollywood has given us of course in many individuals. Time, here again the psychological opposite of the principle of precipitation, is a predominant element in the double-take, and it is likewise a predominant element in the secret work of the inventor who may seem to be wasting time, whereas in the end, according to legendary examples, he proves the time well spent. The preoccupied business man has a plethora of engagements and memoranda, thus a redundance of riches that reflects the redundance of his economic profits. Hugh Herbert, as a parody of the busy executive, becomes a parody also of the intensified powers of the inventor genius, for whose intrinsic richness the comedian can show only a spluttering intrinsic sterility. The hero of this comedy must now take on the full mantle of the American male, exclusively distinguished during peacetime by his interest in two types of power, business and sex. As Neff of *Double Indemnity* he is the megalomaniac salesman of sexual power who through neurosis is driven to crime. But like Bell, Ehrlich, Morse, Pasteur, the Curies, and so on, he is blessed by the genius of creative thought, which justifies his apparent abuse of time through neglect of the conventional forms of self-seeking. In the middle ground he is Hugh Herbert, with his burlesque of the frenzied businessman whose financial ambitions may lead to economic power but have no necessary spiritual content. Hugh Herbert is thus a Neff whose neurosis turns into harmless idiocy rather than murderous psychopathism.

At this crucial point of the comedy, when we cannot tell whether it may not all be too sordid even for ironic laughter, our hero and heroine blossom into the amusingly marionette persons of Jean Arthur and Joel McCrea, the lovers of the Washington steps in *The More the Merrier*, whose motor reflexes in the lady's case show a laughable schizophrenia; for while she does not denounce Joel, she mechanically rebuffs his caresses if he seems to be going too far, yet on the whole permits them while she chats of things alien to his physical maneuvers. A spatial definition now applies to the motif of schizophrenia, a definition indeed already implicit in previous discussion, for when a retarded mental reflex occurs, it means that for the moment there is insufficient room for it. Now the "room" is physically defined, for, the apartments of Jean's apartment building being full of cots and her own parlor rented, she has no place a decent young woman may entertain a gentleman friend; hence the love-making on the steps outside. Jean and Joel, in contrast with Judy and Robert, exist in pure space rather than in space directly modified by time (the clock). Schizophrenia in Jean's case indicates two levels of desire, one negative, the other positive. Yet in this particular situation the relation is not vertical or one-dimensional on two levels but horizontal or two-dimensional on one level—since the lovers are outside (in public), not inside (in private). Jean is enough of a modern young woman to allow a young man certain preliminary privileges of love-making in her own parlor but not in public even in the shadows. Hence the loving hero and heroine, stripped of anything so unpleasant as introversive vices, are faced with one obstacle only, the housing problem. They have been in hell, purgatory, and a hallucinated paradise (Riverside Drive); now a real, *durational* paradise is nigh, if only the national housing problem can be solved! By the strangest of coincidences Joel comes to Washington as an inventor whose genius will enrich the war effort. . . .

And now Our Heroine merits capital letters for her cognomen because she arrives in a vehicle honoring her own name—Mildred Pierce. Played by Joan Crawford, she is a young mother—a mother in the midst of her daughter's affairs and thus peculiarly modern. She is, however, quite the opposite of Lana Turner's mother in *Marriage Is a Private Affair*, even though she has the same strategic position in the drama. The hint of the Electra complex in Lana's picture comes into full bloom in Joan's, although Joan plays a mother in whom the complex has survived. Hence she is actually a familial extension of Lana's character, there being nothing in her to invalidate our playful assumption that she is Lana's young woman married to her soldier home from the war and herself become a mother —a mother fanatically fond of a daughter whom she cherishes in order specifically to encourage her toward the incest crime of which she herself was deprived. Indeed, since Lana hardly knew her father until she was quite grown and already married, she was in an ideal position to feel a profound and mysterious uneasiness.

Mildred Pierce is heroine of a triple-barreled story involving a murder committed by her daughter, her own disguised incest tragedy, and the melodramatic struggle of humble Americans to win commercial fortunes by individual effort. The manner in which Mildred, whose dramatic poker face is Joan's contribution to Hollywood histrionics, is enmeshed in the mystery, incest, and success-story plots, distinguishes her as a typical dreamer, a kind of heroine who reflects, despite her exceptional character and extreme type of experience, the character habits of her audience. When finally, after Mildred's daughter, Veda, has murdered Mildred's second husband, Veda's stepfather, and Mildred and her exonerated first husband walk out of the police station free to seek a new life together, the happy ending becomes in this phase of the comedy the ordinary dream climax of waking up to a guiltless reality from a nightmare of horrors. Of course everything is presumed to be quite real in *Mildred Pierce*. But the mock-incestuous Veda in the arms of her stepfather is but the hallucinated or dream version of Mildred herself. When Veda kills her stepfather, she is Mildred killing her own father husband in mythical terms. Dream and myth here are identical. And since the crime is a twin affair of incest and murder, Mildred must be cleansed by the converse of dream, reality— thereby illustrating the same sort of cleansing reached by dreamers who dream of murder and incest but wake up to guiltless consciousness.

The induplicable Hollywood touch is supplied Mildred's character by her rating as individual breadwinner for her children and herself and later for her second husband. That, near the climax, she is cheated of her handsome restaurant chain by a conspiracy between her male partner in business and her second husband is a daring way of combining the success dream with the dream of sexual guilt. Material success for Mildred is in inverse ratio to sexual satisfaction, and each building, home or restaurant, with which she connects herself has its particular scene of frustration or anticlimax, its peculiar ghosts of aborted desire, the most familiar folk label of which is the skeleton in the closet. The skeleton in the closet is always Mildred's own past self, visibly fleshed in her radiant if ungrateful daughter. If Mildred awakes from the bad dream of her life with her daughter facing prison, she is precisely in the position where she was when her first husband, now reunited with her, deserted her for another woman; she is set to begin baking pies. Inevitably this would be to start the cycle of her life over again with the innocence of someone to whom many things have happened without imparting true experience. People dream during the day of winning fortunes; at night they dream of suppressed desires. These are the waking dreams of American materialism and its myth of a paradisial innocence. Highly significant it is that Joan hands the heroic standard of this fluid comedy to a young man who is much more realistically aware than she of the problem of the ideal home and material success—Tommy Joad.

The final scene of this critico-mythical comedy is played by the Okies of *The Grapes of Wrath,* those unfortunates of the American Dust Bowl—not those fortunates of the American Rose Bowl, some of them incipient Neffs—whose future is rosy with the vision of a proper home, economically stabilized by a permanent relation with fertile land. The fertile land does not exist at home. Therefore it must be sought abroad, for, arid as their home ground is, the Okies are to be evicted from it. The Land of Promise, coincidentally enough, appears as California, which thus repeats its "pot of gold at the end of the rainbow" function that occurred during the days of the Gold Rush. Again there is the historic pilgrimage of the pioneer, this time a pioneer group who are first disillusioned and then find root and flourish in the war industries of the following years.

The immediate emphasis on the economic problems of

the Okie family, the Joads, is directed toward housing, especially sanitation. First they find anchorage in the Hooverville camps of the Sunshine State, and there their miseries are almost too much to allow one to remain in the theater. But finally they reach a clean, modern, sanitation-blessed camp sponsored by the Department of Agriculture. Meanwhile a curious parallel has obtained; as the over-loaded truck with the Joads and all they possess draws nearer and nearer to California, halcyon land of the movies, everything, including the photography and the plot, be-comes neater, cleaner, and more shapely. Therefore the esthetic symbols of plot and technique reflect the modern sanitation which it is an important ambition of Ma Joad's to achieve, for sanitation is the symbol of clean and proper living in the material sense. To a degree more fiction artifices are used as the story reaches the destination of the government-sponsored camp, and in the conventional end-ing of a farewell between mother and son, during which the Reverential Hush prevails, the appeal to the sentiments is in the approved movie tradition, albeit more realistic and relevant than the sentimental-farewell type scene re-peatedly referred to.

. . . How will the gestures of the comedy, the final revelation of its motives, be played? In the person of the climactic hero Tommy Joad elides practically all the youths who have gone before, with the exception that he has rid himself of the narcissistic-professional affectations of Dorian and Danny as well as the esthetic symbology of the chivalrous clown of Chaplin; in brief he seems to have no sex problem. But it is important to note that he remains a *murderer* no less than the sort of *mirage* that a determined and resourceful fugitive is to the vision of his pursuers. So after all Tommy Joad is the solemn-faced champion of a sanitary chivalry and a crusader for the socialization of private property, this being precisely the provisional economic status of the clean Department of Agriculture camps that were multiplied as a result of Steinbeck's novel. If I wanted to make my comedy truly shapely in the romantic Hollywood sense, I should contrive to marry Tommy off to the militant young heroine of *One Third of a Nation,* an urban victim of the housing situation. But let that occur in a story that will earn its author at least a hundred thousand dollars. The important thing is that our hero does not escape the mark of Cain, whereas he is ready to be purified in the crucible of class-conscious endeavor to get better conditions for the human race by making the democratic ideal of clean, modern, economically stable homes for all a reality rather than a hallucination. Thus we may hope that our hero will be forgiven by the ethical experts of the future as well as by those of the present.

That Tommy's mother forgives him his filial fault is evident by her cheerfully assuming the brunt of being the family staff after Tommy informs her that he must abandon the family to fight for all families in the struggle of labor against its economic enemies. Within the immediate focus of the camera our heroine has now become the hero's mother, and in the case of this Okie family the mother is stronger than the father . . . a kind of Madonna, perhaps the very one to whom the sea-trapped marines appealed. However, we see that the facial mask of the hero, while it has no liaison with a mirror, has changed from the one that prevailed during those magical moments in the submarine. The mask is completely stern now, for it is that of a Cain who, being fully aware of the nature of the psychological compulsiveness that drove him to kill, must seek the proper redemption. Being active and free, he does not feel impelled to be passive and beg the favor of benevolent Nature, conceived as the land, the mother, or as the Madonna herself. Tommy Joad is a real man—a walker in the sun, not a Frankenstein's monster—who knows that his way is the independent way of one who renounces the parental shelter in all its senses and sets out to win a home of his own. Yet as such, fundamentally, his texture may still be too romantic and conventional for this comedy. Here Tommy becomes a comic hero because, as Every Worker, still under the *practical* influence of many parental ideas, he mistakes the materialistic ideal for a paradise, whereas as a social foundation it is merely the first stepping stone to what may be termed "supernaturally" the Utopian state of man. So in terms of true art, intellect, and ethics Tommy Joad is not yet, being materialistically handicapped, out of the Frankenstein's monster class nor completely free of the fallacy of thinking, like the depraved Neff, of emotional values in terms of buying and selling commodities.

Tommy vanishes into the night, and on the lips of Ma Joad there appears the "we the people" slogan of official panaceas for proletarian hurts. . . . This slogan is a democratic ghost. It is pure supernaturalism of the twentieth century, and until it is laid, American man cannot be free of the economic fear against which ultimately this slogan, like all others, is a futile antidote. This ghost is not the Virgin or the Madonna and rates neither fear nor a Reverential Hush; in fact there is nothing under its sheet but a tale told by an idiot like Groucho Marx, full of sound and fury, signifying fraud. So, even as Mortimer Brewster's, mine is a somewhat sardonic comedy of critical hallucination . . . and sardonic too in the main, despite its irresponsible fun and its solemn fantasy, is the dubious vision of Bernadette that Hollywood has stamped on the silver-dollarlike surface of its fame.

CHECK LIST
OF PRINCIPAL FILMS REFERRED TO.

ARSENIC AND OLD LACE (1944)
Warner Bros.
With Cary Grant, Priscilla Lane, Raymond Massey. Produced and directed by Frank Capra. Pages 121-131, 259-260

BETWEEN TWO WORLDS (1944)
Warner Bros.
With John Garfield, Paul Henreid, Sidney Greenstreet. Produced by Mark Hellinger. Directed by Edward Blatt. Pages 93-94

CITY LIGHTS (1931)
United Artists
With Charlie Chaplin, Virginia Cherrill. Produced and directed by Charlie Chaplin. Pages 36-38

THE CLOCK (1945)
Metro-Goldwyn-Mayer
With Judy Garland, Robert Walker, James Gleason. Produced by Arthur Freed. Directed by Vincénte Minnelli. Pages 169-170

CRY HAVOC (1943)
Metro-Goldwyn-Mayer
With Margaret Sullavan, Ann Sothern, Joan Blondell. Produced by Edwin Knopf. Directed by Richard Thorpe. Pages 149-150

DAYS OF GLORY (1944)
RKO-Radio
With Toumanova, Gregory Peck. Produced by Casey Robinson. Directed by Jacques Tourneur. Page 150

DOUBLE INDEMNITY (1944)
Paramount
With Fred MacMurray, Barbara Stanwyck, Edward G. Robinson. Produced by Joseph Sistrom. Directed by Billy Wilder. Pages 171, 175-189, 211, 213, 266-270

DRAGON SEED (1944)
Metro-Goldwyn-Mayer
Katharine Hepburn, Walter Huston, Turhan Bey. Produced by Pandro S. Berman. Directed by Jack Conway. Pages 20-21

THE DYBBUK (1938)
Geist

With A. Morewski, R. Samberg, M. Libman. Directed by Michael Waszynski. Pages 88-90, 256

EDGE OF DARKNESS (1943)
Warner Bros.

With Errol Flynn, Ann Sheridan, Walter Huston. Produced by Henry Blanke. Directed by Lewis Milestone. Pages 142, 146

THE ETERNAL MASK (1937)
Mayer-Burstyn

With Peter Peterson, Mathias Wiemann. Directed by Werner Hockbaum. Pages 115-116

THE GHOST CATCHERS (1944)
Universal

With Ole Olson, Chic Johnson, Gloria Jean. Produced by Edmund Hartmann. Directed by Edward F. Cline. Pages 100-101

GILDERSLEEVE'S GHOST (1944)
RKO-Radio

With Harold Peary, Marian Martin, Richard LeGrand. Produced by Herman Schlom. Directed by Gordon Douglas. Page 100

THE GRAPES OF WRATH (1940)
Twentieth Century-Fox

With Henry Fonda, Jane Darwell, John Carradine. Produced by Darryl Zanuck. Directed by John Ford. Pages 230-247, 274-278

GUNG HO (1943)
Universal

With Randolph Scott, Grace McDonald, Alan Curtis. Produced by Walter Wanger. Directed by Ray Enright. Pages 149, 152-157, 262-264

THE HITLER GANG (1944)
Paramount

With Bobby Watson, Roman Bohnen, Martin Kosleck. Produced by B. G. DeSylva. Directed by John Farrow. Pages 136, 139-141, 261

I MARRIED A WITCH (1942)
United Artists

With Fredric March, Veronica Lake, Cecil Kellaway. Produced and directed by René Clair. Pages 85-86, 257

Check List of Principal Films Referred to.

LADY IN THE DARK (1944)
Paramount

With Ginger Rogers, Ray Milland, Jon Hall. Produced by Richard Blumenthal. Directed by Mitchell Leisen. Pages 109-110

THE LOWER DEPTHS (1937)
Mayer-Burstyn

With Jean Gabin, Louis Jouvet, Suzy Prim. Directed by Jean Renoir. Pages 236-238, 242

MAN HUNT (1941)
Twentieth Century-Fox

With Walter Pidgeon, Joan Bennett, George Sanders. Produced by Kenneth Macgowan. Directed by Fritz Lang. Pages 141-142

MARRIAGE IS A PRIVATE AFFAIR (1944)
Metro-Goldwyn-Mayer

With Lana Turner, James Craig, John Hodiak. Produced by Pandro S. Berman. Directed by Robert Z. Leonard. Pages 166-169, 264, 272

MILDRED PIERCE (1945)
Warner Bros.

With Joan Crawford, Jack Carson, Zachary Scott. Produced by Jerry Wald. Directed by Michael Curtiz. Pages 211-229, 271-274

THE MOON IS DOWN (1943)
Twentieth Century-Fox

With Sir Cedric Hardwicke, Henry Travers, Lee J. Cobb. Produced by Nunnally Johnson. Directed by Irving Pichel. Pages 142-146

THE MORE THE MERRIER (1943)
Columbia

With Jean Arthur, Joel McCrea, Charles Coburn. Produced and directed by George Stevens. Pages 191, 194-197, 200-201, 203-210, 270-271

ONE THIRD OF A NATION (1939)
Paramount

With Sylvia Sidney, Leif Erikson. Produced and directed by Dudley Murphy. Pages 230, 235-236, 276

OUR TOWN (1940)
United Artists

With William Holden, Martha Scott, Fay Bainter. Produced by Sol Lesser. Directed by Sam Wood. Pages 92-93

281

THE PICTURE OF DORIAN GRAY (1945)
Metro-Goldwyn-Mayer

With Hurd Hatfield, George Sanders, Donna Reed. Produced by Pandro S. Berman. Directed by Albert Lewin. Pages 55-71, 252-255

THE SEVENTH CROSS (1944)
Metro-Goldwyn-Mayer

With Spencer Tracy, Hume Cronyn, Signe Hasso. Produced by Pandro S. Berman. Directed by Fred Zinnemann. Pages 147-148

THE SEVENTH VEIL (1946)
Universal

With James Mason, Ann Todd. Produced by Sidney Box. Directed by Compton Bennett. Pages 104, 106-109, 258

THE SONG OF BERNADETTE (1943)
Twentieth Century-Fox

With Jennifer Jones, William Eythe, Charles Bickford. Produced by William Perlberg. Directed by Henry King. Pages 94-99, 257-258

SPELLBOUND (1945)
United Artists

With Ingrid Bergman, Gregory Peck. Produced by David O. Selznick. Directed by Alfred Hitchcock. Pages 104, 106-107, 110-115, 258

TO HAVE AND HAVE NOT (1944)
Warner Bros.

With Humphrey Bogart, Lauren Bacall. Produced and directed by Howard Hawks. Pages 21-26, 133

TOPPER (1937)
Metro-Goldwyn-Mayer

With Constance Bennett, Cary Grant, Roland Young. Produced by Hal Roach. Directed by Norman McLeod. Pages 86, 90

TURNABOUT (1937)
United Artists

With Adolphe Menjou, Carole Landis, John Hubbard. Produced and directed by Hal Roach. Pages 86-88, 90, 256

THE UNINVITED (1944)
Paramount

With Ray Milland, Ruth Hussey, Donald Crisp. Produced by Charles Brackett. Directed by Lewis Allen. Pages 91-92

Check List of Principal Films Referred to.

UP IN ARMS (1944)
RKO-Radio

With Danny Kaye, Dinah Shore, Dana Andrews. Produced by Samuel Goldwyn. Directed by Elliott Nugent. Pages 44-45, 52, 251

A WALK IN THE SUN (1945)
Twentieth Century-Fox

With Dana Andrews, Richard Conte. Produced and directed by Lewis Milestone. Pages 157-165, 264

THE WOMAN IN THE WINDOW (1944)
RKO-Radio

With Edward G. Robinson, Joan Bennett, Raymond Massey. Produced by Nunnally Johnson. Directed by Fritz Lang. Pages 171, 173-174, 265, 268

YOLANDA AND THE THIEF (1945)
Metro-Goldwyn-Mayer

With Fred Astaire, Lucille Bremer, Frank Morgan. Produced by Arthur Freed. Directed by Vincente Minnelli. Page 111